LIVES OF THE MASTERS

玄奘法師像

Xuanzang

CHINA'S LEGENDARY
PILGRIM AND TRANSLATOR

Benjamin Brose

Shambhala

Shambhala Publications, Inc.
2129 13th Street
Boulder, Colorado 80302
www.shambhala.com

FRONTISPIECE: Rubbing from a stele erected at
Xingjiao Monastery, Xi'an, China, 1933.

Cover art: Robert Fenwick May, Jr.
Cover design: Gopa & Ted2, Inc.

9 8 7 6 5 4 3 2 1

FIRST EDITION
Printed in Canada

♾ This edition is printed on acid-free paper that meets the
American National Standards Institute z39.48 Standard.
♻ This book is printed on 100% postconsumer recycled paper.
For more information please visit www.shambhala.com.

Shambhala Publications is distributed worldwide by
Penguin Random House, Inc., and its subsidiaries.

LIBRARY OF CONGRESS CATALOGING-IN-PUBLICATION DATA
Names: Brose, Benjamin, author.
Title: Xuanzang: China's legendary pilgrim and translator / Benjamin Brose.
Description: First edition. | Boulder, Colorado: Shambhala, [2021] |
Series: Lives of the masters
Identifiers: LCCN 2020053492 | ISBN 9781611807226 (trade paperback)
Subjects: LCSH: Xuanzang, approximately 596–664. |
Buddhist priests—China—Biography.
Classification: LCC BQ8149.H787 B76 2021 | DDC 294.3092 [B]—dc23
LC record available at https://lccn.loc.gov/2020053492

Contents

Series Introduction

BUDDHIST TRADITIONS are heir to some of the most creative thinkers in world history. The Lives of the Masters series offers lively and reliable introductions to the lives, works, and legacies of key Buddhist teachers, philosophers, contemplatives, and writers. Each volume in the Lives series tells the story of an innovator who embodied the ideals of Buddhism, crafted a dynamic living tradition during his or her lifetime, and bequeathed a vibrant legacy of knowledge and practice to future generations.

Lives books rely on primary sources in the original languages to describe the extraordinary achievements of Buddhist thinkers and illuminate these achievements by vividly setting them within their historical contexts. Each volume offers a concise yet comprehensive summary of the master's life and an account of how they came to hold a central place in Buddhist traditions. Each contribution also contains a broad selection of the master's writings.

This series makes it possible for all readers to imagine Buddhist masters as deeply creative and inspired people whose work was animated by the rich complexity of their time and place and how these inspiring figures continue to engage our quest for knowledge and understanding today.

KURTIS SCHAEFFER, *series editor*

Preface

I FIRST encountered Xuanzang in the city of Nanjing. While doing fieldwork for an unrelated project, I spent a day walking along the old city wall, skirting the southern shore of Xuanwu Lake. On the top of one forested hill stood a five-storied brick stūpa with an inscription informing passersby that the tower contained a portion of the Tang Dynasty monk Xuanzang's skull. There was also a small Buddhist temple about a hundred yards away, and on the altar inside one of its halls, I saw what looked like a champagne flute half-filled with bone fragments. The monk in charge explained that these were shards of Xuanzang's parietal bone. It seemed strange that the same relics would be enshrined at two sites in such close proximity. A few years earlier, on the sprawling grounds of Yakushiji Monastery in Nara, Japan, I had visited a Xuanzang Memorial Hall that also purportedly housed a piece of Xuanzang's skull. How could one relic be in so many different places? I asked the monk at the temple in Nanjing about the relic in Nara and he dismissed it as a fake. "They tried to steal our relic," he said with a twinge of pride, "but we stopped them." This piqued my curiosity and I did a quick internet search the next day. To my surprise, several other sites also advertised reliquaries enshrining a portion of Xuanzang's skull. These were spread not only throughout China and Japan but also in India and Taiwan. How could this be? I started to track down relevant newspaper articles, diaries, and pamphlets. Over time, I visited as many of the sites as I could, and eventually wrote a short essay detailing the many divisions and peregrinations of Xuanzang's relics throughout Asia.

I thought that was the end of the matter but soon came across Xuanzang again. I was living in Taiwan at the time, and at a little park near downtown Taipei where my kids liked to play there was a small temple partway up a hill behind the playground. I walked up one day to take a look around and admired the dozens of statues on the altar of the main hall. The dark, unpainted wood of the central figure was draped in a miniature gold brocade robe. A serene face with downcast eyes gazed out from beneath a five-pointed crown encrusted with jewels. When I asked who this was, the caretaker identified her as the bodhisattva Nine Lotuses and explained that she was an incarnation of Xuanzang. I had never heard anything like this before. The bodhisattva Nine Lotuses is usually identified as the divinized form of a Ming Dynasty empress dowager. I did not mention my interest in Xuanzang, but the caretaker went on to tell me that the abbot of the temple, a laywoman I'll call Ms. Wang, was able to communicate with deities and was in direct and regular contact with Xuanzang.

I returned to speak with Ms. Wang a few days later, and she described how she began having visions as a child. As she grew older, a broad range of divine beings, from Buddhist bodhisattvas to Daoist immortals to Jesus Christ, gave her instructions and invested her with the powers to heal and foresee the future. Her tutelary spirit was Xuanzang. This deity, she explained, originally lived in a heavenly Buddha realm, but because his cultivation was incomplete, he was sent down to earth to perform the meritorious task of bringing Buddhist sūtras from India to China. Once his work was complete, Xuanzang was able to return to the Buddha realm, but out of compassion for the world, he left a portion of his spirit behind in the form of Nine Lotuses. Ms. Wang told me that the bodhisattva now works through her to protect humankind against all manner of illness and natural disasters. After assessing my facial features and interpreting the characters in my Chinese name, Ms. Wang announced that I too had the rare inborn ability to communicate with spirits but would need to study closely with her before I could manifest my potential. She suggested that we begin the following week.

I regret that I never did return to the temple, but I did start seeing Xuanzang nearly everywhere I looked in Taipei. He was in the graphic novels strewn around my local coffee shop. Men and women dressed as Xuanzang to perform in large, dramatic public funeral ceremonies and to march in local temple processions. His statue sat on the altars of some temples. He starred in TV shows, commercials, puppet performances, and movies. An ad campaign for a popular online video game featured scantily clad young women dressed as Xuanzang and holding his golden, ringed staff. The most jarring example was a shrink-wrapped processed meat product labeled "Flesh of the Tang Monk" on sale in supermarkets. I was fascinated by the many different ways modern people thought about this medieval monk.

What began as idle curiosity grew into preoccupation, and I have spent the last few years working on a book that tells the story of Xuanzang's afterlives. But when asked to contribute a volume to the Lives of the Masters series on the historical figure who inspired all these tales, I was initially reluctant. My research looks at how later generations of devotees—most of them not Buddhist in any formal sense—have imagined and invoked Xuanzang, how they have summoned his spirit during rituals and sought his divine intervention during moments of crisis. There are other scholars who are experts in the actual life and teachings of this seventh-century pilgrim and scholar, and I forwarded some of their names to the editors of this series. They were not dissuaded, however, and I am grateful for that. Delving into the details of Xuanzang's life has only deepened my respect and admiration for this remarkable monk. When I first encountered his relics in Nanjing and elsewhere, I wondered why so many people in so many different parts of the world continued to venerate a monk who lived such a long time ago. This book is an attempt to answer to that question.

Acknowledgments

WHILE I ENVY XUANZANG'S twenty-three-person translation team and imperial funding, this book is no less indebted to the labors of other scholars and the financial support of several institutions. Much of the initial research and writing was done during my residence at the Universität Hamburg's Numata Center for Buddhist Studies under the auspices of an Alexander von Humboldt Research Fellowship. I am grateful to Michael Zimmerman for being such a gracious and generous host and to the German taxpayers for their support of the humanities. In Europe and Taiwan, I have been fortunate to know two of the best scholars of Xuanzang's life and legacies: Max Deeg and Liu Shufen. My own work is deeply indebted to their meticulous scholarship and their good-natured willingness to field my many questions. I thank Kurtis Schaeffer for inviting me to write this book. At Shambhala, I benefited from Nikko Odiseos's encouragement and the editorial skills of Matt Zepelin, Emily Coughlin, and Gretchen Gordon. At the University of Michigan, Caitlin Dickinson helped create the maps using ArcGIS® software by Esri. Donald Lopez gave helpful comments and corrections on an early draft of the manuscript. Funding for travel was provided by the Lieberthal-Rogel Center for Chinese Studies. Portions of chapter 24 appeared previously as "Resurrecting Xuanzang: The Modern Travels of a Medieval Monk," in the edited volume *Recovering Buddhism in Modern China*. I remain grateful, as always, to Jennifer, Walker, and Kalina for their companionship, patience, and perspective. Finally, this book was completed under lockdown in the midst of the global COVID-19 pandemic. It is dedicated to the myriad bodhisattvas—the health care professionals, sanitation workers, grocery clerks, schoolteachers, journalists, activists, and others—who continue to work selflessly and tirelessly for the benefit of all beings.

Xuanzang

Introduction

IN THE FALL of 629, Xuanzang (600–662), a twenty-nine-year-old Buddhist monk, left the capital of China to begin an epic pilgrimage. Over the course of the next sixteen years, he walked thousands of miles, visited hundreds of Buddhist monasteries and monuments, and studied with prominent teachers in what are now the countries of Kyrgyzstan, Uzbekistan, Kazakhstan, Tajikistan, Afghanistan, Pakistan, Nepal, Bangladesh, and India. When he finally returned to China in 645, he brought with him 657 texts, 150 relics, and at least seven statues. Xuanzang became a confidant and advisor to two Chinese emperors, and he carried out his translation work at some of the empire's most prestigious monasteries. Seven years after his homecoming, he lobbied for and oversaw the construction of a new library to safeguard the Sanskrit manuscripts he had collected in India and Central Asia. When the towering Great Wild Goose Pagoda was finally completed, Xuanzang wrote a letter to the emperor, thanking him for his support and extolling the new library. "I consider myself unfortunate to live during a time when the Buddha can no longer be encountered," he began. "Still, I have had the small benefit of learning the teachings through images. Living in the Final Age of the Dharma, where else could I take refuge?" This was a common lament. Monks in China not only had the misfortune to live in a place that was geographically distant from the land of the Buddha but they also were born too late. The Buddha entered nirvāṇa long ago and the Buddhist teachings had

1

subsequently entered a period of inexorable decline. During this Final Age, devotees were left only with images: statues, paintings, and words on the page. The teachings of the Buddha and later generations of Indian Buddhist masters, moreover, trickled into China piecemeal. There were gaps in the record and contradicting theories. Different monks, relying on different translations of various texts, preached irreconcilable interpretations of basic Buddhist doctrine. Xuanzang wanted to set the record straight.

> I was determined to go out from the land of my birth and throw myself into the realm of ten thousand deaths. When passing through lands with the Sage's traces, I paid my respects to the numinous [presence] he left behind. If there were people who propagated the Dharma, I sought out their authentic teachings. When I passed through a place, I was moved to see what I had never seen before. When I encountered a word, I rejoiced at hearing what I had never heard before. In this way, I exhausted my life's resources to copy texts that were missing from the imperial palace."[1]

Xuanzang went to study at the source. He visited the places where the Buddha, his disciples, and other towering figures of the Buddhist tradition had lived and taught. He learned the languages, observed regional histories and cultures, apprenticed under learned scholars, and collected as many texts as he could. Back in the Chinese capital, in a rare moment of autobiographical reflection, Xuanzang expressed his hope that the texts, images, and relics he had worked so hard to obtain would not be scattered and lost. The Great Wild Goose Pagoda accordingly had thick, fireproof walls of rammed earth. It was built to last forever, to stand for a "thousand buddhas to see."

Now, nearly fourteen hundred years later, the stūpa is still there. It serves as a monument to China's best-known, most celebrated Buddhist monk. After Xuanzang's death, his extraordinary life became the stuff of legends. It was illustrated in murals, dramatized by storytellers, performed on stage, and immortalized in literature. Xuanzang became something of a saint in China, and his biography quickly assumed the golden glow of hagiography. In contrast to many great religious figures from the distant past, however, we know a great deal about Xuanzang's life. His disciples composed the *Biography of the Trepiṭaka Master of the Great Ci'en Monastery of the Great Tang Dynasty* shortly after his death. At over eighty thousand characters, it is the longest, most detailed biography ever composed in premodern China. The work initially circulated in China, Japan, and Korea. It was later translated into Tibetan and Turkish and, more recently, into French, English, Russian, and German. In addition to his *Biography*, Xuanzang's letters, his memorials to the emperor, his translations, and his remarkable account of the places he visited during his sixteen-year pilgrimage through Central Asia and India, *The Great Tang Dynasty Record of the Western Regions*, have all been preserved. It is an unusually rich body of material from which to reconstruct a medieval monk's life, and yet a number of basic facts about Xuanzang remain unclear. When was he born? When did he leave for India? What route did he take? Which places did he visit? How did the people of China receive his teachings and translations after his return? For someone who is so well known, much about his life remains a mystery.

In the two decades following his return from India, Xuanzang produced an astounding amount of written work, but nearly all of this was translation. He composed very little original material and rarely wrote about himself. His *Record*, while often described as a travelogue or a diary, is in fact an official report, composed by order of the emperor. Its primary purpose, according to Xuanzang, was to "investigate and describe the mountains and rivers [of the Western Regions], examine and gather information on different lands, detail the mountains and valleys [of the Western Regions], investigate and collect data on the conditions in different lands, record the formal and informal customs of different kingdoms, and grasp the climatic conditions of different environments." The Tang Dynasty, which lasted from 618 to 907, controlled a vast swath of territory—roughly equivalent to the modern People's Republic of China minus the regions of Tibet, Inner Mongolia, the southwestern provinces of Yunnan, Guizhou, and Guangxi, and the northeastern provinces of Heilongjiang and Jilin—but its rulers were intent on expanding their borders even farther. Xuanzang's *Record* was written to convey objective information that would be useful for scholars, officials, monks, merchants, and soldiers. It is a work of history and geography, not a memoir or an ethnography. Xuanzang does not delve into his personal experiences on the road, nor does he catalog the works he studied, his daily routines, the people he met, or even his itinerary. His goal was accuracy, not self-aggrandizement or entertainment. "Although it was difficult to exhaustively verify all matters," Xuanzang wrote in a postscript, "I did not resort to speculation."[2] Striving to be comprehensive, however, meant that he freely mixed firsthand observations with secondhand accounts. His *Record* occasionally strains belief, describing incredible distances between locations—five hundred miles in one direction, four hundred miles in another—and routes that are sometimes circuitous or illogical. It is often impossible to distinguish between the places Xuanzang actually visited and those he only heard about.

The biography composed by Xuanzang's disciples fills in some of these gaps. It is much more personal, telling the story of Xuanzang's life from precocious childhood to auspicious death. As the work of devoted students eager to honor and elevate the legacy of their master, however, it is hardly an objective account. It also has a complicated history that raises a number of questions about its accuracy and authenticity. According to the *Biography*'s preface, Xuanzang's disciple Huili (b. 615) wrote the first five chapters, which cover Xuanzang's early life in China and his travels in India. Concerned that his work was inadequate, Huili then reportedly hid the text in an "underground chamber" until, on his deathbed, he sent his own disciples to go and dig up the manuscript. Once retrieved, Huili's chapters were inexplicably separated and dispersed. Only years later did someone track down, purchase, and reassemble the lost pages. Another of Xuanzang's disciples, the monk Yanli, then "mixed the original work with supplementary annotations" and added five more chapters, covering the period from Xuanzang's return to China until his death and funeral. Yanli's preface for the completed *Biography* is dated 688, twenty-four years after Xuanzang's death. By then, many of those who knew him best were already gone. Such a convoluted textual history does not exactly inspire confidence. Why did Huili hide what he had written? Why was such an important account then scattered and lost? How much of the original material was recovered? What exactly was the nature of Yanli's revisions? And why did it take so long to complete the work? Biographies for monks of Xuanzang's stature are typically written immediately after death to be inscribed on stone stelae and displayed at the site of a monk's grave or reliquary. One of the most prominent clerical scholars of the era, the monk Daoxuan (596–667), did in fact write a shorter account of Xuanzang's life shortly after his death. This biography, which was later included in the collection *Further Biographies of Eminent Monks*, differs in small but significant ways from the longer account later published by Xuanzang's disciples. In Daoxuan's version, for example, Xuanzang does not disobey court orders to slip secretly beyond China's borders. Rather, he takes advantage of a government directive for all monks to leave the capital because of a grain shortage.[3] This and other disparities between Xuanzang's earlier and later biographies make it plain that the process of mythmaking was already underway in the decades immediately after Xuanzang's death.

The urge to embellish Xuanzang's life story only accelerated and grew more brazen as time passed. Stories were told and retold. Details were filled in. The bandits became more threatening, the mountain crossings more treacherous, and Xuanzang's triumphs more glorious. Many devotees drew more inspiration from his momentous journey than from his teachings and translations. Today, Xuanzang is mainly remembered as a courageous and intrepid pilgrim, even though travel for him was merely a means to an end. To access the texts, teachers, and sacred sites of India, he had no choice but to undertake a long and arduous journey. Later generations of Xuanzang's admirers, many of whom had no particular interest in the sūtras and commentaries that Xuanzang prized, saw the journey as an end in itself. Travel is a fertile metaphor, and the hero transformed over the course of an epic quest is a timeless plot. People have long projected their own stories and their own journeys onto Xuanzang and his pilgrimage. His travels have variously been interpreted as a passage through danger to a place of safety; as a progression from ignorance to wisdom; as a rediscovery of one's heritage; as a transition from one lifetime to the next; as a journey of personal discovery; or as an effort to bridge political, cultural, and economic divides.

A few modern pilgrims have even been inspired to follow in Xuanzang's footsteps. Men and women from around the world have retraced the long and difficult route leading from China through Central Asia to India. Some have published memoirs documenting their travels—billed as modern-day sequels to Xuanzang's *Record of the Western Regions*. Times have changed, of course. Buddhism has disappeared from Central Asia and has only recently returned to

India. Most modern pilgrims do not intend to study under Central and South Asian Buddhist masters, collect Buddhist texts, learn canonical languages, or master doctrinal positions. They make the journey in part to remember what once was, to mourn the absence of Buddhism in the places it once thrived—the vanished buddhas of Bamiyan, the crumbling stūpas of Sarnath, and so on—but also to learn something about themselves. Many have described their pilgrimages as deeply personal: as an "inner journey" to understand their ancestral identity, as a "spiritual meditation," as a path to recognizing the "passionate idealism" of Communist beliefs, and as a way to discover an "ideological and personal path through life."[4] Reenactments of Xuanzang's pilgrimage now range from journeys of self-discovery to reality-TV endurance competitions. The state-run China Central Television network even sponsors a "Xuanzang Road Business School Gobi Challenge," where teams of MBA students race along a hundred-kilometer stretch of Xuanzang's route through the desert, paying tribute to what they describe as his "commercial wisdom and pioneering spirit."

Xuanzang, in short, has proven a remarkably malleable monk. People recognize themselves in him, and for that reason it can be difficult to locate the man behind all the myth. This presents a challenge for anyone wanting to portray Xuanzang's life, work, and legacy. He is a teacher whose teachings are not much remembered, a scholar whose scholarship is not widely studied, and a traveler whose travels have been invested with a wide range of meaning. As with many premodern religious figures, the legends surrounding Xuanzang's life have taken on lives of their own. His story has been retold, reshaped, and repurposed by generations of devotees, historians, salespeople, and entertainers. Collective beliefs conjure their own realities. The Xuanzang depicted in movies, TV shows, news stories, dramas, and high school history books may be a mixture of fact and fiction, but the iconic form of the pious, resolute

traveler is now far more recognizable and influential than the erudite seventh-century court cleric who devoted his life to studying
Buddhist doctrine and translating Sanskrit texts.

This book charts a course between the earliest, most reliable
accounts of Xuanzang's life and some of the later, more fantastic
legends. It consists of three parts. The first, "Life," is a summary
of Xuanzang's biography as reflected in the *Record* and *Biography*.
I have flagged some of the more improbable elements of both narratives, but my main goal has been to recount and contextualize
Xuanzang's life story as it has traditionally been told. I have not,
therefore, attempted to verify all the information contained in
these accounts or to exhaustively catalog apparent inaccuracies.
In selecting which portions of Xuanzang's writings to include in
the second part, "Translations," rather than rely on secondhand
accounts written by others, I have focused on those texts known
to have been authored by Xuanzang himself—passages from his
Record and some of the letters reproduced in his *Biography*. One
exception is the description of Xuanzang's death, which was written
by his disciple. Of Xuanzang's many translations, I have included
just two: the famous *Heart Sūtra* and the opening section of the
Bodhisattva Vows. Some of his longer translated works have recently
been translated into English and these are listed in the notes. The
final portion of the book focuses on Xuanzang's legacy. While far
from exhaustive, it offers brief overviews of some of the ways that
Xuanzang's teachings, writings, travels, and bodily remains have
continued to circulate in the modern era. Xuanzang and his life
story have been enlisted in the service of several causes, including
nationalism, diplomacy, colonialism, literary reform, and identity
politics. These may not be the legacies that Xuanzang would have
hoped for; they are certainly not ones he would have anticipated.
And yet, it is perhaps a fitting tribute to this extraordinary monk

that so many different people continue to draw inspiration from his life and work.

When the Great Wild Goose Pagoda was finally completed in 652, Xuanzang hoped that it would "endure as long as Heaven and earth." The stūpa now towers above the streets, hotels, and fast-food chains of modern Xi'an, but it stands mostly empty. The palm leaf manuscripts, statues, and relics that Xuanzang acquired in India and Central Asia and carried back to China disappeared long ago. The old tower built to house the treasures now serves as a museum, a monument, and a pilgrimage site. Millions of people from around the world visit every year. Most peruse the displays, climb to the top floor to take in the view, and move on. Some stop to offer incense and bow before the statue of Xuanzang on the altar. Others pick up copies of Xuanzang's translations of Buddhist sūtras or replicas of Xuanzang's statue to pack away for the long journey home.

Life

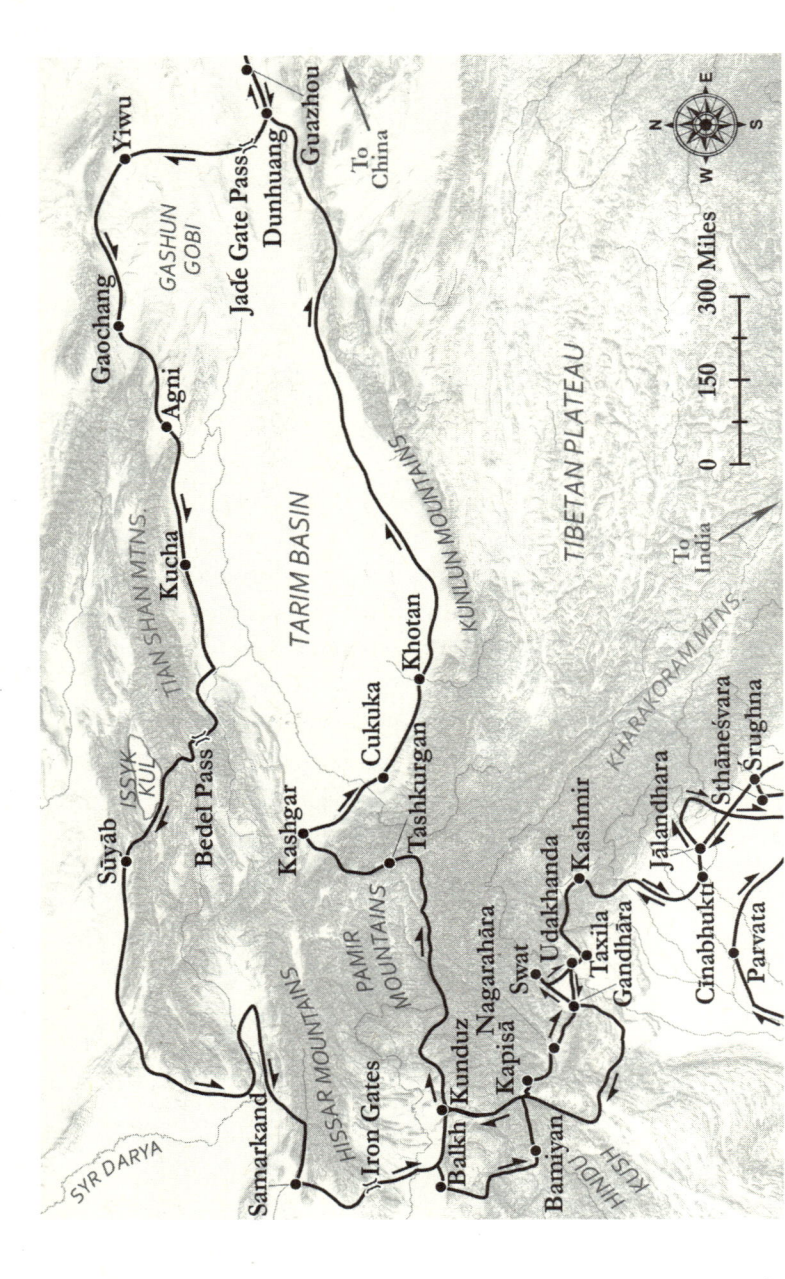

CHAPTER 1

The Journey to Bodh Gayā

XUANZANG almost didn't make it to India. Before setting out on his pilgrimage, his initial request for a travel permit was denied by the court and, after traveling over five hundred miles from the capital to the westernmost Chinese city of Liangzhou, the local governor ordered him to turn back. Hiding during the day and traveling at night, Xuanzang quietly continued on to the desert outpost of Guazhou. There, he learned that the court had issued a warrant for his arrest. The local prefect, it turned out, was a pious Buddhist and urged Xuanzang to leave quickly before he was recognized and detained.

Guazhou lay at the eastern edge of the Tarim Basin, a four-hundred-thousand-square-mile expanse of bleak deserts and barren mountains sparsely supplied with seasonal rivers and small oases. From Guazhou, the route continued northwest, through the Great Wall at Jade Gate Pass and past a series of watchtowers that served as guard posts and garrisons for Chinese soldiers. These towers, set roughly twenty miles apart with neither water nor forage between them, marked the boundary of Chinese territory. All travelers were required to carry detailed official documents recording the name of the issuing official, the name and address of the receiving official, the name of the traveler carrying the pass, a list of the people and animals comprising the party, the specific route they were taking, and the dates of travel. Officials stationed at checkpoints carefully reviewed the information; discrepancies required explanation, verification, and documentation. Anyone traveling without a pass would be held or sent back the way they had come.

Lacking the proper paperwork, Xuanzang did not join a caravan and avoided the most trafficked sections of the route. Instead, he hired a local guide in Guazhou. The young man apparently took Xuanzang for an easy mark and convinced him to trade his young horse for an old nag who, he claimed, was familiar with the route. After dark on their first night out, the guide crept toward Xuanzang with his knife drawn. When Xuanzang quickly got up and began reciting scriptures, the man withdrew. The following day, however, the guide ordered Xuanzang to walk ahead while he followed behind with his bow and sword. Xuanzang refused and the man, citing the dangers ahead, would not go any farther. Xuanzang now had to go on alone, navigating only by means of "skeletons and horse dung."

He eventually reached the first of the five watchtowers and waited until dark to refill his water bag at an outside basin. When arrows began raining down, he called out, "I'm a monk from the capital! Don't shoot!" Fortunately, the captain of the watchtower was sympathetic to Xuanzang's cause, and he fed and lodged him for the night. The next morning, he told Xuanzang of an alternate route that bypassed the second and third towers. The captain of the fourth tower, he explained, was his relative and would treat Xuanzang kindly. Xuanzang arrived at the fourth tower the following night and, as promised, he was given food, water, and a place to sleep. The captain warned him not to pass the fifth tower, whose brash warden might give him trouble. Instead, Xuanzang was advised to travel directly to a spring some twenty miles distant.

Leaving the more established route and chanting the *Heart Sūtra* for protection, Xuanzang walked alone into the Gashun Gobi, one of the largest deserts in the world. Several miles in, his water bag slipped from his hands and his entire supply spilled out and disappeared into the sand. He first decided to turn back and then resolved to press forward. He grew disoriented. During the day, he "saw nothing but the vast desert," and at night, "demonic spirits set fires that burned as bright as stars." After five days without water, Xuanzang could no longer walk.[5] He lay down on the ground and called out to the bodhisattva Avalokiteśvara, protector of travelers and savior of those in distress. That night, a towering figure holding a spear and a flag appeared to him in a dream. The deity admonished Xuanzang for stopping instead of forging ahead. Chastened, he woke and staggered forward. When his horse abruptly changed directions, he struggled to pull him back on course but lacked the strength. It was just as well; the horse had sensed something on the wind and eventually led them to a small oasis with a pool of sweet, clean water.

This is the dramatic beginning of Xuanzang's extraordinary journey from China to India as recounted by his devoted disciple and biographer Huili. The story of Xuanzang braving the dangers of the desert alone establishes a theme that runs throughout this and other accounts of his life: the urbane, learned scholar-monk plunging headlong into the unknown, abandoning comfort and risking death in his single-minded pursuit of the Dharma. Like the Buddha himself, Xuanzang walked away from a life of privilege to pursue the arduous path of liberation. We can safely assume that Huili embellished the account of his master's life, amplifying—perhaps even fabricating—the dangers he faced and inflating his accomplishments, but there is no doubt that Xuanzang was embarking on an exceptionally difficult journey for which he was poorly prepared.

Before leaving the Chinese capital in 629, Xuanzang led a relatively sheltered life devoted to Buddhist scholarship.[6] Born in 602 into an elite, aristocratic family in the city of Luoyang, the eastern capital of China, Xuanzang was the youngest of four boys. His older brother Changjie was a monk and Xuanzang followed his example, becoming a novice at the young age of eleven. Novice monks were called "crow chasers" for their task of driving away the birds before they swooped down and stole older monks' food. They could enter the order as early as seven years old but could not fully ordain until twenty. For the next several years, the novice Xuanzang stayed close to his brother and devoted himself to the study of Buddhist texts.

During Xuanzang's youth, Buddhist monks and nuns interested in doctrine and exegesis tended to specialize in particular sūtras or commentarial traditions. There were six main "schools" of Buddhist scholarship in China at that time: the Three Treatise (Sanlun) tradition, which studied the works of Nāgārjuna (ca. second century), the great Indian philosopher of emptiness; the Establishing Reality tradition, which focused on the scholastic *Treatise on Establishing Reality* (*Tattvasiddhi*) attributed to Harivarman (ca. 250–350); the Abhidharma school, which sought to master Vasubhandu's encyclopedic *Treasury of Abhidharma* (*Abhidharmakośa Bhāṣya*); the Nirvāṇa school, which took the *Great Parinirvāṇa Sūtra* (*Mahāparinirvāṇa Sūtra*) as the final and therefore most complete expression of the Buddha's teaching; the Dilun tradition, which drew inspiration from the *Discourse on the Ten Stages* (*Daśabhūmika Bhāṣya*), Vasubhandu's interpretation of the Ten Stages chapter of the *Flower Garland Sūtra* (*Avataṃsaka Sūtra*); and the Shelun tradition, which upheld Asaṅga's (ca. 320–ca. 390) *Compendium of the Great Vehicle* (*Mahāyānasaṃgraha Śāstra*) as the most comprehensive account of the orthodox teachings. Each of these traditions privileged different sūtras or treatises but they were all devoted to Indian Mahāyāna texts and committed to the faithful implementation of those teachings in China. The goal of most Chinese Buddhist monastics was not reinterpretation or adaptation of the received tradition but fidelity to the intentions of their Indian forebears. Because very few Chinese monks could read Sanskrit, the accuracy of Chinese translations of Sanskrit texts was of paramount importance.

Many monks of Xuanzang's generation lamented China's position on the margins of a Buddhist world centered on India, and they were eager for new texts and teachings issuing from the Buddha's homeland. The traditions of Indian Buddhist thought that had been recently introduced through the translations of Paramārtha (499–569), an influential scholar-monk who arrived in China from western India, were of particular interest. Xuanzang spent his early years as a monk systematically studying Paramārtha's translations and teachings, especially Asaṅga's *Compendium of the Great Vehicle*. This text presented a systematic overview of the Yogācāra teachings, a sophisticated, epistemologically oriented soteriological system that took shape in India during the fourth century.[7] Xuanzang was so taken with Asaṅga's work that by the age of thirteen he had reportedly committed the nearly thirty thousand characters of the *Compendium of the Great Vehicle* to memory.

In search of monks who were expert in these and other teachings, Xuanzang and his brother traveled to the western capital of Chang'an in 618. Their timing could not have been worse. The Sui Dynasty (581–618) had just been overthrown and the capital was in turmoil. The brothers joined a stream of refugees fleeing Chang'an for the relative safe haven of Chengdu in distant Sichuan. It was there that Xuanzang, at the age of twenty-one, finally received full ordination. After several years studying the teachings available in the region, Xuanzang was determined to return to the capital—still a major center of Buddhist learning—to delve into more specialized subjects and resolve his doubts about what he had already learned. Travel at that time was prohibited, however, and his brother refused to let him go. In a move that foreshadowed his later decision to surreptitiously leave China, Xuanzang disobeyed his brother and secretly set sail on a merchant ship down the Yangzi River and through the Three Gorges to a monastery in the city of Jingzhou. From there, he eventually made his way back to Chang'an, where he studied under two learned monks known for their mastery of Asaṅga's *Compendium of the Great Vehicle*.

It was during this period that Xuanzang must have begun to think seriously about traveling to India. He had trained under some of the most prominent clerics in China but remained troubled by their different interpretations of basic Buddhist doctrine. According to his disciple Huili, Xuanzang "often regretted that the books obtained and used by ancient sages contained miswritten words that perpetuated misunderstandings. It pained him that previous scholars heard and then passed on dubious points that compounded people's confusion."[8] Even celebrated exegetes could not agree on basic aspects of the teachings and had different understandings of issues as fundamental as the nature of consciousness, the status of awakening, and the process of purification. Xuanzang worried that something vital had been lost in translation.

In the capital, Xuanzang probably learned two things that strengthened his resolve to travel to India. The first was that a key Yogācāra text translated by Paramārtha, the *Treatise on the Seventeen Lands*, was in fact only a partial translation of the much longer *Discourse on the Stages of Yogic Practice* (*Yogācārabhūmi Śāstra*). The complete version of this work was rumored to be the definitive work on Yogācāra doctrine and practice, but it was not yet known in China. Xuanzang strongly suspected that this text contained the answers to many of his questions. In Chang'an, Xuanzang likely also heard that the *Discourse on the Stages of Yogic Practice* was currently being taught at the thriving Buddhist monastery of Nālandā in northeastern India.[9] As it happened, the elderly abbot of Nālandā, the Venerable Śīlabhadra ("Right Dharma Store"; 529–645), was a leading expert on this very text. The problem, of course, was that Nālandā was over three thousand miles away.

After resting and replenishing his water at a desert spring, Xuan-zang pressed on across the Gobi. In two days' time, he reached the town of Yiwu and lodged in a small monastery. News of his arrival quickly reached the local king, Qu Wentai (r. 623–40), who dispatched an envoy to invite Xuanzang to his palace, promising to provide horses and camels and establish rest stations for the six-day journey. After enduring the deprivations of the desert for weeks, Xuanzang finally arrived in the city of Gaochang (near present-day Turpan), one of the largest and wealthiest outposts along the northern Silk Road. Built around an oasis in a low-lying depression on the northeastern rim of the Tarim Basin, Gaochang had a pop-ulation of roughly thirty-seven thousand people. It was a thriving, self-sufficient city. Farmers grew millet, barley, wheat, grapes, pears, peaches, pomegranates, and dates, while other residents made their living as merchants, soldiers, innkeepers, and craftsmen. Politically, the kingdom was a vassal state of the Western Turkic Khaghanate, a vast confederation of Turkic tribes stretching from Mongolia in the east to the Black Sea in the west. Culturally, however, Gao-chang was more closely aligned with China. Most of the families living there were of Han Chinese descent, Chinese was the official administrative language, and the kingdom's bureaucratic structure mirrored that of the Chinese court. The Chinese presence in the city was so pervasive that Sogdian residents referred to Gaochang simply as "Chinatown."[10]

By the time he arrived in Gaochang, Xuanzang had already traveled nearly fifteen hundred miles from Chang'an, but he was still mostly at home with the region's language, political protocol, and religious culture. The royal family patronized Buddhist monks and monasteries, and the king provided Xuanzang with fine veg-etarian food, lodging in a monastery beside the royal palace, and several eunuchs to look after his needs. After ten days, Xuanzang was rested and ready to leave, but Qu Wentai had grown fond of him and urged him to stay. When Xuanzang politely declined, the king tried again to retain him, promising that all the local people would become his disciples and the several thousand monks living in his kingdom would all become his students. Again, Xuanzang demurred, explaining that the purpose of his journey was not to amass disciples or offerings but to acquire new Buddhist teachings and transmit them back to China. The king was determined, however, and he requested for a third time that Xuanzang abandon the idea of traveling to India. For the third time, Xuanzang declined, reminding Qu Wentai of a ruler's duty to help support the Dharma. Surely, the king would not want to hinder the spread of the Buddha's teachings? Hearing this, Huili reports, Qu Wentai's face darkened and he began to shout. "Your disciple has other ways to deal with the Master! How can you go by yourself? Either you stay here or I will send you back to your country. Please think it over. It is better for us both if you accept my request."[11] Instead, Xuanzang began a hunger strike, taking neither food nor water for four days. As his breathing grew faint, the king, worried he might die, relented and apologized. If Xuanzang broke his fast, the king promised not only to allow him to continue on his journey but also to provide all the necessary support.

Xuanzang stayed in Gaochang for another month, lecturing on the *Sūtra for Humane Kings* and laying in supplies for the next leg of his journey. By way of consolation, he promised Qu Wentai that, after his studies in India were complete, he would return to Gaochang to teach for three years. The king then appointed four monks to serve as Xuanzang's attendants and provided thirty robes and several face covers, gloves, boots, and socks for use during the upcoming mountain traverse. He also issued one hundred taels of gold, thirty thousand silver coins, five hundred rolls of fine and

Mural depicting the Buddhist deity Vaiśravaṇa, from Bezeklik Temple No. 9, near Gaochang, ninth century. Source: Le Coq, *Chotscho*.

coarse silk, thirty horses, twenty-five porters, and twenty-four letters to the rulers of the kingdoms ahead. The most important of these letters was addressed to Tong Yabghu (Tong Yehu, r. ca. 618–30), the khagan, or emperor, of the Western Turkic Khaganate. Qu Wentai was a vassal of the khagan, and along with his letter, he sent gifts of five hundred rolls of silk and two cartloads of fruits and other food. The letter respectfully requested that the khagan offer Xuanzang hospitality and that he instruct rulers throughout his domain to provide the master with safe passage.

The capital of the Western Khaganate was the city of Sūyāb, nearly eight hundred miles to the northwest of Gaochang on the far side of the lofty Heavenly Mountains (Tianshan). To get there, Xuanzang would have to continue west along the northern rim of the Tarim Basin, passing through the cities of Agni and Kucha, and then cross north over the range whose glaciated peaks rose up over twenty-four thousand feet. This was an established route along the so-called northern Silk Road, but it was only one of many possible paths. Despite its name, the Silk Road was not really a road but rather a series of frequently shifting, often unmarked trails that crossed the deserts, mountains, and valleys of Central Asia.[12] As political and environmental conditions changed, so too did the routes followed by travelers. Xuanzang is often depicted as a solitary trailblazer, but official envoys and traders dealing in everything from spices to metals, glass, paper, medicines, slaves, animals, and chemical compounds had been traversing various routes through the mountains and deserts of Central Asia and China for hundreds if not thousands of years. Most gathered in small caravans of four or five people, and together with their pack animals they probably averaged around thirteen miles a day. During difficult stretches, over high passes or in areas where banditry was rampant, smaller groups might band together for greater safety. After his troubles in the Gobi, Xuanzang and his entourage of attendants and porters regularly joined larger parties of merchants or soldiers traveling in the same direction. Over the next sixteen years, he almost never traveled alone.

Many of those traveling in caravans were familiar with the terrain and could serve as informal guides, but Xuanzang almost certainly already had a basic understanding of the region. A voracious reader, he would have sought out and studied accounts of the "Western Regions" available back in Chang'an. Some of these works, like the official Pei Ju's (547–627) *Illustrated Record of the Western Regions* and the monk Yancong's (557–610) *Account of India*, were secondhand accounts, compiled on the basis of testimony provided by traders and monks from Central Asia and India who had come to China. Others, like the travelogue of the Buddhist monk Faxian (337–422) and the accounts of official envoys like Song Yun (active 519–22) and Wei Jie (ca. 604–17), contained more detailed firsthand descriptions of routes traveled and sites visited, but these were dated.[13] Faxian's account was already over two hundred years old and even Wei Jie's text was written nearly twenty-five years earlier. Conditions changed quickly and Xuanzang, like travelers everywhere, gathered critical information about the road ahead—river crossings, mountain passes, places to stay, and places to avoid—from the people he met along the way.

The letters of introduction from Qu Wentai proved invaluable throughout Xuanzang's early travels, but not in the city of Agni (present-day Yanqi). The king there bore a grudge against Qu Wentai and refused Xuanzang's request for fresh horses. Xuanzang stayed only one night and continued directly on to Kucha, where he received a warmer welcome from the king, his ministers, and several thousand local clerics. These were monks of the Sarvāstivāda tradition—literally, "Teaching that All Exists"—one of the most prominent schools of mainstream, or non-Mahāyāna, Buddhism at the time. Like Gaochang, Kucha was a major city along the northern Silk Road with a large Chinese population.[14] Xuanzang lingered there for two months, waiting for the mountain passes to clear of snow, passing the time visiting some of the city's hundred-plus monasteries and debating with local clerics.

Kucha was Xuanzang's last long stop before crossing the Tianshan Mountains. Even rested and supplied with fresh packhorses and porters, the trip, as recounted by Huili, was harrowing.

The mountains are precipitous, rising abruptly up to the sky. Since the route was first opened, the icy snow has accumulated, piling up in passes, melting in neither spring nor summer. Solid blocks of dirty ice are strewn about, reaching up to the clouds. The snow is so blindingly white that one cannot see where it ends. Ice cornices fall and block the trail. Some are a hundred feet long, others dozens of feet wide. It is difficult to proceed along these rugged and choked paths. With the wind-blown snow flying in all directions, even thickly lined fur garments and boots cannot ward off the frigid cold. Whenever one wants to sleep or eat, there is never a dry place to stop. One can only hang a caldron to cook and lay on the ice to sleep.

It took the group a full week to cross the mountains, with one third of the party reportedly dying of starvation or exposure.[15]

By the time Xuanzang descended the northern slope of the Tian-shan range, he had been on the road for nearly six months. He was now entering the heartland of the Western Turkic Khaganate, where he had scant knowledge of the language or culture. After skirting around the southern shores of the massive lake Issyk Kul, he made his way to the capital city of Sūyāb (near present-day Tokmok, Kyrgyzstan). There Xuanzang encountered the khagan himself, Tong Yabghu (d. 628), dressed in a lustrous green silk robe, his head wrapped in a white silk band and his long hair falling down his back.[16] At that moment, the khagan was preparing to leave on a hunting expedition, and his two hundred attendants were arrayed with spears, banners, and bows. Xuanzang was directed to the khagan's official residence to await his return. At their first official audience three days later, Tong Yabghu sat flanked by officials dressed in magnificent brocade, armed guards at his back, in a tent filled with golden flowers. Although he was merely "a lord living in a tent," Huili reported that the scene was nonetheless "dignified and beautiful."[17]

Following a lavish meal of wine, fish, lamb, and veal for the khagan and his men and grape juice, fruits, milk, rice, and honey for the monks, Xuanzang was invited to preach. He spoke about the Ten Good Deeds, the Buddhist perfections (*pāramitā*), and compassion for all sentient beings. The khagan and his people followed the teachings of the ancient Iranian prophet Zoroaster, so the broad, moralistic, and nonsectarian message offered by Xuanzang was well chosen. In a scene that is something of a recurring trope throughout Huili's biography of Xuanzang, the ruler is so impressed that he urges Xuanzang to abandon his mission to India and remain with him instead. Xuanzang, here as always, declines, and the khagan, determined to support the mission regardless, appoints a young man who had lived in China for several years to join the party as an official translator. Tong Yabghu also presents Xuanzang with a set of robes made of red damask silk, fifty bolts of fine silk, and, most valuably, more letters of introduction for the many kingdoms that lay ahead.

The next major city on Xuanzang's route, Samarkand, lay nearly six hundred miles to the southwest of Sūyāb, a journey of roughly six weeks. Situated between the rivers Syr and Amu in the middle of the Kyzylkum Desert, Samarkand was the political, economic, and cultural capital of the region known as Sogdiana. The Sogdians were an Iranian-speaking people, culturally aligned with Persia but under the control of the Western Turks. With the Eastern Roman and Sassanid Empires to the west, the Western Turkic Khaganate to the north, China to the east, and India to the south, Samarkand stood at a critical crossroads, and profit from trade had made it the richest city in Central Asia. The people of Sogdiana were so closely associated with trade that in the kingdom of Khotan all merchants were called Sogdians regardless of their actual ethnicity.[18]

Emissaries and merchants regularly traveled the roughly two thousand miles between Samarkand and Chang'an. Murals depicting Chinese envoys decorated the walls of affluent homes in Samarkand, and Sogdian merchants were a familiar presence in the western market of the Chinese capital. Although people and products had been flowing between the two cities for over six hundred years, the Sogdians and Chinese remained wary of one another. Chinese observers sometimes accused Sogdian merchants of placing profit above all else, and Xuanzang echoes this stereotype in his *Record*, reporting that Sogdians were "slippery and dishonest. They frequently cheat and swindle, so greatly do they covet wealth."[19] The people of Samarkand, for their part, appear to have been uneasy with the Buddhist practices performed by members of Xuanzang's party. Sogdians revered an eclectic array of deities, many of which, like the creator god Ahura Mazda and his darker counterpart Angra Mainyu, derived from Zoroastrian traditions imported from Persia. Unlike in Persia, however, in Samarkand Zoroastrian gods were not part of an organized state religion but belonged to a complex of popular cults that blended Hindu, Greek, Buddhist, and Manichaean traditions. Although Huili reports that the king of Samarkand, whom he describes dismissively as a "fire worshipper," was so delighted by Xuanzang's description of the merits of Buddhism that he asked to receive the precepts, other residents of the city were clearly less enthusiastic. When monks in Xuanzang's party attempted to venerate the Buddha in a local temple, men brandishing torches chased them away. The culprits were arrested and the king ordered their hands cut off as punishment, but Xuanzang mercifully intervened and they were spared. Huili, incredibly, claims that thereafter "all the people, high and low, respectfully inquired about the faith. The master then held a ceremony and those he converted went to live in monasteries."[20] Needless to say, there is no evidence of any mass conversion in Samarkand, and, as far as we know, the people there continued to follow their traditional ways until the region was conquered and converted by the Islamic Umayyad Caliphate (661–750; the second major caliphate after the death of Muhammad) a few decades later.

Leaving Samarkand, Xuanzang traveled south for several hundred miles, passing through the Iron Gate defile that marked the boundary between Sogdiana in the north and Bactria to the south. Descending from the snow-capped Hissar Mountains into the lush Kunduz River valley, in what is now northern Afghanistan, Xuanzang expected to be well received by the regional governor, known as the Tardu Shad, who was the son of Tong Yabghu and the brother-in-law of Qu Wentai. He arrived at a tense moment, however. While Xuanzang was in the city, the governor was poisoned by his current wife at the direction of his former queen. The former queen's son, the Tagin prince, then assumed control and married the murdered governor's wife, his stepmother. After waiting patiently for the month-long funeral and installment ceremonies to conclude, Xuanzang set out, at the new governor's urging, for the nearby city of Balkh.

Alexander the Great had conquered Bactria in 327 B.C.E., and from the third through the second century B.C.E. Balkh served as the capital of Hellenistic Bactria. Xuanzang noted that the Greek language, with its twenty-five phonetic letters and its left to right horizontal writing, was still used for official record keeping in the city. He also would have seen the Greek goddess Aphrodite and the gods Atlas and Triton mingling with Greco-Roman-styled buddhas and bodhisattvas in local murals and sculptures. Balkh was a major cultural crossroads but the primary draw for Xuanzang was the city's Buddhist institutions. According to Buddhist tradition, the Greek king of Bactria, Menander I (r. 165/155–130 B.C.E.), converted to Buddhism in the second century B.C.E., and the region had remained a Buddhist stronghold ever since.[21] When Xuanzang arrived in the city, he found a hundred monasteries occupied by thousands of monks.

In Balkh, Xuanzang met the first of his many teachers outside of China. Under the erudite monk Prajñākara, Xuanzang began reading Sanskrit treatises—particularly the massive *Great Exegesis of Abhidharma* (*Abhidharmamahāvibhāṣā Śāstra*), an influential Sarvāstivāda work that records and refutes different interpretations of the Abhidharma. The Abhidharma comprised a detailed and definitive interpretation of the fundamental teachings contained in mainstream Buddhist sūtras. It was, after the sūtras and the vinayas, the third of the three "baskets" (*tripiṭaka*) of the Buddhist canon. After a month of study in Balkh, Xuanzang and Prajñākara set out together across the Hindu Kush mountain range. Passing through Bamiyan, they found several thousand monks studying in the Lokottaravāda tradition, an early Buddhist school that was unique in its acceptance of the validity of Mahāyāna sūtras.[22] In addition to the famous monumental rock-cut standing buddhas (destroyed by the Taliban in 2001), Xuanzang also marveled at a hundred-foot-tall standing image of the Buddha cast in bronze and a beautifully adorned recumbent parinirvāṇa statue of the Buddha one thousand feet in length.[23]

From Bamiyan, Xuanzang and Prajñākara continued south to the city of Kapisā. Xuanzang found the place "windy and cold" and the people "rude and rustic," but he nonetheless remained in the city for several months. It was midsummer and monsoon season was about to begin. Since the time of the Buddha, monks and nuns had been required to stop their wandering for three months during the rainy season, lest they trample on and inadvertently kill the worms and insects that surfaced on muddy paths. During the retreat, monastics were expected to engage in intensive study and practice and were not supposed to leave the monastery for longer than seven nights. Those who maintained the residency requirement were eligible to receive donations, such as cloth for new robes, from lay devotees at the conclusion of the retreat. Throughout his travels, Xuanzang regularly observed the rains retreat, and in Kapisā, he and Prajñākara passed the three months at Sālāka Monastery.

It was Prajñākara who made the decision to stay at Sālāka. According to Huili, Prajñākara was not willing to lodge at any of the city's Mahāyāna monasteries. This reluctance suggests that he shared the widespread critique that the Mahāyāna was not an authentic form of Buddhism. According to this view, Mahāyāna sūtras were created long after the Buddha's death and thus did not

Sketch of the Bamiyan Buddhas drawn by Alexander Burnes in 1832.
Source: *Travels into Bokhara.*

record his actual teachings, despite Mahāyāna Buddhists' emphatic claims to the contrary. The Buddhist councils, moreover, had never sanctioned Mahāyāna sūtras, and their content often contradicted traditional Buddhist teachings. Mahāyāna monks, for their part, could likewise be dismissive of "Hīnayāna" (Small Vehicle) monks. Clerics who self-identified as members of the Mahāyāna (Great Vehicle) believed they followed the most advanced and therefore most authentic form of the Buddha's teaching, but the monks and nuns who adhered to the older, more conventional teachings chafed at the idea that their tradition was somehow "smaller" or "lesser" than these new interpretations. (For this reason, modern scholars refer to non-Mahāyāna teachings by more neutral labels like "mainstream" Buddhism rather than "Hīnayāna" or the anachronistic "Theravāda.") Despite differences in doctrine and practice, however, Mahāyāna and mainstream monks often lived together in the same monasteries and observed virtually the same monastic rules and routines. There were disagreements and heated debates to be sure, but the two groups appear to have existed in relative harmony. Xuanzang's own assessment of mainstream monks and their teachings was mostly positive. He clearly felt that Mahāyāna represented the ultimate expression of the Buddha's teaching and lamented the fact that mainstream monks were "stagnating in the stage of the gradual teaching," but he recognized the importance of earlier forms of the teaching as the foundation of the Mahāyāna. Xuanzang's *Biography*, his *Record*, and his translations all highlight his far-ranging, ecumenical interests. He was a serious student of both Mahāyāna and non-Mahāyāna texts, and he clearly held several mainstream teachers, like his friend Prajñākara, in high regard. While Xuanzang was staying in Kapisā, the king staged a five-day debate between Mahāyāna and mainstream monks. Huili relates with characteristic hyperbole that, although there were many monks well-versed in the theories of their own particular traditions, "Only the Master had studied all the different theories and could answer any question asked based on the teachings of different schools."[24] Xuanzang, in other words, defended the superiority of the Mahāyāna at the same time that he aspired to an encyclopedic knowledge of the entire Buddhist tradition.

After Xuanzang and Prajñākara passed the summer retreat together at Sālāka Monastery, they parted ways. As Xuanzang continued southeast, he sought out the traces left behind by Śākyamuni Buddha and the places where other eminent monks of the past had lived and taught. His purpose in traveling to India was not only to study doctrine and gather texts but also to come into contact with the sites and objects that retained the Buddha's numinous presence. Śākyamuni had died roughly a thousand years earlier, but his life force could still be accessed in various ways. There were his bodily relics—the bones, hair, teeth, and fingernails that remained after his cremation—and there were what are sometimes called his contact relics—the places where he stood or sat, the objects he had touched, or even shadows he had cast. There were also miraculous images that replicated his form and were reportedly endowed with his miraculous powers. Xuanzang traveled great distances to see and touch these objects and sites, and his *Record* recounts the life of the Buddha and the history of Indian Buddhism as he encountered it embedded in the landscape. In Nagarahāra, for example, he visited the place where the Buddha-to-be encountered the previous buddha Dīpaṃkara. Xuanzang later prostrated himself and recited sūtras in the cave where the Buddha left his shadow, and he was rewarded with a vision of the Buddha's body. In the nearby city of Hilo, Xuanzang was shown a piece of the Buddha's skull, which resident monks, for a fee, used to tell fortunes. After grinding some incense into powder, wrapping it in a piece of white silk, and pressing it onto the yellowing bone, Xuanzang received an impression that resembled the Bodhi Tree. The brahmin in charge enthusiastically snapped his fingers and scattered flowers, saying that this meant that Xuanzang would one day be awakened. The rocks, trees, temples, and bones of northern India were saturated with traces of the Buddha, a presence that was painfully absent in China.

The wealth of Buddhist legend and lore Xuanzang encountered in northern India often contrasted starkly with the derelict state of the Buddhist temples and monuments he visited. In places where Buddhism had once flourished, he found only the crumbling foundations of abandoned monasteries. This was in some ways to be expected. Xuanzang knew that Śākyamuni's teachings were prophesized to decline as time progressed. According to tradition, the period of "true Dharma," when the Buddha's original teachings are accurately transmitted and practiced, would be followed by a period of "semblance Dharma," when the teachings would only vaguely resemble what the Buddha had taught. This in turn would be followed by the period of the "final Dharma," when the teachings enter a precipitous decline and eventually disappear completely. Different traditions calculated the dates differently but most commentators in China agreed that the time of "true Dharma" had passed and the era of dissolution had begun. This was a regrettable but natural progression. The Buddhist teachings, like all conditioned things, are impermanent. All traces of the Buddha and the tradition he inspired will eventually vanish from the earth. In the distant future, the next buddha, Maitreya, will be born in India, the Buddhist teachings will once again flourish in the world, and the cycle will begin anew. Until then, Maitreya waits in Tuṣita Heaven for his time to come. The people of the present age can only do their best to follow Śākyamuni's example and hope that, through the sincerity of their practice and the virtue of their actions, they will be reborn in the same time and place as the future buddha.

In northern India, Xuanzang saw many signs that the Dharma was beginning to decay. The formerly thriving Buddhist center of Gandhāra once had "over a thousand monasteries, but they are deserted and desolate now, overgrown with weeds. The stūpas are also in ruins. There are about a hundred deva-temples where various non-Buddhists dwell."[25] In Pāṭaliputra, the former capital of the quintessential Buddhist King Aśoka (r. ca. 273–232 B.C.E.), there had once been several hundred monasteries but now only two or three remained. It was the same in Śrāvastī, the city where the Buddha had passed twenty-five rains retreats. Although there were still several hundred monasteries when Xuanzang passed through, most were dilapidated. In these and other abandoned sites, Xuanzang dutifully describes places of historical significance but says little about what existed at the time of his visit. He moved quickly through Nagarahāra, Gandhāra, up and down the Swat Valley, and through Taxila. These regions, once major enclaves of North Indian Buddhist culture, had recently fallen under the control of the Alchon Hun tribes of Central Asia, who, according to Xuanzang, attempted to "destroy whatever was connected with Buddhism and to expel all monks."[26]

Buddhism in India appeared to Xuanzang to be in a state of slow, inexorable decline. The golden age had passed, many major monasteries had been abandoned, and brilliant monks were few and far between. Still, several strongholds remained and Xuanzang's itinerary maps the landscape of Buddhist learning in northern India during the first half of the seventh century. Kashmir remained the preeminent center of Sarvāstivādin Abhidharma studies, the most influential tradition of mainstream Buddhism in India at that time. There, Xuanzang found one hundred temples with a total of five thousand monks. In addition to Sarvāstivāda specialists, Kashmir was also home to experts in Mahāyāna sūtras and commentaries as well scholars of the Mahāsāṃghika ("Great Congregation")— another influential early school of mainstream Buddhism.[27] Not only were there excellent scholars of "lofty character" and "outstanding intelligence" in Kashmir, but there were also libraries stocked with Buddhist manuscripts. The king generously appointed twenty scribes to copy scriptures and commentaries for Xuanzang and sent five other men to serve as his attendants. The conditions for study were ideal, and Xuanzang remained in Kashmir for a full two years.

Xuanzang spent the next three years traveling relatively short distances and pausing for long stretches to study under prominent monks and, more rarely, lay scholars. As was his habit, he sought out specialists in both Buddhist and non-Buddhist texts, from the treatises and commentaries of different mainstream Buddhist schools to works on the Vedas, logic, and language. He stayed in Cīnabhukti for over a year and in the cities of Jālandhara, Śrughna, Matipura, and Kānyakubja for several months each. Traditions of Buddhist scholasticism remained strong in these places. Kānyakubja, near present-day Kannauj, for instance, had thousands of Mahāyāna and mainstream monks living in more than a hundred monasteries. The city served as the political capital of northern India and its ruler, King Harṣa (aka Harṣavardhana, r. ca. 608–47), was an open-handed patron of both Buddhist and non-Buddhist monks and ascetics.

By the early seventh century, the long period of political unity that prevailed in northern India under the Gupta Dynasty (ca. 320–550) had come to an end. The subcontinent was divided into a series of rival kingdoms: the Pallava Empire continued to control much of the southern part of the peninsula; the Chalukya Empire occupied the center of the continent; the small Maitraka Empire held the northwest, in present-day Gujarat; and the Gauḍa Kingdom dominated the northeast, in present-day Bengal. The rich Gangetic plain of northern India, the heartland of Buddhist culture, had only recently come under the sway of King Harṣa. According to Xuanzang, Harṣa rose to power at the beginning of the seventh century after leading an army of five thousand elephant-mounted soldiers, twenty thousand cavalrymen, and fifty thousand infantry-men. Following brutal wars to pacify the five parts of India, which in truth only succeeded in consolidating control in the north, Harṣa reportedly transformed himself from a fierce military commander into a benevolent, pacifist king. Under his watch, "the weapons of war were not raised and the government was fair and just. [Harṣa] was frugal in his affairs and sought after fortune and goodness with such determination that he forgot to eat and sleep. He ordered that within the five parts of India nobody could eat meat. If anyone took life, they would be executed without mercy."[28] Like Aśoka, Harṣa atoned for the blood he shed by embracing piety and self-restraint. Xuanzang accordingly portrays Harṣa as a righteous ruler who built thousands of stūpas, established and supported countless monasteries, and regularly convened great convocations of monks. Xuanzang stayed in Harṣa's capital for three months, but it would be several more years before he met the king face to face.

From Kānyakubja, Xuanzang traveled southeast, following the course of the Ganges River. By this point, he had been on the road for six or seven years, and he had collected a sizable store of texts, images, relics, gifts, and other supplies. He would have required several porters to carry the weighty load and the many bundles would have attracted thieves. In one of the more dramatic episodes from the *Biography*, Huili describes the day when Xuanzang and his party, sailing down the Ganges, are overtaken by several boatloads of pirates. The group is first forced to the riverbank and then strip-searched for valuables. Making a bad situation even worse, the thieves turn out to be devotees of the bloodthirsty goddess Durgā, the fearsome consort of Lord Śiva. The time of Durgā's autumn sacrifice is approaching and handsome, exotic Xuanzang makes for an irresistible offering. The pirates set to work constructing a makeshift sacrificial altar. Xuanzang, unperturbed, asks for some time to prepare for his death. He visualizes Maitreya Buddha and prays to be reborn in Tuṣita Heaven, where he might finally receive the object of his pilgrimage: the *Discourse on the Stages of Yogic Practice*. Lost in his meditative trance, Xuanzang is no longer aware that he is seated on an altar, and he cannot hear the anguished weeping of his fellow travelers. It is then that a black wind begins to howl through the forest, toppling trees, throwing up clouds of sand, and roiling the river. The bandits are terrified and, fearing that Durgā is displeased with their offering, call off the sacrifice. They beg Xuanzang to absolve them but cannot penetrate his *samādhi*. Finally, they touch him, breaking his trance. Xuanzang opens his eyes, looks around, and asks, "Is it time?"

Whether or not depraved Śaivite bandits nearly burned Xuanzang alive, the episode makes for a fitting metaphor. In Xuanzang's view, Buddhism was under siege in India. Learned monks were losing ground to charlatans, false sages who engaged in practices that

Xuanzang found delusional and disturbing. In the *Biography*, Huili quotes Xuanzang's description of the various non-Buddhist practices he encountered in India:

> The Bhūtas smear their bodies with ash as a means of practicing the Way. Their bodies are pale white like cats who sleep in stoves. The Nirgranthas [Jains] practice nudism and have strange appearances. They pull out their hair as an act of virtue. Their skin is cracked and their feet are chapped. They look like rotting trees beside a river. The Kāpālikas make garlands of skulls to adorn their heads and hang around their necks. Shriveled and withered like piles of stone, they resemble *yakshas* beside tombs. The Jūtakas wear soiled clothes, drink urine, and eat filth. They have a foul stench like wild pigs wallowing in a latrine.[29]

Only a fool, he goes on, would regard these practices as admirable or efficacious.

Buddhist monks were no strangers to ascetic practices, of course, but the Buddha expressly forbade certain acts. According to the *Nirvāṇa Sūtra*, Śākyamuni did not allow his monks "to hold one leg in the air and remain silent, to jump into an abyss, to lay down upon fire, to let oneself fall from a cliff, to remain in painful circumstances, to take poison, to fast, to lie face down in ashes, to bind their own hands and feet, to kill living beings, to practice geomancy, and to cast spells."[30] Non-Buddhist renunciants in India engaged in acts of self-mortification to eradicate negative karma through physical suffering and thus obtain liberation. Jain monks and nuns, the devotees of the "destroyer" god Śiva and the "preserver" god Viṣṇu, and other ascetics all competed with Buddhist monastics for the support of the laity. Xuanzang reports that these "heretics," or "people outside the way," outnumbered Buddhists in many places.

The capital city Kānyakubja, for example, had twice as many "deva" temples as it did Buddhist monasteries. Even King Harṣa, whom Xuanzang wishfully portrays as a committed Buddhist, was more likely a devotee of Śiva, the same deity venerated by the Kāpālikas with their grisly necklaces made of human skulls.[31]

It was further evidence of the decline of the Dharma that some of these heretics had taken over formerly Buddhist sites. On Vipula Mountain, the peak outside of Rajgir where the Buddha once preached, naked ascetics now practiced punishing austerities, blinding themselves by staring at the sun. In the country of Udyāna (present-day Swat), where fourteen hundred Buddhist monasteries once stood, Xuanzang reports that only a few ignorant monks remained. The temples of non-Buddhists, however, were proliferating. In Sthāneśvara, Xuanzang likewise found just three Buddhist monasteries stranded in a sea of deva temples. The band of Shaivite pirates might not have succeeded in sacrificing Xuanzang on the banks of the Ganges River, but non-Buddhists seemed well on their way to destroying Buddhism in India.

Recovered from the attempted robbery, on guard against heretics and thieves, Xuanzang continued on. He was now entering the cradle of Buddhism, passing through the places where Śākyamuni Buddha had lived and taught. These sites were charged with heightened significance for Xuanzang. Just before he died, the Buddha explained to his attendant Ānanda that there were four places that pious monks, nuns, and laypeople should visit during their lives: the place where the Buddha was born, the place where he awakened, the place where he first turned the wheel of the Dharma, and the place where he entered nirvāṇa.[32] These four sites had long been major destinations for Buddhist pilgrims, and Xuanzang visited them each in turn. Many, however, had fallen on hard times. At Lumbinī, where the infant Buddha emerged from his mother's right

side, Xuanzang found two stūpas, but the tree under which the
Buddha had been born had withered and a greasy film covered the
pool of water where the Buddha's mother had bathed after giving
birth. Even the Aśokan pillar that celebrated the Buddha's birth had
been broken in half. Nearby Kapilavastu, where the young Buddha
grew up as a privileged prince, was deserted. Only the ruins of his
father King Śuddhodana's palace remained. The old foundations
of a thousand monasteries littered the ground but just one Buddhist monastery and two deva temples occupied the site. Jetavana,
where the Buddha had lived much of his adult life, now had only
a single dilapidated monastery to memorialize the place where the
Buddha delivered so many teachings to his disciples. The forest
where the Buddha entered nirvāṇa, near Kuśinagara, was likewise
abandoned. The road leading there, according to Xuanzang, was
rough, dangerous, and crawling with bandits.

Fortunately, other major sites associated with the Buddha's life
were still thriving. The Deer Park in Sarnath, where the Buddha
delivered his first sermon on the four noble truths, had a massive monastic complex housing fifteen hundred monks. In Bodh
Gayā, the site of the Buddha's awakening, the towers of the great
Mahābodhi Temple rose up behind the famed Bodhi Tree (p. 39).
The extensive monastic complex housed nearly one thousand
monks, who studied both Mahāyāna and mainstream teachings
and ministered to the tens of thousands of pilgrims who descended
on the site each year. The region radiating out from the Bodhi Tree
was so densely populated with Buddhist sites that it took Xuanzang
eight or nine days to visit them all. His great joy at finally arriving
at the seat of awakening and walking in the footsteps of the Buddha
was tempered by a melancholy sense that the place, and the Buddhist teachings in general, would not last much longer. The Bodhi
Tree itself was diminished. When the Buddha sat beneath it, it had
towered up for several hundred feet. Now, having been hacked down

Watercolor of the Mahabodhi Temple at Bodh Gayā in Bihar,
by James Crockatt, c. 1800. Source: British Library.

by heretical kings, it was a mere fifty feet high. More ominous were
the two statues of the bodhisattva Avalokiteśvara that marked the
southern and northern boundaries of the site. According to local
lore, the Buddha Dharma would vanish from the world once the
earth swallowed up the statues. One of the bodhisattvas, Xuanzang
observed, had already sunk up to its chest. The Buddhist presence
at Bodh Gayā seemed to be slipping away.

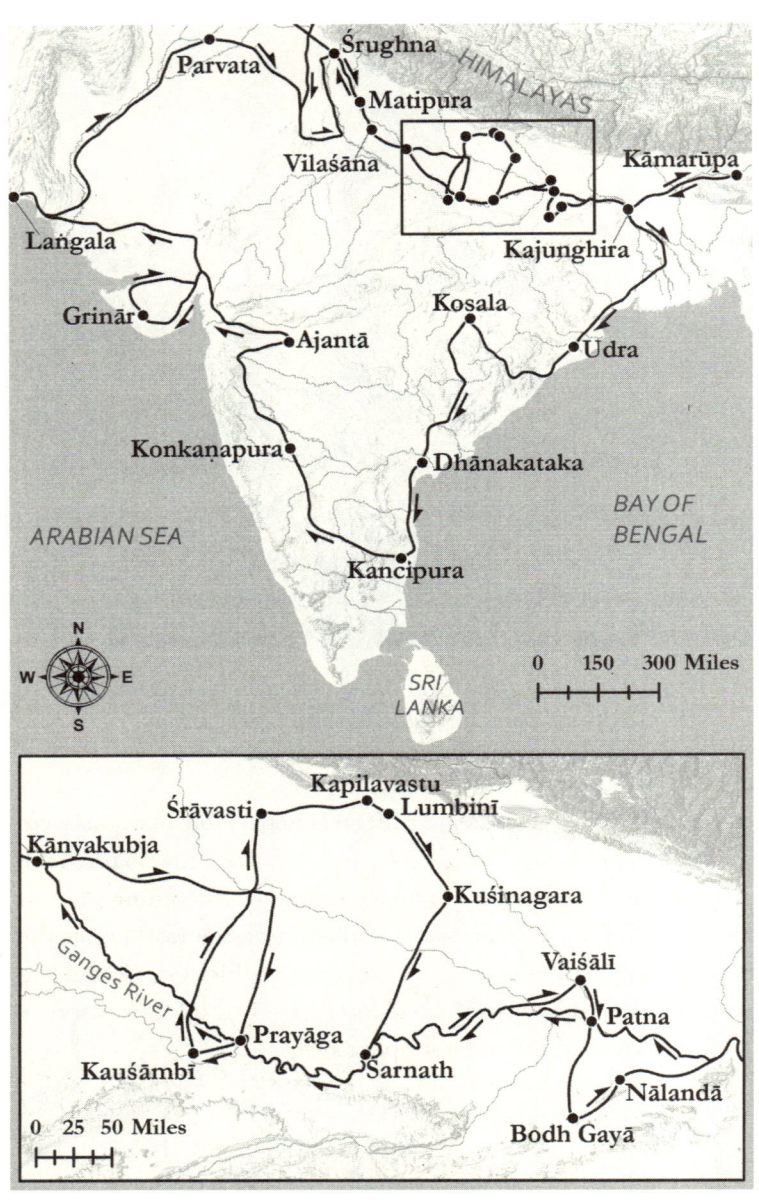

CHAPTER 2

Nālandā to Chang'an

WHILE XUANZANG was staying at Bodh Gayā, four monks came from Nālandā—the great center of Buddhist learning in northern India—to escort him back to their monastery. There, Xuanzang was met by hundreds of monks and over a thousand laypeople holding banners, canopies, flowers, and incense. After he had greeted the resident clerics and officially received permission to stay at the monastery, he was taken to see the Venerable Śīlabhadra, one of Nālandā's most senior monks and the famed specialist in Yogācāra whom Xuanzang had long sought to meet. Following custom, he crawled on his knees and elbows to approach the master, kissing his feet and prostrating before him. Śīlabhadra then invited Xuanzang to sit. With a crowd of curious monks looking on, Śīlabhadra asked where Xuanzang had come from and he explained that he had traveled from China specifically to study the *Discourse on the Stages of Yogic Practice* under the master. Śīlabhadra reportedly began to weep and called on his elderly nephew, the monk Buddhabhadra, to describe what had transpired three years earlier. Buddhabhadra, wiping away his own tears, explained,

In the past, the master suffered from wind disease. Whenever it flared up, his hands and feet seized up and felt as though they were being stabbed with burning knives. It came and went over the course of more than twenty years. Three years ago, the pain was especially severe. He became disgusted with his body and wanted to starve himself. In the middle of the night, he dreamt of three heavenly beings. The first was the color of gold, the second was the color of lapis lazuli, and the third was the color of silver. They had a dignified appearance and their clothes were light and luminous. They asked the master, "You want to abandon this body? The [*Vimalakīrti*] *Sūtra* says, 'Say that the body suffers but do not say that the body can be abandoned in disgust.' In a past life, you were a king who caused great trouble to living beings. That is why you have received this recompense. Now you should examine your faults and sincerely repent. Endure your suffering patiently. Diligently expound on the sūtras and treatises and the symptoms will vanish. Abandoning your body will not put an end to your suffering." Hearing this, the master bowed before them. The golden being pointed to the blue one and said to the master, "Do you recognize him? This is the bodhisattva Avalokiteśvara." Then he pointed to the silver being, saying, "This is the bodhisattva Maitreya." The master then bowed to Maitreya and said, "I have always vowed to be born in your realm but I do not know if I will obtain it." Maitreya responded, "If you broadly proclaim the true Dharma, you will certainly obtain rebirth there." The golden being said, "I am the bodhisattva Mañjuśrī. We observed that you vainly wanted to abandon your body, which would be of no benefit. Therefore, we came to advise you. You should rely on our words and propagate the true Dharma of the *Discourse on the Stages of Yogic Practice* and other texts. Spread these teachings to those who have not heard them and your body will gradually be at peace. Do not worry! There is a monk from China who takes pleasure in the great Dharma and who wants to study with you. Wait for him to arrive and then teach him. After hearing these words,

Śīlabhadra bowed and responded, "I will respectfully abide by your esteemed instructions." When he finished speaking, the beings disappeared. Since that time, the master's painful illness has been cured.[33]

Hearing that his arrival at Nālandā had been prophesized by Mañjuśrī himself, Xuanzang was deeply moved. He venerated Śīlabhadra again and vowed to be diligent in his studies if the master would accept him as his disciple. Śīlabhadra agreed and Xuanzang was given a room on the fourth floor of one of Nālandā's monastic complexes. He also received provisions and unfettered access to Nālandā's extensive resources. After traveling roughly four thousand miles over the course of nearly seven years, Xuanzang had finally arrived at his destination.

At that time, Nālandā was perhaps the most prestigious and affluent monastery in all of India. Xuanzang traces the history of the monastery back to the time of Śākyamuni, when five hundred merchants purchased a mango grove and presented it to the Buddha. Only much later did the king Śakrāditya (r. ca. 415–55) build a permanent temple on the site (see "Nālandā"). Xuanzang's account in his *Record* tallies with the earliest archaeological evidence for a permanent Buddhist presence at the site, which dates to the fifth century. No temple of significance appears to have existed at the location prior to this. When the Chinese Buddhist monk Faxian (337–422) visited the region in the early fifth century, he only noted a large stūpa, suggesting that the monastic complexes were constructed at some later date.

By the seventh century, Nālandā was an extensive and influential center of Buddhist scholarship and practice. It comprised eight monastic complexes, built of brick and lined up side by side with east-facing entrances. Each monastery contained thirty individual cells arranged around a central courtyard. Four temples faced the

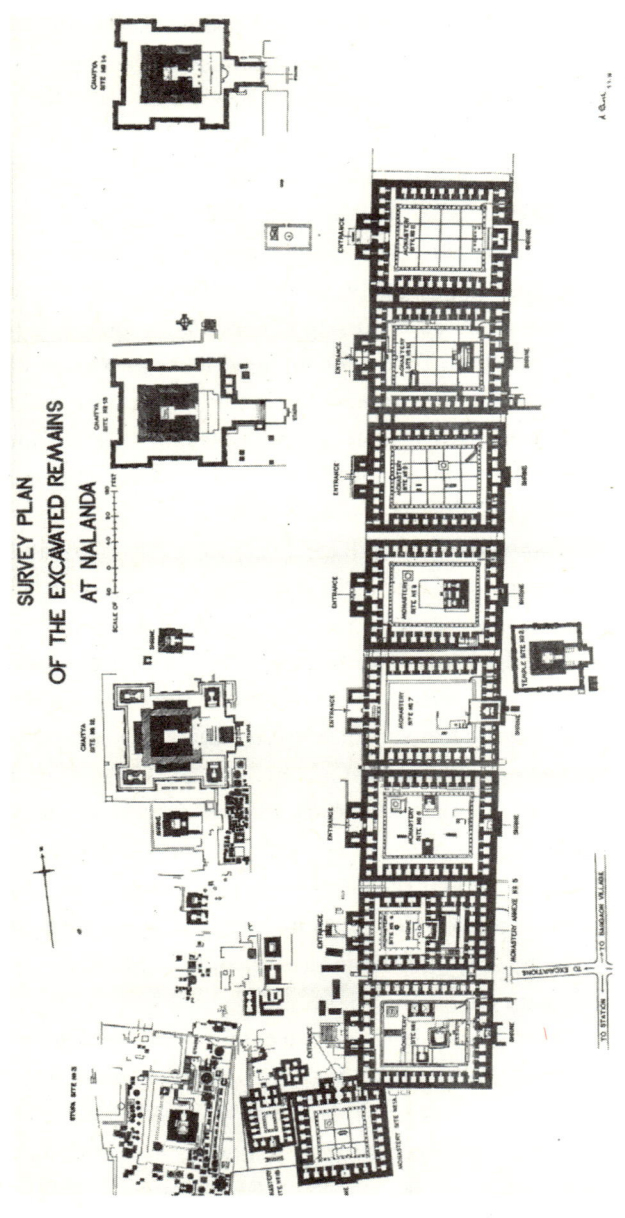

Survey plan of the excavated remains of Nālandā. Xuanzang lived at monastery site number one, the leftmost complex along the bottom row of eight structures.

Source: Ghosh, *A Guide to Nālandā*.

monasteries in front, and a fifth was positioned behind (p. 44). The buildings were brightly painted and their columns and railings elaborately carved. Streams ran through the grounds, feeding ponds filled with blue lotuses and water lilies. The entire complex, nearly thirty acres in total, was enclosed by a thick brick wall and was off limits to the public.

Xuanzang reported that he joined an assembly of several thousand monks living at Nālandā. The Chinese Buddhist monk Yijing (635–713), who spent ten years at Nālandā some four decades after Xuanzang, estimated that there were about three thousand resident monks. The logistics of maintaining such a large population of clerics must have been daunting. Aside from administering the affairs of the monastery, monks at Nālandā were expected to focus entirely on their studies. They did not beg for their food, as was customary, nor did they farm the land, which the monastic code prohibited. To supply the monastery, King Harṣa decreed that more than a hundred nearby villages would be responsible for provisioning Nālandā. Two hundred families from each village were required to provide daily supplies of rice, butter, and milk. The allotments of individual monks were determined by rank. As an eminent guest, Xuanzang received more provisions than most other clerics. These included a daily supply of one hundred and twenty betel leaves, twenty areca nuts, twenty nutmegs, over an ounce of fine incense, a half-liter of rice, and an unlimited supply of butter and milk. Every month, he also received an additional liter and a half of oil.[34] Xuanzang was further exempted from administrative duties, had two servants, and was given an elephant for his personal travel. According to Huili, only nine other monks at Nālandā enjoyed this level of privilege.

Xuanzang made Nālandā his home for the next five years. Like other monks, he slept in one of the ten-by-ten-foot cells surrounding the central courtyard of his cloister and was awakened before dawn by the beating of the great drum. He bathed in the nearby pools in the morning and attended chanting services in the evening. During the day, he was free to attend the many lectures that were regularly held in the various monastic complexes. These presentations covered all aspects of Buddhist thought as well as important non-Buddhist topics such as logic, grammar, medicine, divination, and the Vedas. In the *Biography*, Huili provides a rough outline of Xuanzang's course of study:

> In the monastery the master listened to [lectures on] the *Discourse on the Stages of Yogic Practice* three times; the *Abhidharma According with Reason Treatise (Abhidharmanyāyānusāra Śāstra)*, *Exposition of the Ārya Teachings (*Prakaraṇāryavāca Śāstra)*, and the *Exposition on the Collection of Mahāyāna Abhidharma (Mahāyānābhidharmasamuccaya Vyākhyā)* one time each; the *Introduction to Logic (Nyāyapraveśa)*, *Treatise on Grammar (Vyākaraṇa)*, the *Compendium on Valid Knowledge (Pramāṇasamuccaya)*, and so forth, two times each; and the *Exposition of the Middle Way (Madhyamaka Śāstra)* and the *Exposition of the Hundred Verses (Śata Śāstra)* three times each. As for the *Treasury of Abhidharma (Abhidharmakośa Bhāṣya)*, the *Great Abhidharma Commentary (Abhidharma Mahāvibhāṣa)*, the *Six Part Abhidharma (Abhidharmaṣaṭpāda Śāstra)*, and other texts, which he had already studied in Kashmir and other kingdoms, he merely reread them to resolve questionable points.[35]

These works, which range from Yogācāra doctrine to Abhidharma exegesis, Madhyamaka theory, and logic, highlight the ecumenical offerings available at Nālandā. In addition to his doctrinal studies, Xuanzang also necessarily spent considerable time mastering Sanskrit grammar, honing skills he would later use when translating many of the treatises he studied at Nālandā and elsewhere into Chinese.

Xuanzang extolled Nālandā's teachers and his fellow students as both brilliant scholars and extraordinarily disciplined monks who upheld the monastic regulations without fail. "They ask for instruction and have profound discussions all day long. Day and night they admonish each other with young and old supporting one another."[36] The quality of Nālandā's training was such that outside scholars frequently came to test their mettle against the monastery's monks. To limit time spent in pointless debates, entry to the monastery was restricted to those who were already well versed in both traditional and contemporary teachings. Despite this screening, Xuanzang noted that most of those who did manage to gain entry and engage in debate usually ended up slinking away in defeat.

Xuanzang says very little about his personal relationship with his teacher Śīlabhadra, but when Yijing reported on his time at Nālandā in the late seventh century, he described the intimacies of the master-disciple relationship. The disciple was expected to meet with his master on a daily basis, inquiring after his needs and performing a variety of tasks, including massaging him, folding his clothes, and cleaning his cell. The teacher, in turn, would treat his student as a father would care for his child. As surrogate parents, they not only instructed and guided their wards but also cared for them when they became sick.[37]

Śīlabhadra had been born into the Brahmin caste in the northeastern Indian kingdom of Samatara and he later studied at Nālandā under the eminent monk Dharmapāla (530–61). After Śīlabhadra gained some renown from defeating a South Indian "heretic" in debate at the age of thirty, the king awarded him a monastery in Magadha that was supported by the revenues of a nearby village. When Śīlabhadra later moved back to Nālandā, he taught his disciples the stages of the Buddha's teachings revealed in the *Scripture*

on the Explication of the Underlying Meaning (Samdhinirmocana Sūtra).
According to this work, there had been three turnings of the wheel
of the Dharma. The first and earliest of these turnings was the teaching of the four noble truths, which the Buddha intended for the
śrāvakas, or disciples. The second was the Madhyamaka teachings,
which revealed the truth of emptiness to bodhisattvas. Both the
first and the second turnings of the wheel were perfectly true and
accurate for those for whom they were intended, but they required
interpretation and thus could lead to disputes. The third turning
was available to all—disciples, *pratyekabuddhas* (solitary buddhas),
and bodhisattvas. Because these teachings represented the Buddha's
unvarnished view, interpretation was not necessary. These were the
Yogācāra teachings, which Śīlabhadra heralded as the highest, most
complete expression of the Buddha Dharma.[38]

Xuanzang had been alarmed by the contradictory teachings he
heard as a young monk in China, but he was not overly concerned
with the doctrinal diversity he encountered in India. In his view,
"The sages established each of their teachings with a single intention. There is no disagreement or obstruction among them. Deluded
people who are unable to comprehend them call them contradictory.
This is the fault of transmitters. What does it have to do with the
Dharma?"[39] Despite his commitment to the underlying unity of all
Mahāyāna teachings, Xuanzang clearly shared Śīlabhadra's view
that Yogācāra occupied the apex of Buddhist thought. Together
with Madhyamaka ("Middle Way"), Yogācāra was one of the two
primary strains of Mahāyāna Buddhism in India during the seventh
century.[40] Its name, which literally means "practice of yoga," was
synonymous with the doctrine of "mind-only" or "representation
only." (In China, Yogācāra accordingly went by names that translate
as "Consciousness Only" and "Dharma Characteristics.") Some of
the central concepts of Yogācāra doctrine appear in early Mahāyāna

sūtras, but they were elaborated and systematized by the two Indian half-brothers Asaṅga and Vasubandhu sometime during the fourth or fifth century. Both men were prolific authors, touching on nearly every aspect of Buddhist thought and practice in their writings, but for Xuanzang and many others, Asaṅga's *Discourse on the Stages of Yogic Practice* represented the pinnacle of their teachings. Xuanzang accepted the prevailing view in East Asia that Asaṅga had in fact received his teachings in Tuṣita Heaven from the future buddha Maitreya. As divine revelation, the *Discourse on the Stages of Yogic Practice* provides detailed, authoritative descriptions of the various stages on the path to buddhahood, distinguishing between the lesser stages of the disciple and the more demanding and lofty stages of the bodhisattva. The text also outlines the distinguishing doctrines of the Yogācāra tradition—the three natures (*trisvabhāva*), mind-only (*cittamātra*), and the storehouse consciousness (*ālayavijñāna*).

These three doctrines are presented as aspects of a single, integrated system that seeks to describe and transform consciousness. The three natures refer to the distinct ways people experience the world. The first nature is "constructed." Because our mental processes color all our experiences of the world, we are unable to see things as they really are, viewing them instead through the filters of our language, learning, past experiences, and inherent biases. We erroneously perceive a world consisting of distinct objects endowed with specific qualities, even though those objects and qualities are in fact mere constructs of our consciousness. The second nature, "dependent," describes the processes that give rise to our ordinary, constructed experiences. The interdependent, interconnected flow of all phenomena and the temporary arrangement of matter into distinct forms gives rise to the illusion of enduring, independent entities even though none actually exist outside of the mind. Our experience of the world is in fact a creation of our own consciousness.[41] The mental projections that we perceive as objective reality are rooted in ignorance, particularly the delusion of an independent self, and ignorance is the origin of suffering. The goal for Yogācāra practitioners is to transform the mind so that it is no longer fooled by the distortions of conventional consciousness and can instead experience the world as it truly is: empty, devoid of self, and dependently arisen. This is the third, "perfected" nature, the ultimate reality realized by buddhas and bodhisattvas.

The Yogācāra theory of mind explains how our experiences come to be misconstrued and, more importantly, how practitioners can purify their perceptions. The mind, according to this analysis, consists of eight types of consciousness. The first five belong to the familiar five senses of sight, sound, smell, taste, and touch: our eyes are conscious of sight, our ears are conscious of sound, and so on. The mental consciousness, the sixth, is conscious of mental activity, such as thoughts. Unlike the first five, which can only perceive objects as they are, the mind consciousness is able to draw on past experiences, anticipate future experiences, and evaluate present experiences. These six types of consciousness are common to all Buddhist schools, but the seventh and eighth consciousnesses are unique to the Yogācāra tradition. The eighth, or "storehouse," consciousness retains all the wholesome, unwholesome, and neutral seeds of our past deeds and memories. When conditions are right— which might take a moment or multiple lifetimes—these seeds will sprout, develop, and bear fruit in the form of experience. The storehouse consciousness is also sometimes known as the "foundational consciousness" because it forms the foundation of people's experiences throughout their lives and carries their karmic imprint over into future incarnations. It thus accounts for the continuity of a person, their sense of self, not only from moment to moment but also from year to year and lifetime to lifetime. What has happened in the past affects a person's experience of the present and will play a part in determining their future. Although it is regularly mistaken for a self, the storehouse consciousness is in fact in a constant state of flux as seeds are planted, germinate, reproduce themselves, and are exhausted in rapid succession.

The seventh consciousness takes the storehouse consciousness as its underlying basis. It is sometimes referred to as the deluded consciousness because it observes the storehouse consciousness and mistakenly perceives it to be an enduring self. This false sense of self compels people to act based on ignorance and attachment, thus generating more karma and more seeds and perpetuating the cycle of suffering. Once a person becomes aware of how this consciousness functions, however, they can work to disrupt the process, transforming a defiled consciousness into a purified consciousness. For this reason, the seventh consciousness is also known as the liberating consciousness. It has the potential to subvert the ordinary functioning of the mind by directly seeing the conditioned nature of thought. This realization puts an end to erroneous perception, which gradually empties the storehouse consciousness. Vacant, the storehouse becomes like a mirror, impartially and perfectly reflecting what it encounters without impediment or distortion. In this luminous, clarified state, the distinction between perception and perceiver vanishes, ignorance is eradicated, and liberation is attained.

Śīlabhadra was an expert on Yogācāra doctrine and practice, and Xuanzang studied under him longer than any other Indian teacher. Xuanzang's later writings make clear that he viewed Śīlabhadra as his master, but he did not conclude his studies after his years at Nālandā. Instead, he continued to search for additional teachers who could clarify aspects of Yogācāra thought that continued to elude him. Xuanzang's first destination after departing Nālandā was the island of Sri Lanka, where he had heard there were unparalleled scholars of the *Discourse on the Stages of Yogic Practice* and the works of the Sthavira (School of the Elders), an influential tradition of early mainstream Buddhism.[42] As he traveled south through eastern India, Xuanzang paused along the way to consult with prominent scholars. In Kosala, he spent a month with a learned Brahmin studying Dignāga's *Compendium on Valid Knowledge* (*Pramāṇa-samuccaya*), a Yogācāra interpretation of causation and logic. In Dhānakataka, he spent two months with a pair of Buddhist monks who were expert in the Mahāsāṃghika teachings—the primary rivals of the Sthaviranikāya school.

When Xuanzang finally reached the port city of Kancipura, from where he intended to sail to Sri Lanka, he learned that the island's king had recently died and the island was in the midst of a devastating famine. Hundreds of Sri Lankan monks were fleeing to the mainland in search of food and shelter. Xuanzang questioned these refugees and, judging that their understanding did not surpass what he had already learned at Nālandā, he abandoned his plan to visit the island. Instead, he set out on a long circuit across the southern tip of the subcontinent and up the western coast until, after several months, he reached the country Parvata in what is now northwestern Pakistan. Xuanzang describes Parvata as an active center of Buddhist learning with more than ten monasteries and over a thousand monks. According to his *Biography*, he remained in the city for a full two years studying the teachings of the Saṃmitīya (School of Correct Logic).[43]

His tour of India nearly complete, Xuanzang returned to Nālandā in 641. Over the next few years, he maintained his close connection with the monastery but pursued his studies primarily with local scholars living outside Nālandā's walls. After two months at nearby Tiladhāka Monastery, refining his understanding of grammar and logic under the monk Prajñābhadra, Xuanzang moved to Stickwood Hill, where he apprenticed himself to a lay scholar named Jayasena (aka Prasenajit). Jayasena was a former student of Śīlabhadra and an expert in a wide range of Buddhist and non-Buddhist theories.[44]

Although he never ordained as a monk, Jayasena lived as a renunciant hermit devoted to doctrinal study and merit-making activities. In his spare time, he sculpted small stūpas from clay and filled them with hand-copied sūtras—a practice that Xuanzang would also take up in his later years. After two years of study at Stickwood Hill, Xuanzang's lingering questions about the *Discourse on the Stages of Yogic Practice* and other treatises were finally resolved. His studies in India were drawing to a close.

It was during this time that Xuanzang had a dream portending his imminent return to China. According to Huili, Xuanzang saw a vision of Nālandā in ruins. Entering the abandoned monastery, he beheld a golden figure emanating light. The deity, who identified himself as the bodhisattva Mañjuśrī, showed Xuanzang that the villages around Nālandā had been burned to the ground and explained that in ten years the ruler of northern India, King Harṣa, would die and India would descend into chaos. If Xuanzang did not leave soon, the bodhisattva warned him, he might come to harm. After delivering this prophecy, the apparition vanished.[45] Years earlier, Mañjuśrī had appeared to Śīlabhadra in a dream to say that Xuanzang would soon arrive at Nālandā. Now he was alerting Xuanzang that it was time to go.

After nearly sixteen years away, Xuanzang must have been ready to return home. A series of events that were unfolding while he was on Stickwood Hill, however, would delay his trip back to China for another year. King Harṣa was traveling in the country of Udra (present-day Odisha) when local monks, adherents of mainstream Buddhist teachings, openly mocked the Mahāyāna monks of Nālandā as "sky flower" heretics—a slur aimed at people who mistook illusions for reality. The clerics in Udra promoted a text with the combative title of the *Treatise That Destroys the Mahāyāna*. The author of this anti-Mahāyāna tract, Prajñāgupta, was a prominent cleric who had consecrated the king of southern India. Not only were the monks in Udra outspoken critics of northern Mahāyāna monks, but they were also aligned with Harṣa's political rival in the south. When they challenged Harṣa to find a Mahāyāna monk who could refute their treatise, the king was happy to comply. Harṣa sent a letter to Śīlabhadra at Nālandā requesting that he dispatch his best monks to put this matter to rest:

> The Hīnayāna teachers here, relying on their limited views, have composed a treatise slandering the Mahāyāna with cutting language and harmful theories. Disregarding the feelings of others, they want to broadcast this dubious work and hold a debate with other teachers. Your disciple knows that within your monastery there are monks with virtue and talent to spare who have mastered all they have studied. I have therefore agreed to their request and I respectfully order you to accept and respond to their challenge. Select four great worthies who are versed in the inner and outer teachings of their own and other schools to come to my residence in Udra.[46]

On receiving the letter, Śīlabhadra appointed Xuanzang and three other senior monks to represent Nālandā—and thus the Mahāyāna tradition—in the debate.

In debates between rival groups, the stakes could be quite high. These were public events, often attended by current and potential patrons, and the winners were richly rewarded. According to Xuanzang, monks who had mastered the teachings and who were able to eloquently and convincingly express their understanding were treated like royalty, amassing countless followers and abundant offerings. "Those whose teachings are empty and elusive," on the other hand, would be publicly humiliated. They had "their face smeared with red mud, their bodies covered in dust, and they were banished to the wilderness and abandoned in ravines." The terms of some debates could be more even extreme. The loser might have his tongue cut out, Xuanzang reported, or be put to death. These contests, particularly when convened by kings, were not for the faint of heart.

While Xuanzang was preparing to respond to the summons, a non-Buddhist brahmin of the materialist Lokāyata school arrived at Nālandā and brashly challenged the monks to a debate. Adherents of the Lokāyata held that a person's body and mind were made up entirely of physical elements that would disperse after death. One should, they argued, fully indulge the senses while alive, for there would be no transmigration after death. This ran counter to long-established Buddhist positions on self-restraint and the workings of karma, but the brahmin was so confident in his position that he staked his life on it. "If anyone is able to refute any point of my argument," he announced, "I will cut off my head to apologize!"[47] According to Huili, Xuanzang alone accepted the challenge and debated the brahmin in front of an audience that included his teacher Śilabhadra and other resident monks. After Xuanzang effortlessly exposed the logical inconsistencies in the positions of the Lokāyatas and other non-Buddhist schools, the brahmin had no choice but to concede defeat. Xuanzang mercifully spared the man's life, but he did make him his servant. The services rendered were primarily exegetical. After obtaining a copy of the *Treatise That Destroys the Mahāyāna*, Xuanzang asked the brahmin, who had attended several lectures on the text, to walk him through its arguments. Once Xuanzang understood the critique and its weaknesses, he composed his own refutation in sixteen hundred stanzas. When Śilabhadra and other Nālandā monks read the work, simply titled the *Treatise That Eradicates False Views*, they were confident that the upcoming debate was all but won.

Once his treatise was complete, Xuanzang released the brahmin from his service and the man returned to his home in Kāmarūpa, a kingdom that occupied present-day Bengal, Bhutan, and Assam. When Kāmarūpa's king, Kumāra (aka Bhāskaravarman; 600–650), heard about the learned foreign monk residing at Nālandā, he dispatched an envoy to go and request that Xuanzang visit his capital. His mind already turning toward home and his talents already committed to the upcoming debate in Udra, Xuanzang declined the invitation. King Kumāra wrote again, however, this time threatening Śīlabhadra, "If [Xuanzang] does not come, your disciple could become fierce. Recently, King Śaśāṅka was poised to ruin the Dharma and destroy the Bodhi Tree. Does the master think his disciple does not have the same power? I will surely array my elephant troops to gather like clouds and march on Nālandā, smashing it to dust!"[48] It was an unsubtle reminder that Buddhist institutions thrived or perished at the pleasure of regional rulers. Kumāra was raising the example of King Śaśāṅka (r. ca. 590–625), the ruler of the Gauḍa Kingdom, who had attacked Magadha not long before. During the offensive, Śaśāṅka destroyed the monasteries at Bodh Gayā, cut down the Bodhi Tree, set it on fire, and then soaked what remained in sugarcane juice to accelerate rot. Reading the letter, an uneasy Śīlabhadra asked Xuanzang to reconsider: "If you refuse to go, something dreadful could happen."

It was a journey of nearly five hundred miles, across the broad Brahmaputra River and through the dense forests of Assam. Upon Xuanzang's arrival in the capital, the king feted him with fine food, music, and an array of offerings. He passed a leisurely month in this way, but he was surrounded by nonbelievers and there was little to engage him. Kāmarūpa had several hundred deva temples, Xuanzang observed, but "since the rise of Buddhism to the present day, no monastery has been built to invite Buddhist monks. Those who follow the pure faith only do so in private."[49] He gently tried to convince the king of both the efficacy of the Buddhist teachings and the virtues of the Chinese emperor (whose territory lay just two months of hard mountain travel to the northeast), but his sojourn with King Kumāra was unexpectedly, perhaps mercifully, cut short.

Word had reached King Harṣa that Xuanzang was in Kāmarūpa, and he was not pleased. Kumāra and Harṣa were both sovereign kings, but Harṣa held the superior position, and *primas inter pares* protocol dictated that his interests take precedent. Harṣa had already extended an invitation to Xuanzang. Why had that request gone unanswered while Kumāra's was accepted? Kumāra was thus ordered to send the "Chinese monk" to Harṣa immediately. He initially balked at the demand. Xuanzang had traveled such a long way and had stayed only a relatively short time. Even if it cost him his own head, Kumāra told Harṣa's envoy, he would keep Xuanzang in Kāmarūpa for a while longer. By the time the envoy returned with Harṣa's icy response—"Hand over your head"—Kumāra was having second thoughts. Anxious about the consequences of his disobedience, he quickly set out with Xuanzang to meet King Harṣa in the city of Kajunghira (present-day Rajmahal). As a precaution, Huili tells us, they traveled with no less than twenty thousand elephant-mounted troops and thirty thousand boats.

Kumāra's delegation set up a temporary encampment on the northern bank of the Ganges River outside of Kajunghira and waited for King Harṣa to arrive. That evening, torches and candles were seen in the distance. The clamor of hundreds of metal drums marked the footsteps of the approaching king. By the time Harṣa arrived, his anger had apparently dissipated. He made obeisance to Xuanzang and inquired about his home country. Xuanzang delivered a lengthy but apparently convincing paean about the great Tang emperor and his flourishing empire. The following morning, it was Xuanzang's turn to visit the king in his temporary palace. There, he presented Harṣa with his *Treatise That Eradicates False Views*.

The king, according to Huili, was so impressed that he proceeded to berate the mainstream monks in his entourage, declaring, "All your theories have now been refuted!" Harṣa then ordered a great assembly convened at the capital so that all the monks, brahmins, and ascetics throughout India could learn the subtle truth taught by Xuanzang and thus have their arrogant attitudes debunked once and for all.

The camps were broken down and the elephants were saddled for the long journey back to the capital. It must have been an extraordinary sight:

> With the river flowing between them, the two kings proceeded by land and water, leading four divisions of disciplined soldiers. Some rode in boats, some rode on elephants. They were beating drums, blowing conchs, plucking stringed [instruments], and sounding pipes. After traveling for ninety days, they arrived at Kānyakubja and stayed in a great flowering grove west of the Ganges River. At that time, more than twenty kings of various countries, who were the first to receive the summons, gathered for the great assembly with their kingdoms' most talented monks, brahmins, officials, and soldiers.[50]

In his *Record*, Xuanzang gives a detailed description of the elaborate assembly (see "King Śīlāditya"). Its focal point was a golden statue of the Buddha, which a grand procession of hundreds of armored elephants carried to a raised, bejeweled terrace at the beginning of each day (p. 59). After ritually bathing the Buddha, King Harṣa ceremonially distributed offerings of food, jewels, and silk to the thousands of people in attendance. This went on for several days until disaster suddenly struck. The jeweled terrace erupted in flames and the king leapt into the blaze to extinguish it. The fire

The procession at Kānyakubja depicted in a fourteenth-century illustrated biography of Xuanzang from Japan. Source: Minamoto, *Genjō Sanzō e.*

was snuffed out and the king emerged unharmed, but it was an ill omen. Shortly thereafter, while Harṣa was descending the stairs of a stūpa, a man brandishing a knife attacked him. In the ensuing struggle, the king apprehended the culprit and once again escaped without injury. When the assassin was interrogated, he revealed a plot by jealous brahmins to murder the king. They felt Harṣa's faith in the Buddha and Buddhist doctrines had blinded him to the truth of their own teachings and caused him to lose sight of his more deserving non-Buddhist subjects.

In Xuanzang's *Record*, this dramatic episode concludes the assembly; the offenders are banished, the king returns to the capital, and Xuanzang resumes his travels. According to the *Biography*, however, the grand procession and almsgiving (the assassination attempt is not mentioned) were merely a prelude to the main event: the great debate. In Huili's triumphant account, thousands of monks, heretics, and laypeople solemnly gathered to hear a monk from Nālandā read aloud Xuanzang's *Treatise That Eradicates False Views*. A written copy was also posted for all to read. If anyone present could refute a single word of the *Treatise*, Xuanzang would be beheaded. The work, however, was so perfectly conceived that no one could find any flaws. The first day, the crowd sat in silence until nightfall and then adjourned for the evening.

The next day proceeded in the same way—procession, meal, offerings, challenge, and silence. After five days of this, some in the assembly were growing irritated. Who did this foreign monk think he was? Rumors began to spread of a plot to murder Xuanzang. Hearing of this, Harṣa announced that anyone who attempted to harm his guest would be summarily executed, and anyone who so much as slighted him would have his tongue cut out. Unsurprisingly, nobody dared challenge Xuanzang for the remainder of the debate. After eighteen days, he was declared the victor and awarded gold, silver, ornate robes, and other gifts, all of which he modestly declined. The Mahāyāna clerics praised him as "Lord of the Mahāyāna," and even the mainstream monks dubbed him "Lord of Emancipation." It was an extraordinary accomplishment. Xuanzang, a forty-two-year-old monk from China, had bested all of India in debate.

Or had he? There is no other record of Prajñāgupta's *Treatise That Destroys the Mahāyāna* or Xuanzang's rebuttal, the *Treatise That Eradicates False Views*. If this text was the definitive Mahāyāna refutation of Hīnayāna teachings, surely Xuanzang would have carried a copy with him back to China. In a letter written after he had returned home, Xuanzang does mention his participation in a debate in Kānyakubja, but he only alludes to a heated exchange with his friend, the mainstream monk Prajñādeva (see "Letter to Prajñādeva"). He says nothing to indicate that the debate centered on a treatise he had composed or that he alone emerged victorious. Perhaps Xuanzang was too humble to mention such things. It is also possible, of course, that his star-struck disciples inflated his role in the debate. Whatever the case, in all subsequent accounts of his life, Xuanzang's triumph in the great debate stands as the crowning achievement of his studies in India. It was a vivid illustration that although he had arrived in India as a student troubled by doubts, he left as an accomplished master whose knowledge surpassed that of India's most erudite monks. There was, in short, nothing left for Xuanzang to learn in India.

The debate was followed by a great almsgiving festival farther down the Ganges River in Prayāga (near present-day Allahabad). Since becoming king, every five years Harṣa had distributed his accumulated wealth to monks, brahmins, and the poor over a period of seventy-five days. This elaborate display of imperial largess, known as Pañcavārṣika (quinquennial festival), was a long-standing tradition dating back to Aśoka in the third century B.C.E. Xuanzang had probably witnessed something similar in China. "Dharma assemblies without discrimination," as they were called, were introduced to China during the sixth-century reign of the famously pro-Buddhist Emperor Wu (r. 502–49). Later generations of Chinese rulers followed Emperor Wu's example, and several assemblies had been staged in the capital by the time the young Xuanzang left for India. Harṣa's festival, however, was of a different order.

At the confluence of the Ganges and Yamuna rivers, the king had dozens of thatched halls built to store

> gold, silver, pearls, red crystals, emeralds, and sapphires. Beside the halls were several hundred long buildings containing thin silk clothes, clothes made of fine cotton, gold and silver coins, and other things. Kitchens were built separately outside the fence. In front of the treasure storerooms, more than a hundred long buildings were arranged in lines like the rows of stores on the streets of the capital. Each building could seat over a thousand people.[51]

Many of those who had attended the debate in Kānyakubja, including various regional kings and their entourages, came to participate. The distribution of alms proceeded according to rank: offerings to a statue of the Buddha came first. On the following day, the kings honored the God of the Sun, while Śiva was venerated on the third day. Subsequent offerings then flowed to monks, brahmins, ascetics, ordinary people, and the poor. After two and a half months, Harṣa had emptied his treasury, save for his elephants, horses, and weapons, which he prudently retained in case of rebellion or invasion. Even his own clothing and jewelry had been given away, though by tradition these were bought back by other kings and ministers and subsequently returned to him.

When the festival concluded, Xuanzang announced his intention to return to China. For many of the monks he had befriended, the decision was hard to fathom. "India is the birthplace of the Buddha," they reminded him. "Although the Great Sage is gone, his traces remain. To travel around and venerate them is enough to make one's life content. Why would you want to give this up after having come here? China is a barbarian land where people are neglected, and the Dharma is despised. That is why no buddhas have ever been born there. The people have narrow aspirations and deep impurities, so sages do not go there. The air is cold and the land is dangerous. How can you think of returning there?"[52] Xuanzang reportedly responded by quoting an exchange from the *Vimalakīrti Sūtra*, where the noble layman Vimalakīrti asks Śāriputra, "Why does the sun come to Jambudvīpa?" The answer: "To illuminate it and eliminate the darkness." If Xuanzang remained in India, the true Dharma might never be known in China.

Declining Harṣa's and Kumāra's requests for him to remain and live a comfortable life supported by their generous patronage, Xuanzang said his final farewells and joined the northbound army of a regional ruler named Udita. Harṣa supplied him with an elephant, three thousand gold coins, and ten thousand silver coins to cover his traveling expenses. The king also dispatched four of his officials with letters to the rulers of the kingdoms through which Xuanzang would pass, requesting that they provide him with fresh horses and an escort for each leg of his journey. Although Xuanzang had traveled to India with only a small bundle of belongings, he was leaving with hundreds of texts, dozens of statues, relics, and count-less other articles accumulated over the course of his sixteen-year stay. It would take many men and pack animals to safely transport those items thousands of miles over rivers, through mountains, and across political borders.

After two months in the city of Vilaśāna and another month in Udita's capital of Jālandhara, Xuanzang set out with a party of more than one hundred other monks who were also traveling north. Like Xuanzang, many of these monks had come to northern India to study under prominent masters and acquire scriptures and images not yet known in their homelands (see image on p. 65). A large convoy of unarmed clerics transporting so much cargo made a tempting target for bandits. To be on the safe side, the group sent one monk ahead with a message to would-be-robbers: the group had "come from far away in search of the Dharma. What we carry now are scriptures, statues, and relics. We hope you benefactors will protect us and not entertain any other thoughts." Abstruse Buddhist manuscripts and bits of bone were of little value to thieves, and the monks were largely left alone.

The trip was not without its hazards though. When the caravan reached the southern bank of the great Indus River, Xuanzang had his luggage loaded onto boats for the crossing. One of the longest rivers in Asia, the Indus drains nearly half a million square miles and is prone to severe flooding. Xuanzang waded through the swiftly flowing water on the back of his elephant, but a strong wind kicked up waves that upset the boats. The man in charge of Xuanzang's belongings fell overboard along with a portion of the baggage. The man was rescued but the torrent washed away fifty bundles of scriptures and several packets of seeds. So many hard-won texts destroyed so quickly. Xuanzang was devastated and later spent years trying to replace the lost works.

The king of Kapisā, who Xuanzang had met nearly fifteen years earlier, happened to be in the city of Udakhanda, on the northern side of the Indus River. He came to commiserate about the accident, explaining that everyone who attempts to take seeds across meets with the same fate. (The culprit, it seems, was a possessive dragon who lived in the river.) The king, who was preparing to return home and would be traveling in the same direction, offered to accompany Xuanzang on the next leg of his journey. Following more than a month of travel, Xuanzang, the king, and the rest of their entourages reached the capital of Lampāka (present-day Laghmān), a dependency of Kapisā, where thousands of monks and laypeople turned out to welcome them. Xuanzang stayed in the city to attend another seventy-five-day almsgiving festival before continuing northwest. Passing through the foothills of the Hindu Kush mountains, the caravan arrived in Kapisā, where Xuanzang had passed a rains retreat many years before. The king ordered yet another almsgiving assembly, this one lasting just seven days. Laden with offerings, outfitted with provisions for the long journey ahead, Xuanzang finally took leave of the king and set off into the Hindu Kush.

Xuanzang and more than a hundred porters began their ascent, following the same route taken by Alexander the Great nine hundred years earlier. Huili described the hardships of their traverse:

> Traveling for seven days, they came to the summit of a great mountain. The mountain had precipitous cliffs and danger-

Itinerant monk carrying scrolls, ninth century.
Source: *Saiyūki no shiruku rōdo.*

ous, jagged peaks. Some were flat, others were steep—they all had different forms. It is hard to describe how difficult they were to climb. They could not ride their horses so used walking sticks to forge ahead. After another seven days, they reached a high ridge with a village of about a hundred houses at its base. The sheep they raised were as big as donkeys.

They spent a day in the village and then set out again in the middle of the night with a villager riding a mountain camel leading the way. This area had many snow-filled ravines and river crossings. Without the help of their guide, they feared they might fall into them. The next day, they made it out of this dangerous area. At that time, only seven monks and over twenty porters remained. They also had one elephant, ten mules, and four horses. The following day, they reached the base of the range. Following a winding path, they climbed another range. It looked to be covered in snow but it was all white rock. This was the highest range. Although clouds of snow flew past, no snow accumulated here. Reaching the summit at dusk, the wind was so bitterly cold that no one could stand upright. The mountain had neither grass nor trees, only piles of rock rising into peaks like a bamboo forest. The mountain was so high and the wind so strong that birds were unable to fly across it. They could only spread their wings several hundred paces away from the northern and southern ranges. Of all the mountains in Jambudvīpa, none surpasses this one in height.[53]

The group descended from the high country into the lush Kunduz River valley. This was the place where, years earlier, Xuanzang had attended the funeral service of the poisoned Tardu Shad and the installation of his son. Now, Xuanzang gratefully accepted the hospitality of that new ruler, resting for over a month at the king's compound.

Up until this point, Xuanzang had mostly been retracing the route he had taken on his way to India. In the early months of that journey, while waylaid in the city of Gaochang, Xuanzang had promised the king Qu Wentai that he would come back for several years to teach before returning home to China. By the time he reached Kunduz, however, news must have reached Xuanzang that Qu Wentai was dead; in 640, Chinese forces attacked and annexed Gaochang. Instead of backtracking the way he had come, Xuanzang opted for the shorter but more difficult route along the southern Silk Road. Turning east, he entered the foothills of the Pamir Knot, where the Himalaya, Tianshan, Kharakorum, Kunlun, and Hindu Kush ranges meet in a jumble of alpine ridges and deep, maze-like canyons.

Known as the "roof of the world," the Pamirs are one of the highest mountain ranges on earth. With multiple peaks topping twenty-three thousand feet, the range is extensively glaciated and blanketed in snow year-round. Xuanzang entered the mountains together with a caravan of merchants and escorts provided by the king of Kunduz. The group proceeded up the rocky and treeless Great Pamir Valley, on the border of present-day Afghanistan and Tajikistan. At the head of the valley was Lake Zorkul, which Xuan-zang calls "Great Dragon Lake" and describes as an otherworldly place: "The water is as clear and as bright as a mirror. Its depth is unfathomable. The water is bluish-black and has a sweet and refreshing taste. Hidden within are sharks, fish, dragons with and without horns, soft-shelled turtles, alligators, and tortoises. On its surface swim mandarin ducks, swans, geese, cranes, and bustards. All the birds lay giant eggs whose shells are left in the marshes and on the sand."[54] This lake, according to Xuanzang, sat at the very center of the world.

Climbing out of the Pamir River watershed, which drained into the mighty Amu-Darya River in the west, Xuanzang and his party crossed over a high mountain pass, probably Wakhjir (16,152 ft.), and descended into the valley of the Tashkur River, whose waters flowed east toward the Tarim Basin, toward home. Following the river, they reached the country of Kabhanda (present-day Tashkur-gan) and rested for several weeks. Amazingly, the elephant Harṣa had given Xuanzang survived the months of mountain travel. After leaving the village, however, the entire party panicked on encountering a group of bandits and the terrified elephant plunged into the river and drowned. The elephant's salvaged cargo was off-loaded onto horses—the bandits, apparently, were uninterested in their books and buddhas—and the group moved on. Xuanzang and his companions eventually emerged from the mountains several days later and made their way to the city of Kashgar, on the western rim of the Tarim Basin.

It had to be a welcome sight. The hardest travel was now behind them. Kashgar was a major city with a supply of fresh fruits, vegetables, and all manner of provisions to replenish the stores and satisfy the appetites of the weary travelers. The people of Kashgar also supported several hundred Buddhist monasteries and more than ten thousand resident monks, all of whom were students of the Sarvāstivāda school. Xuanzang was still nearly twenty-five hundred miles from the capital at Chang'an, but he had finally returned to Chinese territory. A series of campaigns carried out by Emperor Taizong in the 630s had brought the entire Tarim Basin, including Kashgar, under Chinese control.

After resting and resupplying, Xuanzang and his party followed the established route southeast through the desert to the settlement of Cukuka (present-day Kargilik). The monks in this place were all adherents of the Mahāyāna, but most of the dozens of monasteries lay in ruins with only about one hundred monks left to care for what remained. Despite this decline, Xuanzang reports that a large number of Mahāyāna scriptures were stored in the area: "Of all the places where Buddhism has prevailed, none can surpass this country in its collection of scriptures. Books consisting of one hundred thousand stanzas each amount to more than ten titles, and those of fewer stanzas are widely circulated."[55]

When Xuanzang reached the city of Khotan, he stopped. Khotan was a prosperous, bustling city whose "genial and polite" population included over five thousand Mahāyāna monks who oversaw several hundred monasteries. (Archaeological work carried out in the early twentieth century has confirmed the existence of multiple temples, living quarters, irrigated orchards, and tree-lined avenues.) Xuanzang notes that locals were skilled in spinning and weaving silk and one of the major monasteries, Maza, was built to commemorate the introduction of sericulture to the region. According to local legend, Khotan was one of the first kingdoms outside of China to acquire the jealously guarded silkworms and the seeds of the mulberry trees on which they fed. The contraband was reportedly smuggled into the kingdom by a Chinese princess who had been promised to the king of Khotan in a politically arranged marriage.

Khotan, with its thriving Buddhist culture and its rich local traditions, intrigued Xuanzang and in his *Record* he provides detailed accounts of local legends—some of which mirror those told by the ancient Greek historian Herodotus (484–425 B.C.E.).[56] Practical matters also extended his stay in the area. In an attempt to recover some of the texts that he lost while crossing the Indus River, Xuanzang dispatched emissaries to travel to back to Kashgar and Kucha to seek out and make copies of the missing manuscripts. While waiting for the men to return, he also composed a letter to the Chinese court, confessing that sixteen years earlier he broke the law to travel to India. He duly informed the authorities that he was currently in Khotan making arrangements for the final leg of his return journey (see "Letter from Khotan"). He entrusted the letter to a layman from the kingdom of Gaochang who was en route to the Chinese capital in a caravan of merchants. Xuanzang would not risk returning to China until he received a reply from the court.

He surely knew that word of his travels had already reached the capital and that news of his arrival in Chinese territory would quickly be conveyed to the authorities. If Xuanzang had indeed left China illegally, he could potentially be arrested on his return; his letter was testing the waters. Would he be punished or would he be welcomed home? He had reason to be optimistic. His travels and diplomacy in India had already borne fruit for the emperor. After Xuanzang met with King Harṣa in 641, Harṣa sent envoys to establish formal diplomatic relations with China. The Chinese court responded that same year, sending a Chinese official to accompany Harṣa's envoys back to India. Shortly thereafter, in 642, monks from the Mahābodhi Monastery, where Xuanzang had spent time, traveled to Chang'an to offer Buddhist texts and other artifacts to the Chinese court. The following year, two more Chinese officials made the long trip to India to meet with King Harṣa and King Kumāra—both of whom were supporters of Xuanzang. After visiting Vulture Peak, Mahābodhi Temple, and other Buddhist sites in northern India, the two envoys came back to the Chinese capital in 645 or early 646, shortly after Xuanzang himself returned.[57] Xuanzang had laid the groundwork for a series of diplomatic exchanges and could reasonably assume that his intimate knowledge of western territories, his connections to foreign leaders, and his linguistic skills would place him in good stead with the Chinese emperor.

After waiting seven or eight months, a reply to his letter finally arrived:

> We are extremely happy to hear that the master is coming back after seeking the Way in foreign lands. He may come speedily to see us. Let him bring back those foreign monks who understand the Sanskrit language and the meanings of the scriptures. We have already instructed the authorities of Kustana and other countries, asking them to escort

the master, so that porters and horses may not be lacking. The governor of Dunhuang has also been ordered to receive the master in the desert and the governor of Shanshan will receive him at the Jumo River.[58]

Xuanzang immediately resumed his journey. He still had two thousand miles to cover and the route, which led through pathless marshes and barren deserts, was rough going. He describes a vast wilderness marked only by the bones of the dead and scoured by a burning wind that rendered people and animals faint and hallucinatory. "One sometimes hears singing, screaming, or wailing, but when one goes looking for the source of the sounds they suddenly become lost," he explained. "Many people have died in this way, the victims of ghosts and demons."[59]

After several months, Xuanzang and his party arrived in the outpost settlement of Shazhou. Nearby was the site of the spectacular Buddhist cave complex of Dunhuang, with its exquisite murals, fine sculptures, and well-stocked Buddhist libraries. It is telling that neither Xuanzang nor Huili make any mention of the sights around Dunhuang, which today is designated a UNESCO World Heritage Site. Xuanzang had his sights set on home. From Shazhou, he wrote again to the emperor, letting him know that his return was imminent. At that moment, the emperor was mounting a military campaign against the Koryo Kingdom in present-day Korea, but he dispatched his ministers to arrange for Xuanzang's arrival in the capital. Xuanzang, however, traveled so quickly that he arrived before officials could properly prepare. Traveling by boat along the Wei River and its canal, he approached the outskirts of the capital and was soon mobbed by crowds of curious onlookers. After more than sixteen years and thousands of miles, Xuanzang had returned home.

CHAPTER 3

China

WORD SPREAD QUICKLY through the capital that a native son had returned to Chang'an after nearly seventeen years in the "Western Regions" of India and Central Asia. At dawn on February 8, 645, thousands of people gathered along the capital's tree-lined avenue, Vermillion Bird Street, vying for places with a clear view of the grand procession scheduled for later that day. The broad avenue, as wide as a forty-lane highway running down the center of the walled city, was festooned with hanging banners, colorful canopies, fine tables, and elaborately decorated chariots all supplied by Buddhist temples from the capital. Xuanzang had entered the capital two days earlier and was formally received by several high-ranking court officials. He had remained secluded in a courier station on the outskirts of the city while preparations were made to escort him to one of the capital's most prestigious monasteries, Hongfu ("Vast Blessings") Temple.

Curious crowds were eager to see the exotic treasures that had arrived in dust-covered bundles on the backs of twenty horses. Their first glimpse came the day before the procession, when a great exhibition was held at the southern end of Vermillion Bird Street. One hundred and fifty grains of relics, the physical remains of Śākyamuni that many believed still radiated the force of his awakening, were put out on display. Multiple statues, large and small, some carved of sandalwood, some cast with precious metals, were placed on makeshift altars. These images, which depicted key moments in the Buddha's life, were based on originals created by Indian artisans who, according to tradition, had seen Śākyamuni while he was alive. They were as close as anyone in China would ever come to beholding the appearance of the historical Buddha. In addition to the Buddha's remains and replicas of his body, the Buddha's teachings were also on display. Although almost no one could read any of 657 texts that Xuanzang had collected during his travels, they all understood that these palm-leaf manuscripts contained teachings and techniques that were not yet known in China. Their physical presence alone conveyed a kind of unearthly power, and, once translated, they had the potential to revolutionize everything from medical knowledge to meditation practices.

On the morning of the procession, monks and nuns from the capital's monasteries dressed in their finest robes and flowed slowly up Vermillion Bird Street. From the massive Mingde Gate, with its five passages tunneling more than fifty feet through the heavily fortified city wall, the group walked roughly three miles through the center of the city. Some carried Xuanzang's texts, statues, and relics. Others scattered flowers, held incense censors, beat drums, or sounded bells. Walking north toward the imperial compound, they passed in front of walled aristocratic residential quarters as well as Buddhist monasteries and Daoist temples painted bright red and gold. The procession turned left in front of the Gate of the Vermillion Bird—the main entrance to the inner Imperial City—and continued toward the Western Market with its neighboring Nestorian, Manichean, and Zoroastrian temples. The crowds had grown so thick that officials, fearing a stampede, ordered everyone to remain in place and not attempt to follow the monks. When they arrived at the gates of Hongfu Monastery, Xuanzang's long journey finally came to an end. It was an extraordinary homecoming for a formerly unknown monk who had quietly left the capital many years before.

Xuanzang's new home, Hongfu Monastery, was just west of the thirty-three-foot-tall walls that enclosed the imperial palace compound. The reigning emperor, Taizong (r. 626–649), had built the monastery ten years earlier as a memorial to his late mother. Spacious, well provisioned, and situated in the midst of a bustling city of nearly a million people, Hongfu was a prestigious appointment for Xuanzang. It was also a burden. Life in such a prominent monastery inevitably involved constant official obligations and a host of other distractions. When he first met with the emperor in the weeks following his return, Xuanzang delicately expressed his reservations and requested permission to relocate to the more remote Shaolin Monastery on Mount Song, 260 miles outside the capital. "The common people do not understand," he explained. "They know that I have come from the west and will presume to come to see me, turning my residence into a marketplace."[60] Shaolin Monastery, by contrast, was nestled in the mountains and thus removed from the inevitable interruptions of city life. Emperor Taizong, however, was determined to keep Xuanzang close at hand. Hongfu Monastery was quite peaceful, the emperor countered. Nobody would bother him there. In the end, it mattered very little where Xuanzang wanted to live. He served the emperor now.

Shortly after the master had settled in at Hongfu, Emperor Taizong, as if confirming Xuanzang's concerns, gave him his first assignment. He was to write a detailed account of all the places he had visited and all the things he had seen and heard during his years on the road. The purpose of the work was not just to satisfy the court's curiosity about exotic, little-known lands in the "Western Regions." Emperor Taizong was then in the midst of a protracted military campaign against the Western Turkic Khaganate that controlled territories and lucrative trade routes along China's northwestern borders. Chinese troops had already attacked and occupied some of the cities Xuanzang had visited on his way to and from India. As Xuanzang was readjusting to life in the capital, the court was laying plans for the pacification of the entire Western Khaganate, including the overthrow of its capital at Sūyāb. Xuanzang had been to this and other strategically important cities and could describe the types of crops they grew, the products they traded, the size of their militaries, and the state of their defenses. His *Record of the Western Regions* thus occasionally reads like an intelligence report, particularly when he is describing territories adjacent to China's western frontier.[61] While reporting on the political and economic conditions of western cities, Xuanzang was also careful to assure Taizong that the people beyond China's borders recognized the moral authority of the Chinese emperor and stood in awe of his extraordinary military power. Chinese troops and administrators, he implied, would be welcomed in these foreign lands as liberators. Emperor Taizong is said to have been so impressed with Xuanzang's diplomatic and linguistic skills that he twice asked him to renounce his monastic vows and serve instead as a member of the imperial court. Both times, Xuanzang declined, but he nonetheless remained a loyal servant of the emperor and his administration for the rest of his life.

The *Record of the Western Regions,* the most extensive and detailed account of seventh-century Central Asia and India ever produced, is one of the only original works Xuanzang composed. Its historical value is unparalleled, but it was probably a low priority for Xuanzang. The twelve-fascicle text was completed quickly, in just over a year, and Xuanzang never again wrote about his travels abroad, though later generations never tired of retelling (and embellishing) the story. For the remainder of Xuanzang's life, he focused his considerable energy on the translation and explication of Buddhist texts. He had gone to India to acquire and study major Buddhist treatises, and he was now committed to translating these works and introducing their contents to the people of China. To that end, one of his first tasks was to assemble an elite translation team. In the summer of 645, learned monks were recruited from through-out the empire based on their area of expertise. There were twelve "theory verifiers," clerics whose expertise in Mahāyāna and mainstream teachings qualified them to assess the accuracy of doctrinal interpretations. To help polish the prose, there were nine "literary composers." Further editing was handled by one linguist and one proofreader of Sanskrit. In addition to these twenty-three monks, there were several additional scribes and assistants on hand to manage logistics and oversee the supplies of ink, paper, and brushes that the court regularly provided.

The team was composed of some of China's brightest monks, and they worked at a brisk pace. Xuanzang's own work ethic was legendary. According to his disciple Yancong,

> Every day he made a schedule. If his work was not finished during the day, he would continue during the night. He would put down his brush only after the second watch (9–11 p.m.). After studying sūtras, he would venerate the Buddha and practice the Way, going to sleep at the third watch (11 p.m.–1 a.m.). Rising during the fifth watch (3–5 a.m.), he read Sanskrit texts, marking sections to be translated that day in red. Every day after eating, for two hours in the early evening he lectured on new sūtras and treatises to the monks who had come from every province to resolve their doubts and inquire about the truth.[62]

Translating, attending obligatory events in the monastery, lecturing, meeting with other monks, entertaining dignitaries—Xuanzang had little time to rest. His disciples marveled that, whether working with his students or conversing with guests, he could sit for hours without moving. He never seemed to tire.

By the summer of 648, three years after his translation team began their work, they had translated 175 fascicles of texts. The most highly anticipated was the first complete Chinese edition of the *Discourse on the Stages of Yogic Practice* (*Yogācārabhūmi Śāstra*), the hundred-fascicle text that Xuanzang considered the most complete and perfect expression of the Dharma. Even Emperor Taizong, who seems to have had little genuine interest in Buddhist doctrine, was impressed. After reading Xuanzang's translation, according to Yancong, the emperor remarked that compared with these teachings, "Confucianism, Daoism, and the Nine Schools of Thought are like small pools beside the vast sea. It is absurd to say that the three teachings are equal."[63] This would have been a radical declaration for an emperor who claimed descent from the Daoist sage Laozi and whose officials were deeply steeped in Confucian learning. If Taizong ever did render such a controversial judgment, it was in private; his public pronouncements were far less polarizing. When, at Xuanzang's repeated request, the emperor composed a preface for the new translations, he began by praising the Buddha and the Buddhist teachings. He then extolled Xuanzang for making the arduous journey across mountains and rivers, through bitter cold and sweltering heat, all for the sake of benefiting others. Because of Xuanzang's heroic efforts, Taizong declared, "The teachings of the Sage that were lacking were again made complete, and suffering people once again knew good fortune."[64] Buddhism was not necessarily superior to native Chinese traditions, but now, thanks to Xuanzang, it was more complete and therefore more effective at improving the lives of ordinary people. To speed the spread of these new teachings, Taizong ordered nine copies of Xuanzang's new translations readied for distribution throughout the empire. For the first time, the teachings of *Discourse on the Stages of Yogic Practice*, translated by the empire's most celebrated monk and endorsed by the emperor himself, were available all across China. The problem that Xuanzang had encountered as a young monk—confusion stemming from partial translations and contradictory interpretations of Yogācāra teachings—was now much closer to being resolved.

Xuanzang's work, however, was just beginning. He had hundreds more fascicles of texts to translate and, as a cleric of influence at court, he shouldered the heavy responsibility of shoring up imperial support for Buddhist monks and monasteries. Emperor Taizong had been a stalwart supporter of Xuanzang in the years since his return, but by 648 the emperor's health was failing. Fearing the worst, Taizong asked Xuanzang what meritorious act he could perform to improve his fate. Xuanzang replied that the ordination of monks and nuns would be most effective, and the emperor subsequently called for each of the 3,716 monasteries in the empire to ordain five new monastics. Hongfu Monastery, Xuanzang's residence at the time, was given a special dispensation to ordain fifty clerics. With a single decree, the number of monks and nuns in China grew by over 18,500. The emperor's health, however, continued to decline. When later that year official envoys returned to the Chinese capital from a diplomatic mission to India, they brought with them an Indian physician with a reputation for compounding powerful, life-prolonging elixirs. The doctor was housed in the Office of Precious Metals and appointed a team of assistants to acquire and compound medicinal minerals and plants from throughout China, Central Asia, and India. Emperor Taizong dutifully ingested the resulting concoctions, but his condition only worsened.

With the emperor's death appearing imminent, his ninth son and appointed successor, Li Zhi (628–83), began taking steps to shore up his own position. Modeling himself on his father, Li Zhi threw his support behind Xuanzang and his work. With Xuanzang stationed

at Hongfu, the monastery Emperor Taizong had built in memory
of his late mother, Li Zhi now began construction on a new, even
larger monastery in honor of his own deceased mother. Called Ci'en
("Compassionate Kindness"), it would have ten courtyards and
1,897 bays and was designed to be the largest, most opulent monastic
complex in the empire. Once construction of Ci'en was complete,
Xuanzang was ordered to move from Hongfu to a specially built
cloister within the sprawling new complex. This was a promotion for
Xuanzang—he and his team would have more resources and more
space in buildings specifically designed for translation work—but
it was also a highly visible, carefully choreographed changing of
the guard. In moving from a temple built by Emperor Taizong to
one built by Taizong's soon-to-be successor, Xuanzang was playing
his preordained part in the transfer of imperial authority. The court
accordingly staged the move as a grand public spectacle. Fifteen
hundred carriages, some carrying the relics, images, and texts previously stored at Hongfu, inched their way along avenues lined with
onlookers. Magicians, jugglers, and acrobats performed for the
crowds. Hundreds of bright banners swayed from long poles. Three
hundred newly ordained monks and fifty eminent clerics recruited
to reside at the new monastery walked together with other monks
from the capital, holding incense braziers and flowers. Behind the
clerics came civil and military officials with their attendants and
bodyguards. These in turn were flanked by nine bands of musicians,
playing pipes, sounding bells, and beating drums. The emperor,
the heir apparent, and members of the imperial household watched
from a high tower as the procession passed by the imperial palace.
The main Buddha image from Hongfu arrived at the gates of Ci'en
and was ceremoniously received by high officials and conveyed to
the main hall, as if the Buddha himself were accepting a new post
and serving a new lord. Five months later, Taizong was dead and

the twenty-one-year-old Li Zhi ascended the throne as Emperor
Gaozong (r. 649–83).

For the next eleven years, Ci'en Monastery was Xuanzang's primary home and the center of his translation work. As the preeminent center of Sanskrit studies and Buddhist translation in China,
it housed an unparalleled collection of Sanskrit and other non-
Chinese Buddhist texts. Xuanzang maintained ties with monks
in India and Central Asia, and the hundreds of volumes of Indic
manuscripts he had carried to China were augmented by additional
works donated by monks and emissaries arriving from the Western
Regions. To accommodate this growing collection and protect it
from fire, Xuanzang requested the construction of a massive tower
built of rammed earth. In what must have amounted to one of
the greatest estate sales in recent memory, the costs of construction were covered by selling the clothing and other belongings
of deceased members of the imperial household. The newly built
210-foot-tall library, known as the Great Wild Goose Stūpa, was the
tallest structure in the capital. A later poet marveled that "its four
corner eaves blot out the bright sun, its seventh story rubs the blue
sky's vault."[65]

Ci'en was a thriving hub of Buddhist activity in the heart of the
Chinese capital, and Xuanzang stood at its center. Talented and
ambitious clerics from throughout China and from as far away as
Korea and Japan gravitated to Ci'en to study with Xuanzang and
immerse themselves in the new Indian Buddhist doctrines that he
was teaching. A handful of these monks, following long apprentice-
ships on the translation team and personal instruction by Xuanzang,
fanned out to other temples within the capital and in the provinces,
helping to establish Xuanzang's interpretation of Yogācāra as the
preeminent Buddhist tradition in the empire. Xuanzang's foreign-

born disciples later carried his teachings and translations back to their native countries, establishing Yogācāra temples in the cities of Nara and Gyeongju. In this way, in relatively rapid succession, Indian Buddhist texts and teachings spread thousands of miles from Nālandā to the capitals of China, Korea, and Japan.

The intricacies of Yogācāra theory were of paramount importance to Xuanzang and his close disciples, but they were far too arcane for all but the most scholarly of Xuanzang's lay devotees. These men and women were attracted to Xuanzang's reputation as a cosmopolitan traveler, learned scholar, and disciplined cleric. He also cut an exotic figure. According to his disciples, Xuanzang was an extraodinary seven feet tall and "liked to wear clothes from Gandhāra cut from fine cotton cloth and tailored to fit just right."[66] Xuanzang was surely an object of fascination, but laypeople were also intrigued by the promise of new, more efficacious techniques for securing health, happiness, and security in this life and the next. Several prominent laypeople, along with hundreds of monks and nuns, formally committed themselves to the path leading to buddhahood by receiving the bodhisattva precepts from Xuanzang. The bodhisattva precepts, unlike the conventional *prātimokṣa* precepts observed by all monks and nuns, were exclusive to Mahāyāna traditions and could be received by monastics and laypeople alike. These vows committed the recipient to working for the liberation of all beings rather than their own personal salvation. The standard form of these precepts in China was based on what modern scholars regard as an apocryphal text, the *Brahmā's Net Sūtra* (*Fanwang jing*), but Xuanzang had received a somewhat different set of vows from his teacher Śīlabhadra while studying at Nālandā. This new version of the bodhisattva precepts, derived from the forty-first fascicle of *Discourse on the Stages of Yogic Practice*, was promoted as particularly powerful. According to Xuanzang, these precepts were one thousand times more efficacious than the *prātimokṣa*.

Xuanzang seated. 13th–14th c., Japan. Source: *Tenjiku e.*

In the spring of 651, several prefectural governors arrived at Ci'en Monastery and formally requested the bodhisattva precepts from Xuanzang. During the ensuing ceremonies, they each bowed before a buddha image, bared their right shoulders, and knelt on the ground. Xuanzang instructed them on the meaning and import of the vows and warned against committing any of the four grave offenses: benefiting oneself at the expense of others; being stingy with material possessions or with the teachings; harboring ill will or acting out of anger; and criticizing the bodhisattva teachings or promoting false doctrines (see "Bodhisattva Precepts"). If any of these offenses were committed, the bodhisattva vow and the merit it generated would be nullified. Forty-five additional minor rules accompanied these commitments. If violated, these could be redeemed through repentance. After vowing to live in accord with these strictures, the governors bowed, presented offerings, and thanked Xuanzang for conferring on them "the Dharma that was previously unknown and giving rise to the supreme mind of the Way."[67]

The governors who received the bodhisattva precepts were laypeople. After the ceremony, they returned to their homes and continued to support their families and serve in their official capacities. But many other people went further, abandoning the life of a householder and entering the monastic order as monks and nuns. Xuanzang personally oversaw the ordination of hundreds of new clerics, swelling the ranks of the sangha and, in the process, often strengthening ties that bound powerful aristocratic families to the Buddhist order. Xuanzang's most influential patron was undoubtedly Emperor Gaozong, and on at least two occasions he personally ordained members of the imperial family. In 656, Xuanzang was summoned to the newly constructed Helin nunnery to preside over the state-sponsored ordination of the late Emperor Gaozu's concubine—Emperor Gaozong's own former tutor, Née Xue (fl. 626–56). Another major ordination took place later that same year, when Emperor Gaozong's wife, Empress Wu (aka Wu Zetian; 623 or 625–705), was recovering from a difficult pregnancy with her third son. Earlier, when problems first became apparent, she formally took refuge in the Buddha, Dharma, and Sangha and asked Xuanzang to confer divine protection on her and her unborn child. Xuanzang reassured the empress that all would be well but asked that in return, if the baby was born a boy, he be given to Xuanzang to raise as a monk. The empress agreed, and Xuanzang proceeded to pray for a safe delivery. Writing to the emperor and empress shortly before the birth, Xuanzang was delighted to report the appearance of an unusual red bird hopping up and down near the imperial throne. He explained to the bird that the empress was at risk of a premature birth and asked for a sign indicating a smooth delivery. The bird then walked toward Xuanzang and allowed him to stroke it. "To repay its kindness, I tried to have it receive the three refuges," Xuanzang wrote. "I followed it back and forth but it flew off before I could catch it."[68]

After a healthy baby boy was born to the empress, Xuanzang wrote again to the emperor, reminding him of his promise. "I humbly wish that your earlier command will not be violated and [the prince] will immediately be allowed to leave home [and become a monk]. He will be transformed from an heir of the people's king to a son of the Dharma king."[69] The child was accordingly named Prince Buddha Light and symbolically entrusted to Xuanzang's care, making Xuanzang an honorary member of the imperial family. At the age of one month, Xuanzang tonsured the baby and presented him with gilded copies of the *Perfection of Wisdom Sūtra*, the *Illustrated Sūtra of Requiting Kindness*, a Buddhist robe, and other monastic implements. Someday, Xuanzang predicted, all Buddhist monks would seek his protection and scholars would hang on his instruction. The young monk prince later became Tang Emperor Zhongzong (r. 694, 705–710). He was only eight years old when Xuanzang passed away, and although he never seems to have seriously pursued monastic life, he did become a great champion of Buddhist monks and monasteries.

Xuanzang's close relationships with the emperor and aristocrats brought tremendous benefits. Not only was his work fully supported and sanctioned by the court, but he was also able to influence governmental policy for the benefit of the sangha. Conditions for Buddhist monks and nuns improved, Buddhist teachings were promoted and distributed, new Buddhist temples were constructed, and influential members of the court were converted to the faith. These were extraordinary successes for the sangha, but in the diverse religious culture of the capital, every gain for Buddhists monks and laypeople was a potential loss for their rivals. Not everyone was convinced that Buddhist monastics should have the ear of the emperor, enjoy the privileges of tax exemption, or depend on hard-working laypeople for their support. For those committed to the infallibility of Daoist or Confucian teachings, the promotion of Buddhist doctrines was a dangerous mistake and the construction of extensive monastic complexes was a waste of resources. For all the allies that Xuanzang won over to his cause, he inevitably enflamed the ire of his opponents.

Buddhism held a precarious position in mid-seventh-century China. After Buddhist texts, images, and devotees first began to trickle into China from India and Central Asia via trade routes during the first century, there followed a long period where the tradition was practiced primarily by immigrant populations and the Chinese-born children of non-Chinese families. Only later, after the first sūtras were translated, did some Han Chinese make the leap from disinterest and confusion to curiosity and devotion. A small but growing minority were attracted to the exotic, sophisticated philosophical system with its rigorous and highly organized regimes of self-cultivation. Buddhist texts and their proselytizers held out enticing promises of prosperity and protection in this life and lives to come. They also introduced a vast and colorful pantheon of buddhas and bodhisattvas, imbued with extraordinary power and boundless compassion, who were committed to safeguarding the faithful. Some influential members of the court saw Buddhism as an important supplement to the power of the state. Imperially sanctioned and supported monasteries, established throughout the empire, performed ceremonies for the protection of the people, the long life of the emperor, and the well-being of deceased imperial ancestors. They fed the poor, instilled morality, provided lodging for travelers, and held memorial rites for those who died during military campaigns. The Buddhist tradition, many believed, helped maintain peace and stability within the realm.

The enthusiastic reception the Buddhist teachings received in some quarters was countered by fierce opposition in others. The Buddhist tradition of "leaving home" to become monks and nuns, for example, was anathema to fundamental Chinese notions of filial piety. Law required children to support their parents and paternal grandparents or suffer penal servitude. Buddhist monastics were not only accused of abandoning their responsibilities to their parents—they were also labeled social and economic parasites for living off the donations of others while contributing nothing of material value to the communities that supported them. China, moreover, already had its own highly developed cosmological, philosophical, and soteriological systems that often ran counter to basic Buddhist tenets. The Buddhist positions that our ordinary perceptions are flawed, that the world as it ordinarily appears is in fact illusory, and that life is characterized by suffering contradicted basic Chinese cosmogonic principles based on the notion of the Dao, or Way—the origin and animator of all things. The Dao was the very substance of reality made manifest in both the material and immaterial realm. While many people celebrated the Buddhist teachings as a powerful new technology for salvation, others saw it as an existential threat to the foundations of Chinese civilization. During the turbulent centuries that preceded the Tang Dynasty, public sentiment vacillated between the extremes of pious devotion and patronage and virulent opposition and persecution.

When the founder of the Tang Dynasty, Emperor Gaozu (r. 618–26), overthrew the short-lived Sui Dynasty (581–618), he and his ministers were determined to reverse the pro-Buddhist policies of their predecessors and reestablish indigenous Chinese systems of thought and practice. Emperor Gaozu himself claimed descent from Laozi, the mythical figurehead of the Daoist tradition, and when he pronounced on the relative rankings of the three teachings in China, Daoism was accorded pride of place at the top. Confucian teachings were a close second and the teachings of Buddhism were relegated to the bottom. Court officials under Gaozu regularly accused Buddhist monks of arrogance, avarice, tax evasion, and social subversion. One of the most virulent anti-Buddhists among Gaozu's advisors, the Daoist priest Fu Yi, submitted a memorial to the throne calling for the eradication of the barbarian tradition:

[In the era before Buddhism came to China] there were no barbarian deities within the emerald seas...Everyone revered the teachings of Confucius and Laozi because there was no barbarian Buddha...From that time forward, the evil barbarians multiplied and flourished, and the majority of them mixed with the Han...The dissolute language of the evil barbarians was even used in the study of Confucius. It is warped like the singing of frogs, and in listening to it the root of Confucianism was lost...Corvée laborers and skilled craftsmen do nothing but set up mud barbarians [statues of the Buddha]. They strike Chinese bells and gather together false crowds of barbarian monks to dazzle the eyes and ears of innocent folk...I ask that the heretical teachings of the barbarian deity [the Buddha] return to India and all the monks be sent back to their hometowns...In the Western Regions barbarians are born from mud. Therefore they naturally worship pagodas and statues made from mud and tiles...Today they still have the stench of fur and the faces of men but the hearts of beasts. The four categories of monks, owls, donkeys, and mules are the evil spawn of greed and contrariness...If we were to transmit the teachings of

Confucius to the Western Regions, the barbarians would certainly be unwilling to practice them . . . The Buddha is a household ghost of one particular clan and cannot simultaneously act as a ghost for other lineages. How can a living Han be urged to give offerings to a dead barbarian?[70]

Fu Yi's xenophobic diatribe was circulating while Xuanzang was still living in Chang'an before leaving on his pilgrimage to India. Even Confucian officials found it too extreme, but the sentiments that it expressed—that the Buddhist teachings posed a threat to Chinese culture—were widely shared by many both during Gaozu's time and during the reign of his son and successor, Emperor Taizong. Gaozu's proclamation that the number of Buddhist monasteries in the capital be reduced from 120 to just three was later rescinded. However, in 631, after five years on the throne, Taizong officially forbade the practice of monks and nuns receiving homage from their parents, which he and his advisors saw as a perverse inversion of the ethos of filial piety. Following protests by prominent Buddhist clergy, that edict too was later retracted, but it was followed by a series of declarations that officially elevated the doctrines of Daoism above those of Buddhism and gave Daoist priests precedence over Buddhists monks during state ceremonies.

The court delivered these blows to the Buddhist clergy while Xuanzang was away in India. After his return, Xuanzang's erudition, experience, and political savvy won him the favor first of Emperor Taizong and then of his son and later successor, Emperor Gaozong. No other Buddhist monk enjoyed this level of access and influence at court, and Xuanzang felt an obligation to use his position to lobby for greater imperial support for Buddhist monks and monasteries. He successfully petitioned Gaozong to rescind an earlier order that crimes committed by Buddhist and Daoist monks be tried in secular courts, convincing him instead to reestablish hybrid lay-monastic courts to try serious monastic offenses. Xuanzang's repeated request to eliminate the preference for Daoist over Buddhist priests, however, was never granted, and he and his disciples remained on the defensive against accusations that Buddhist teachings were inferior to or derivative of Daoism.

Daoist critiques of Buddhism ranged from the historical—claiming that Laozi traveled west to India after writing the *Daodejing* and his teachings there became the basis for Indian Buddhism—to the metaphysical. According to this latter line of reasoning, because all things originate from the Dao, it stands to reason that the Buddha and his teachings must also issue from that same source. The Buddhist tradition, then, is merely a second-order teaching, and just as the Buddha and his teachings flow from the Dao, Buddhist monastics necessarily follow behind Daoist masters. Many officials also felt passionately that rather than passively allow Indian Buddhist traditions to influence the culture of China, the government should be more active in spreading Chinese thought abroad. The court accordingly dispatched missionaries to the Tang's neighbors and political rivals, the kingdom of Koguryo (modern North Korea), in 626 and 643 in an effort to spread the teachings of the *Daode jing*. When Emperor Taizong, on the advice of an official who had recently returned from India, requested that Xuanzang translate the *Daode jing* into Sanskrit so that the people of India could appreciate the wisdom of the Dao, Xuanzang begged off. The language of the text was too difficult to translate into Sanskrit, he protested, and the people of India would not be able to make sense of it anyway. It would be confusing at best, the object of ridicule at worst.[71]

There were different opinions about the relative merits of Buddhism and Daoism in the capital. Some officials wanted to include the *Daode jing* as a compulsory text in the imperial exams, an honor that had never been considered for Buddhist works. Others challenged Buddhists on theoretical grounds. When Emperor Gaozong staged a series of public debates between Buddhist monks and Daoist masters, Xuanzang's disciples, trained in the rigorous Indian method of "elucidating the cause" logic, were regularly appointed to represent the Buddhist side. According to records of these debates—composed, not incidentally, by a prominent Buddhist cleric—Xuanzang's disciples were easily able to demonstrate the logical inconsistencies of the Daoists' theses and thus were consistently declared the winners.[72] Xuanzang was not personally involved in these debates, which must have seemed beneath a monk of his lofty status, but when attacks on his Buddhist teachings issued not from minor Daoist priests but from influential court officials, he was compelled to defend himself.

The controversy, recorded in detail in Xuanzang's biography, was sparked by Xuanzang's recent translation of the eminent Indian Buddhist epistemologist Dignāga's *Gateway to the Correct Procedure for Elucidating the Cause (Nyāyamukha)*.[73] This work, which presented a detailed exposition on the principles of logic and the criteria for constructing and refuting proofs, was famously difficult to penetrate and no fewer than three of Xuanzang's disciples had composed commentaries attempting to clarify its meaning. When the chief of the Imperial Medical Bureau, Lü Cai (606–65), read Xuanzang's translation of the *Gateway* together with his disciples' commentaries, he detected inconsistencies and errors of interpretation and so decided to write his own, definitive commentary on Dignāga's treatise. His work, he explained, would "follow the good opinions of the three teachers as explained in their works but refute their doubtful views with my own standpoint."[74] Lü Cai was well versed in Daoist metaphysics, and he argued that the theories underlying the *Gateway* were simply variations on ideas already expressed in native Chinese texts. The form of Buddhism Xuanzang and his disciples promoted, in other words, was essentially a convoluted variation of principles expressed with greater eloquence and clarity by ancient Chinese philosophers. The people of China, Lü Cai pronounced, need not bother trying to make sense of these repetitive and unnecessarily complicated foreign doctrines.

Such a direct challenge to the Buddhist tradition in general and to Xuanzang's disciples in particular could hardly go unanswered. When Huili, Xuanzang's loyal disciple and biographer, wrote an uncharacteristically angry letter to the left premier, he protested that Lü Cai "with his mediocre talent" had arrogantly misconstrued the meaning of the text in a shameless attempt to curry favor with government officials. A series of rebuttals and counter-rebuttals followed in quick succession. One of Lü Cai's colleagues, a scholar from the Board of Rites, responded that Lü was a philosopher known for his eloquence, virtue, and penetrating insight. Lü Cai's interpretation of the *Gateway*, he pointed out, was shared by several other prominent officials, and Buddhist monks were simply upset that lay scholars' understanding of Buddhist texts surpassed their own. The monk and translator Mingjun, after politely conceding that Lü Cai was indeed an erudite and accomplished official, charged that he and his colleagues' attempts to paint the Buddhist teachings as poorly executed copies of Daoist and Confucian theories were not only demonstrably wrong but also arrogant in the extreme. "What Lü Cai says is wrong is not wrong," Mingjun wrote. "What he says is right is not right."[75] As the insults mounted, Emperor Gaozong intervened, suggesting that the matter be settled once and for all with a public debate between Lü Cai and Xuanzang. It would have been an extraordinary event—prominent scholar-official squares off against learned Buddhist monk—but it never happened. Recognizing the futility of debating Buddhist logic with China's foremost expert on the topic, Lü Cai, according to the undoubtedly biased account preserved in Xuanzang's biography, issued a bland apology and withdrew from the debate.

As Xuanzang was defending his new teachings against attacks from Daoists and officials, he was also facing some opposition from prominent members of his own Buddhist community. Some monks disapproved of his style of translation, which privileged fidelity to the Sanskrit original over fluency of the Chinese prose. They preferred the more eloquent, if less precise, translations of the Central Asian monk Kumārajīva (344–413). Even more controversial, however, were the selection of texts Xuanzang chose to translate and the doctrinal positions those treatises and commentaries expressed. The teachings of Yogācāra were known in China prior to Xuanzang's pilgrimage to India—exposure to Asaṅga's work was, after all, the initial inspiration for his journey—but they were understood somewhat differently. Previous interpretations of Yogācāra doctrine supported the widely accepted Mahāyāna position that all beings shared a universal buddha nature. This doctrine, evocatively referred to as the "Womb of the Thus-Come Ones" (tathāgata-garbha), holds that all people contain within them the potential for awakening, envisioned as an embryo of a buddha. Properly nurtured, this embryo could be brought to term, a new buddha could be born, and liberation attained.

The interpretation of Yogācāra that Xuanzang learned at Nālandā and subsequently introduced to China was more complicated and, for many, more difficult to accept. According to this view, there are in fact two different types of buddha nature. The first, "buddha nature in principle," is inherent in all beings. The second, "buddha nature in practice," refers to the potential to manifest buddhahood, which is determined by the presence or absence of untainted seeds within our consciousness and is not available to everyone. Those who possess the proper seeds are able, through many lifetimes of practice, to become buddhas. Those who lack these pure seeds will never be awakened no matter how long and how faithfully they follow the bodhisattva path. These unfortunate people are *icchantikas*, beings condemned to wander in *saṃsāra* for eternity.

The very idea that some people are predestined for buddhahood while others are forever damned flew in the face of Chinese indigenous thought, which took for granted an underlying unity and equality of all things. Chinese readings of Mahāyāna Buddhism sometimes went so far as to assert that not only did all *people* have the potential for awakening, but indeed all *things*—animals, grasses, pebbles, and tiles—were imbued with a single, all-pervading buddha nature. Xuanzang's so-called "new Yogācāra" challenged deeply held convictions about the structure of the world in general and human potential for liberation in particular, and many monks rejected his teachings as both mistaken and dangerous. While the sangha as a whole was undoubtedly pleased to see one of their own wield his influence at court to spread the faith and secure stronger support for Buddhist monks and monasteries, Xuanzang's teachings were not universally accepted and his position as the most prominent cleric in the empire was not without controversy.

Positions of power in imperial China conferred privilege and for that reason they could be extremely precarious. The court of the Tang Dynasty was divided into factions of ideological allies and influential families vying for advantage. As Xuanzang drew closer to members of the imperial family and elite aristocratic clans, he inevitably became entangled in the political intrigues that were endemic to the inner court. Even the position of the emperor could be fraught—Emperor Taizong had imprisoned his own father in order to secure his path to the throne—and the question of succession was always open ended. Emperor Taizong had at least fourteen sons, most of whom came from different mothers. Which of those boys would become the next emperor? Mothers tried to position their sons to inherit the throne and groups of officials accordingly cast their lots with different candidates. The stakes were high. Those who backed the right prince would have their fortunes elevated overnight. Those who chose poorly ran the risk of ruin. Once a new emperor was finally enthroned, rivals needed to be contained or eliminated, and the allegiance of the old guard to the new regime could not be in doubt.

Emperor Gaozong, Taizong's ninth son, rose to power only after a protracted and bitter struggle with his older brothers. Once on the throne, he launched a purge of officials deemed insufficiently loyal. Among those demoted, exiled, or killed were members of the court who had closely served his father as well as those who had backed one of his brothers in the struggle for succession. Xuanzang, a close ally of Taizong, might have initially been viewed as suspect, and some scholars have suggested that Gaozong initially took steps to restrict Xuanzang's freedom and limit his influence.[76] Any doubts Gaozong might have harbored about Xuanzang's reliability were soon put to rest, however, and he maintained his position as one of the most prominent clerics in the capital. Imperial favor notwithstanding, incessant court intrigues and official obligations took a toll on Xuanzang and he began looking for a way to extricate himself from the burdens of imperial patronage.

The atmosphere in the capital grew considerably more tense in the winter of 655, when one of Emperor Gaozong's concubines, Wu Zetian, was installed as empress. Empress Wu moved quickly to consolidate her position. Later historians would judge the first and only woman to serve in the capacity of emperor harshly. Empress Wu was accused of murdering her own child to gain political advantage, torturing and mutilating her opponents, having affairs with underlings, and relying on superstition rather than reason. Her most egregious crime in all likelihood was to be a woman with the audacity and intelligence to rule over a deeply patriarchal bureaucracy. In the face of fierce opposition, she tolerated no dissent. Officials suspected of opposing the empress were demoted, exiled, or killed. The heir apparent—the son of another of Gaozong's consorts—was deposed and Empress Wu's eldest son, Li Hong (652–675), was named the new crown prince. The purges sent a chill through the court, and Xuanzang, who had extensive connections with a wide range of officials, had reason to be concerned. In the span of a few years, most of Xuanzang's allies at court had either died or been demoted. Xuanzang survived the transfer of power, maintaining his close relationship with Emperor Gaozong and eventually winning the favor of Empress Wu, but his work suffered. In 656, Gaozong declared that henceforth, a group of officials would supervise all of Xuanzang's translations and would be at liberty to "polish and improve them as required." This announcement, framed as a gift of assistance but surely intended and understood as an effort to monitor and control the team's work, greatly slowed their progress. The famously prolific group produced just four fascicles of texts between 655 and 658.

In the midst of this difficult period, during the fall of 657, Xuan-zang once again requested permission to leave the capital and relo-cate to Shaolin Monastery on Mount Song. He was getting old, he pleaded, and his strength was failing. Ever since his travels in the high mountains of Central Asia, he had suffered from a mysterious "cold disease," which caused intense pain in his heart when it flared up. He also suffered back pain, bone and muscle aches, appetite loss, insomnia, and trouble breathing. What he wanted now was a quiet place to work and recuperate far from the stresses and distractions of the capitals. Mount Song had remote monasteries that had long served as centers for Buddhist translation. When he first returned to China from India, Xuanzang had asked Emperor Taizong to allow him to settle on Mount Song but he was refused. Now, over a decade later, he begged Emperor Gaozong to "make an exceptional show of virtue and allow me to quit the common world of dust and noise, to sweep away the traces of the human realm. Allow me to go among the deer and follow the flocks of ducks and cranes; to perch myself atop rocks and shelter my shadow in the shade of a tree" (see "Letter to Emperor Gaozong"). The emperor denied the request and warned him not to ask again.

Disheartened, Xuanzang remained a virtual hostage in the imperial palace in Luoyang. His illness returned, and he was forced to sneak out of the palace to seek medical treatment in a monastery. Leaving the palace without permission was a crime and when he was discovered and reported to the emperor, Xuanzang expected to be punished. The emperor merely ordered him to return to the palace to continue his translation work. It may have been punishment enough. Xuanzang was trapped in the capital, unable to leave the palace, and cut off from his library and his translation team at Ci'en Monastery over two hundred miles away.

In 658, Emperor Gaozong announced that Xuanzang would relocate to yet another newly constructed imperial monastery back in Chang'an. Ximing ("Western Brightness") Monastery was built to celebrate the recovery of Empress Wu's son, the crown prince Li Hong, from a serious illness. As the ceremonial monastery of the future emperor, the complex was meant to surpass temples built in honor of previous rulers, and Ximing's ten courtyards and four thousand bays were spread over half a city block. The court staged another grand ceremony to inaugurate the new complex. According to one account, "the sounds of flutes and drums shook the earth. Incense and flowers filled the air. From the northern part of the city to the monastery in the south, crowds filled the streets for several miles."[77] Despite the pageantry and the palatial setting, the working conditions at Ximing were hardly ideal. Members of Xuanzang's translation team from Ci'en Monastery were not among the fifty monks selected by the emperor to relocate to Ximing, and no translation ever seems to have been produced there. Instead, Xuanzang spent his time entertaining a steady stream of palace messengers and courtiers. With all the offerings he received, he paid to have stūpas constructed, sūtras copied, images cast, alms given to the poor, and resources provided for visiting monks from India. What he wanted most, however, was to quit the capital and resume his translation work.

Emperor Gaozong refused to let Xuanzang relocate to a remote Buddhist monastery, but when, in the winter 659, Xuanzang asked permission to move to the emperor's secluded summer palace, his request was granted. Yuhua ("Jade Flower") Palace was in the mountains roughly eighty miles to the north of Chang'an, and Xuanzang had previously accompanied the emperor there during the hot summer months. At Yuhua, Xuanzang would have the quiet he had long sought, and the emperor still could keep him within his orbit. The timing was also fortuitous. Just one year later, Gaozong suffered a paralyzing stroke that left him partially blind and unable to function. Empress Wu, who had been steadily accumulating power for years, stepped in to fill the void, becoming the de facto ruler of the empire, a position she would hold until just before her death in 705. The empress was a great patron of Buddhism—she was the first Tang ruler to formally elevate Buddhists above Daoists and even claimed to be an incarnation of the future buddha Maitreya—but the public ascent of the first female ruler in China sent shockwaves through the exclusively male bureaucracy.[78] Many members of the court viewed her as an illegitimate usurper whose time on the throne was a disastrous but temporary interruption of the glorious patriarchy of the Li family's Tang Dynasty.

Safely settled in the mountains several days' journey from Chang'an and Luoyang, Xuanzang was spared much of the intrigue that preoccupied people in the capitals. He no longer needed to publicly perform his allegiance to the empress and her inner circle; he was liberated from entertaining guests and donors; and he was no longer expected to manage the affairs of a bustling imperial temple. At that time, hundreds of monks from Ximing were protesting new imperial edicts requiring them to bow down before their parents and members of the imperial family, but Xuanzang was at Yuhua, quietly and methodically pursuing his translation work. In the five years between 660 and 664, Xuanzang and his team translated an astonishing 670 fascicles of texts, an average of 134 fascicles each year. These included two of the texts that are among the most influential works of the East Asian Yogācāra tradition: the *Treatise Establishing Consciousness Only* (*Cheng weishi lun*) and the *Treatise on Twenty Verses of Consciousness Only* (*Viṃśatikā*).[79] The crowning achievement of this period was the massive *Great Perfection of Wisdom Sūtra* (*Mahāprajñāpāramitā Sūtra*) in six hundred fascicles. The daunting length of this work initially tempted Xuanzang to dispense with his usual method of carefully comparing different editions, researching unfamiliar phrases, correcting textual errors, and then translating verbatim. Instead, he briefly experimented with the approach taken by translators like Kumārajīva, who famously left out repetitive or superfluous sections in an effort to render his translations more concise and easier to read. However, after a nightmare in which he saw himself adrift in a leaky boat and then walking along a precipitous ridge, Xuanzang concluded that altering the words of buddhas and bodhisattvas was simply too dangerous. He would translate accurately or not at all. For Xuanzang's disciples at least, there was no doubt which approach was superior. Xuanzang, they said, was like a great lake or river. As for Kumārajīva and others, they were more like "ditches by the side of the road."[80]

With the completion of the *Great Perfection of Wisdom Sūtra* in 663, Xuanzang's energy, which once seemed boundless, was depleted.

The following year, he and his team finished translating two shorter works and were preparing to begin another major project: the 120-fascicle *Great Sūtra of Accumulated Treasures* (*Mahāratnakūṭa Sūtra*). Xuanzang dutifully started the project but after translating just a few lines, he set down his brush. He was done. All he wanted now, he told his fellow monks, was to "practice the Way." Xuanzang had spent his entire life traveling, studying, and translating. Despite all that he had accomplished, he regretted that he never had sufficient time to "practice meditation, to clarify my mind and still its waves, to control the untamed ape of my emotions and restrain the charging elephant of my will." Now, sensing the approach of death, he set aside all other matters and spent the following weeks venerating stūpas, making buddha images, and engaging in meditation.

One winter night, nine days into the new year, while Xuanzang was crossing a drainage ditch behind his quarters, he fell and injured his leg. Confined to bed, his body began to fail and his breathing grew labored. His disciples compiled a list of all the things he had accomplished over the course of his life and read it aloud: he had translated a total of 74 texts in 1,338 fascicles; made one thousand images of Maitreya and hundreds of thousands of clay images; hand-copied the *Diamond Sūtra*, the *Original Vows of the Medicine Master Tathāgata of Lapis Light*, *Dhāraṇī of the Six Gates*, and other sūtras ten times each; given alms to over ten thousand poor people and monks; lit hundreds of thousands of lamps and redeemed countless beings. Reminded of all he had accomplished and all the people he had helped, Xuanzang felt a sense of peace. He made a final confession and then gave away his robes and other possessions. Before an image of the Buddha, he made a vow to be reborn in Tuṣita Heaven, where he hoped to join the inner circle of the future buddha Maitreya until the time when they would descend again into the world to continue the work of saving all beings. Then, at midnight,

Xuanzang's stupa (center) at Xingjiao Monastery flanked by the stupas of his disciples Ji (left) and Wŏnch'ŭk (right), photographed in 1906. Source: Tokiwa Daijō, et al. *Wan Qing Minguo shiqi Zhongguo mingsheng guji tuji.*

on the fifth day of the second month of 664, Xuanzang laid down on his right side—the posture of the dying Buddha—and stopped breathing. At that moment, disciples outside the hall reported seeing four white auroras arch across the starry sky.

Xuanzang's body was brought back to Chang'an to lie in state in the Sūtra Translation Hall of Ci'en Monastery. Hundreds of thousands of people came to pay their last respects. On the day of the state-sponsored funeral, a grand procession, like the one that welcomed Xuanzang back to the capital nearly twenty-years earlier, snaked through the capital and out into the suburbs. Nearly a million people reportedly lined the roads to watch the bier pass. Another thirty thousand spent the night at the gravesite. If anyone delivered a eulogy, it was not recorded. But the words of Xuanzang's colleague and former member of his translation team, the eminent monk Daoxuan (596–667), would have been appropriate.

> I listened to Xuanzang's words and observed his actions, and he lived up to his reputation. His extraordinary energy lasted from morning to night. Scheduling his time according to the work to be done, he was diligent and untiring in applying his mind in service of the Dharma. He did not speak of fame or profit. In his actions, he cut off the superficial and understood perfectly how to make the most of opportunities and penetrate to the heart of matters. He was neither arrogant nor obsequious, but always acted in accord with the moment. His words were profound and his discourses resolved people's doubts. He was not only a virtuous hero of our generation but also a Dharma general of the Buddhist tradition.[81]

Translations

CHAPTER 4

Buddhism in India

from the *Record of the Western Regions*

Shortly after Xuanzang returned to China in 645, Emperor Taizong asked him to write a comprehensive account of the places he had visited. The resulting text, *The Great Tang Dynasty Record of the Western Regions*, was completed the following year. Xuanzang wrote the work not as a travelogue but rather as a report on lands and peoples not well known in China. He included information on climate, crops, local products, language, social structure, political conditions, and, especially for kingdoms close to China, defense capabilities. At the beginning of the second chapter of the *Record of the Western Regions*, Xuanzang provides a long, detailed account of the history, culture, and language of India. The section translated here includes his descriptions of architecture, fashion, and education as well as his observations on Indian Buddhist monks, monasteries, and teachings. Xuanzang was careful to point out those aspects of the Indian Buddhist tradition that previous generations of monks in China had mistranslated or misunderstood. Given the dearth of other historical materials, and given Xuanzang's careful attention to what local people would have considered mundane, insignificant details, this section of the *Record of the Western Regions* remains one of the most valuable accounts of the history and culture of seventh-century India.

———

In accordance with the Buddha's teaching, monks in India undertake two retreats. These are held during either the first three months or the later three months [of the rainy season]. The earlier three-month period runs from our sixteenth day of the fifth month to the fifteenth day of the eighth month. The later three-month period runs from our sixteenth day of the sixth month to the fifteenth day of the ninth month. When translating scriptures and vinayas, earlier generations referred to this [retreat] as the "summer sitting," or "annual sitting." Because they followed the peculiar customs of remote regions and either did not understand the correct pronunciation of central [India] or were not familiar with the dialect, their translations contain mistakes. There are also discrepancies regarding the dates of the Tathāgata's entry into the womb, birth, leaving home, becoming the Buddha, and nirvāṇa. These will be discussed later.

As for cities and villages, they have a square [layout enclosed] by a tall, thick wall. Streets and alleys wind throughout, with shops lining the main roads and taverns set along the narrow lanes. The homes of butchers, fishmongers, entertainers, actors, executioners, and night soil collectors are marked with flags and relegated to outside the city. When these people come and go from the village, they must stay far to the left of the road. As for the construction of houses and city walls, since the terrain is low and damp, city walls are built of brick. The walls of buildings are constructed of woven bamboo or wood. Dwellings and viewing platforms are usually made of boards, plastered with lime, and covered with fired or sun-dried bricks. Various tall buildings are made in the same way as in

China, using thatch, grass, bricks, and boards. They differ in the way that the walls are covered with lime and the ground is purified with cow dung and a scattering of seasonal flowers.

All the monasteries are of extraordinary construction, with towers rising from their four corners. The main buildings have three stories, and their rafters, eaves, ridgepoles, and beams are carved in marvelous shapes. The doors, windows, and walls are covered with colorful paintings. The homes of common people are luxurious on the inside but spartan on the outside. Interior rooms and main halls are built to different heights and widths. There are no restrictions on the number of levels in a building. Doors open to the east and thrones also face east. As for sitting, everyone uses a rope chair. Members of the royal family, great men, scholars, common people, and people from powerful families adorn [their chairs] in different ways, but there is no difference in how they are made. The monarch's throne, which is lofty, wide, and inlaid with gems, is called the lion seat. It is covered in fine cloth and mounted by means of a jeweled footrest. All the various officials, in accord with their tastes, carve [their own seats] with different designs and decorate them with precious stones.

As for clothing and adornments, they are not tailored. Pure white is valued while mixed colors are not. Men wrap themselves with a long cloth around their waist and armpits, leaving their right shoulders bare. Women's skirts hang down and completely cover their shoulders. They wear their hair in a small bun atop the head with the remaining hair hanging down. Some men have trimmed moustaches and some adopt peculiar fashions [like] wearing garlands of flowers in their hair or decorating their bodies with jeweled ornaments. Cloth is known as *kauśeya*, "fine wool," and so forth. *Kauśeya* is wild silk. *Kṣauma* cloth is a type of hemp. *Kambala* cloth is finely woven sheep's wool. *Harali* cloth is woven from wild animal hair. Fine and soft animal hair that can be spun and woven is treasured and used for cloth. In northern India, where it is intensely cold, the clothing is short and tight fitting. It is very similar to the clothing worn by northern barbarians. The clothing and ornaments of non-Buddhists are a jumble of different styles. Some dress in peacock feathers, some wear skull necklaces, some go naked, some cover their bodies with grass mats, some pull out their hair and cut their mustaches, some draw their abundant hair up into a topknot. The clothing is not consistent; sometimes red, sometimes white, it is not always the same.

The robes of monks consist of only three garments, [as well as] a *saṃkakṣikā* and a *nivāsana (sangkasa)*.[82] Different groups cut the three garments differently. Some have broad or narrow edges and some have small or large folds. The *saṃkakṣikā* (called "armpit concealer" in Tang China; formerly mistakenly called *sengqizhi*) covers the left shoulder and conceals the two armpits. Open on the left, closed on the right, its length extends past the waist. The *nivāsana* (called a "skirt" in Tang China; formerly mistakenly called *niepanseng*) is not fastened with a belt. This garment is connected to the robe by folding and is secured with a strap. Various groups use different folds and the colors, either yellow or red, also differ.

Kṣatriyas and brahmins live pure and simple lives and are clean and frugal. The dress of kings and high officials is quite different. They adorn their hair with flowers and their heads with jeweled crowns. Their bodies are decorated with bracelets and necklaces. Wealthy businessmen and great merchants can only wear bracelets, no other [jewelry]. Most people go barefoot; only a few wear shoes. They dye their teeth either red or black. The people have neat hair, pierced ears, long noses, and big eyes. This is how they look.

People keep themselves clean and pure of their own accord. Ordinarily, before eating people must first wash their hands. Leftovers are not used again and eating utensils are not shared. Ceramic and wooden utensils are discarded after use. Gold, silver, copper, and iron [utensils] are always kept polished. After eating, [the mouth is] cleaned by chewing a willow twig. No one touches anyone else until after they have cleaned and rinsed their mouths. Every time a person urinates, they must wash themselves. The body is anointed with various fragrances, such as sandalwood and turmeric. When a monarch is about to bathe, there are drums, stringed instruments, and singing. Sacrifices are offered at the shrine and then he immerses himself in the water to bathe.

Brahmā created their written language. When it was originally passed down, it had forty-seven letters. As people encountered things, they composed words [to name them]. As events occurred, [words were] used to describe them. Different branches evolved as the original language gradually spread and different people in different places made small changes. Relatively speaking, these [variations] do not deviate from the original [language]. Middle India is considered to have the most detailed and correct [dialect]. The diction and tone is harmonious and elegant and the sounds are the same as those in Heaven. The style, clear and bright, is the standard among the people. Neighboring territories and different kingdoms have grown accustomed to their mistakes and these have become standardized. In the rush to emulate degenerate forms, the pure style has not been maintained. There are officials in charge of recording words and documenting events. The general term for histories and royal edicts is *nīlapiṭa* (called "Blue Annals" in Tang Chinese). These works consider both the good and the bad and fully document both disasters and good fortune.

The instruction of children begins with the twelve chapters [of the *Siddhavastu*—a syllabary of *siddham* script]. After their seventh year, children are gradually taught the great treatises on the five kinds of knowledge. The first is knowledge of sound, which explains the words in classic texts, details their classifications, and comments on their differences. The second is knowledge of techniques, such as arts, mechanics, *yin* and *yang*, and calendrical calculations. The third is knowledge of medicines, such as incantations, countering evils, compounding medicines, and performing acupuncture and moxibustion. The fourth is called knowledge of logic, which is used to determine right and wrong and to investigate what is true and false. The fifth is called inner knowledge; it thoroughly examines the marvelous principle of cause and effect [as it relates to] the five vehicles.[83] The brahmins study the four Vedas (formerly mistakenly called "Pituo").[84] The first is called "longevity"; it discusses nourishing life and cultivating nature. The second is called "sacrifice"; it discusses making offerings and prayers. The third is called "pacification"; it discusses etiquette, divination, military tactics, and battle arrays. The fourth is called "arts"; it discusses unusual skills, numerology, incantations, and medical practices.

Teachers must have broad learning, deep knowledge, and must be completely versed in the profound mysteries. They instruct others in the great meaning, guide them with subtle words, and skillfully lead them forward, carving out what is rotten and encouraging the weak. If they have penetrating knowledge and a mind set on escape [from saṃsāra], they confine themselves behind a barrier and emerge only after their work is complete. At the age of thirty, with their will established and their studies complete, they take up an official position and begin to repay the virtue of their teachers. These men have broad knowledge about the past and are inclined toward what is proper. They enjoy living in seclusion, drifting along beyond worldly things, and are untroubled by external affairs. They are not motivated by honor or disgrace. Although their fame has spread far and wide, they are not swayed by the fine praise of monarchs. Moreover, the people of this country value profound knowledge and commoners esteem those of lofty brilliance. People of eminent acclaim are treated with utmost respect. Therefore, those who are determined to study diligently forget their exhaustion when exploring their craft. Relying on benevolence to seek the Way, they do not consider one thousand *li* far [to travel].[85] Although a person may be from a powerful and rich family, they live as wanderers and obtain their food by begging. They are rich in knowledge and not ashamed of poverty. Those who travel for amusement, who do careless work, eat for pleasure, and wear beautiful clothing have no great virtue and are out of step with the times. They bring shame on themselves and ruin their reputations.

The teachings of the Tathāgata are explained differently according to people's capacities. Since the Sage left us long ago, the true Dharma is sometimes strong and sometimes weak, but those who apply the mind of understanding will obtain the realization of wisdom. Schools may rise up like mountain peaks and critiques may crash like waves, but specialists of different schools just take different roads to the same destination. All of the eighteen schools have mastered their weapons [of debate]. The residences of the greater and lesser vehicles are separate. Their [approaches to] silent contemplation, moving and staying still, and [developing] concentration and wisdom are distinct. The levels of noise and silence are very different. Each assembly has created its own regulations. It goes without saying that the Vinaya, Abhidharma, and sūtras are the Buddha's teachings. Monks who can recite one section are exempted from monastic duties. Those who can recite two sections are given additional living expenses and necessities. Those who can recite three sections receive attendants. Those who can recite four sections are given a pure person as a servant.[86] Those who can recite five sections can ride in an elephant chariot. Those who can recite six sections travel with an entourage of bodyguards. Their virtue is lofty and they are considered extraordinary.

At gatherings where treatises are presented, the superiority and inferiority of monks is examined. Distinctions are made between skillful and unskillful [teachings]. The obscure are demoted while the bright are promoted. Those who deliberate with subtle words, who invoke the marvelous principle in their criticism and praise, who speak in refined, beautiful language, and who are nimble in debate can ride on bejeweled elephants. Their followers will be as thick as a forest. As for those whose teachings are empty and elusive, whose words are sharp and demoralizing, who have few principles but many words, and whose meaning is clever and words are accommodating, their faces are smeared with red mud, their bodies covered in dust, and they are banished to the wilderness and abandoned in ravines. This is done to distinguish the good from the bad and to identify the wise and the foolish. Wise people delight in the Way. Diligent families are fond of study. One can leave home or remain a layperson as they wish. An internal monastic unit disciplines those who are guilty of violating the regulations. If [the offense] is light, the assembly will have them reprimanded. With the next [degree of offense], the assembly will not speak to the offender. For heavy [offenses], the culprit is not allowed to live among the assembly. They are banished and held in contempt. They search for a place to live but there is nowhere for them to settle down. They either endure the hardships of wandering or return to wearing their former [lay] clothes.

CHAPTER 5

Kapilavastu

from the *Record of the Western Regions*

Kapilavastu is the city where the Buddha's father, Śuddhodana, ruled as king. The Buddha's mother, Mahāmāyā, gave birth to him in nearby Lumbinī. In Kapilavastu, Xuanzang visited many of the key sites associated with the Buddha's life as a young prince—the place where he was conceived, where soothsayers foretold his future, where he studied, where he performed great feats, where he lived with his wife Yaśodharā and their son Rāhula, and where, after encountering old age, sickness, and death, he resolved to seek liberation. Xuanzang's account suggests that, while the ancient city itself had been deserted, the sites associated with the Buddha's life were active places of pilgrimage, with key locations marked by shrines and statues depicting important events in the prince's early life. Modern excavations at Lumbinī date the earliest extant structures to the reign of King Aśoka (d. 232 B.C.E.) and the first major monuments at Kapilavastu probably arose at the same time. The precise location of the city remains undetermined, with some archaeologists identifying Kapilavastu with modern Tilaurakot in southern Nepal and others with Piprahwa in northern India.

───────

The kingdom of Kapilavastu is over four thousand *li* in circumference. It had ten imperial palaces but these are now overgrown with weeds. The capital lies in ruins and its extent is not clear. The imperial palace within [the capital] has a circumference of fourteen or fifteen *li*. It was built of brick and its foundation is still strong. The place has been empty and desolate for a long time and people rarely venture inside. There is no great ruler; each city has its own lord. The land is fertile and crops are sown and reaped at the appropriate times. The seasons are orderly and the customs are gentle and pleasant. There are foundations for over one thousand monasteries, and beside the imperial palace there is one monastery with more than three thousand monks. They all study the Saṃmitīya teachings of the Hīnayāna. There are two deva temples where non-Buddhists live together.

Within the imperial city there is the old foundation of King Śuddhodana's main palace. A temple housing an image of the king has been built on top of it. Not far from the side of the old palace is the old foundation of Lady Mahāmāyā's bedroom. A temple housing an image of the lady has been established on top of it. To the side of this is a temple on the spot where the bodhisattva from the Śakya clan descended into his mother's womb. It contains an image of the incarnated bodhisattva. The Sthaviras say that the bodhisattva descended into his mother's womb on the evening of the thirtieth day of the month of Uttarāṣāḍhā, which corresponds to the fifteenth day of the fifth month in China.[87] Other schools say that this happened on the evening of the twenty-third day of the same month, which is the eighth day of the fifth month in China. Northeast of where the bodhisattva was incarnated there is a stūpa marking the place where the sage Asita observed the prince's appearance. Auspicious signs converged on the day of the bodhisattva's birth. At that time, King Śuddhodana summoned various physiognomers and said to them, "Will this newborn's fortune be good or bad?

If you know, speak frankly." They said, "Based on the records of former sages and our examination of the auspicious responses, if he remains at home he will be a wheel-turning sage king. If he abandons home he will attain complete and perfect awakening." At that time, the sage Asita came from far away. He knocked on the door and asked to see the prince. The king was delighted and welcomed him respectfully. After inviting him to sit on the throne, he said, "The great sage has come to see us unexpectedly." The sage said, "I was quietly sitting in the heavenly palace when I suddenly saw various devas dancing. At that time, I asked, 'Why are you so happy?' They said, 'The great sage should know that in Jambudvīpa the first wife of King Śuddhodana of the Śakya clan has given birth to a prince who will realize perfect awakening and obtain complete omniscience.' I heard these words and came to pay my respects. It grieves me that my old age will prevent me from hearing the Sage's teachings."

At the southern gate of the imperial city, there is a stūpa at the place where the prince wrestled with other members of the Śakya clan and hurled an elephant. The prince was so skilled in various arts that he had no equal. King Śuddhodana, feeling joyful, was about to return home [from a wrestling competition] so the driver of his elephant carriage was preparing to leave the city. Devadatta, who always relied on brute force, came in from the outside and asked the driver, "You have outfitted this elephant. Who wants to ride it?" The driver said, "The prince is planning to return so I have come to prepare his carriage." Devadatta angrily pulled the elephant down. He beat its forehead and kicked its chest until it became stiff and collapsed, blocking the road. With the road cut off, nothing could be transported, and the people were stuck. When Nanda arrived, he asked, "Who killed this elephant?" Someone said, "Devadatta." [Nanda] then dragged it to the side of the road. The prince arrived and he also asked, "Who has behaved badly and hurt this elephant?"

Someone said, "Devadatta injured it to block the gate, and Nanda pulled it aside to open the road." The prince then lifted the elephant high and threw it over the city moat. When the elephant landed, it made a deep pit. Locals call it the "fallen elephant pit."

There is a temple beside the pit with an image of the prince. To the side of this there is another temple where the prince's wife had her bedroom. Inside there are images of Yaśodharā and Rāhula. Next to the palace, there is a temple with an image of [the prince] as a student. This is [located on] the old foundation of the prince's study hall. In the southeastern corner of the city, there is a temple with an image of the prince riding a white horse through the air. This is the place where he crossed over the city wall. There are temples outside each of the four city gates that contain images of an old man, a sick man, a corpse, and a monk. These are the places where the prince went out to look around. Seeing these signs deepened his disillusionment with the dusty world and he was moved to awaken. He ordered his driver to turn the carriage around.

CHAPTER 6

The Bodhi Tree

from the *Record of the Western Regions*

According to the *Mahāparinibbāna Sutta*, just before his death, the Buddha, or Tathāgata (Thus-Come-One), identified four key sites of pilgrimage for his followers:

> These, Ānanda, are the four places that a pious person should visit and look upon with feelings of reverence. And truly there will come to these places, Ānanda, pious bhikkhus and bhikkhunīs, laymen and laywomen, reflecting: "Here the Tathāgata was born! Here the Tathāgata became fully enlightened in unsurpassed, supreme Enlightenment! Here the Tathāgata set rolling the unexcelled Wheel of the Dhamma! Here the Tathāgata passed away into the state of Nibbāna in which no element of clinging remains!" And whoever, Ānanda, should die on such a pilgrimage with his heart established in faith, at the breaking up of the body, after death, will be reborn in a realm of heavenly happiness.[88]

Lumbinī is the place of the Buddha's birth. The site of the Buddha's awakening, the second major pilgrimage center, is the Bodhi Tree, in present-day Bodh Gayā. This was a sacred place for Buddhists not just because of what occurred here in the past but also for what would happen here in the future. The tree and the diamond throne that stood beside it marked the spot where all buddhas, past and future, realize buddhahood. After traveling so far, Xuanzang was moved to be in this place. His joy at seeing the sacred tree and the throne, however, was tempered with a sense of sadness and loss. It seemed to him that the site, and thus the tradition that issued from it, was in decline. The tree had been cut down and statues of bodhisattvas were sinking into the earth. According to the *Biography of the Trepiṭaka Master*, Xuanzang, after bowing down before a statue of the Buddha, expressed his sorrow for arriving at such a late date. "'I do not know where I was wandering in the cycle of existence when the Buddha obtained the Way. I have arrived here only now, during the age of the semblance Dharma.' Recalling the depth and weight of his karmic hindrances, his eyes over-flowed with melancholy tears."[89]

———

Going fourteen or fifteen *li* to the southwest of Mount Prāgbodhi, I arrived at the Bodhi Tree, which is enclosed by a lofty, impregna-ble brick wall. The enclosure is broad from east to west and narrow from north to south, with a circumference of more than five hundred paces. The tree is unusual and has beautiful flowers. It casts contin-uous shade on the ground, which is covered in fine sand and quilted with different green grasses. The main gate of the enclosure opens to the east and faces the Nairañjāna River. The southern gate connects to a great lotus pond. To the west is an insurmountable barrier, while the northern gate leads to a great monastery. The Sage's traces fill the area within the wall. There are also stūpas and temples built by the kings, ministers, and powerful clans of Jambūdvīpa out of their admiration for the teachings bequeathed by the Buddha.

At the center of the Bodhi Tree enclosure is the Diamond Seat. Formerly, at the beginning of the Auspicious Kalpa, it arose together with the Great Earth.[90] Within the great trichiliocosm, it extends to the wheel of metal and rises up from the earth.[91] It is made of diamond and has a circumference of over one hundred paces. During the Auspicious Kalpa, one thousand buddhas will sit here and enter the diamond samādhi.[92] That is why it is called the Diamond Seat. The place where the Sage realized the Way is also called the site of awakening. When the great earth shakes, this place alone does not move. When the Tathāgata was about to realize perfect awakening, he passed by the four corners of this place and the earth was quaking. Then he arrived at this spot and it was peaceful and still. Once we enter the final age, the true Dharma will grow faint. Sand will cover the ground and the site will not be seen again. After the Buddha's nirvāṇa, the kings of various countries, having heard the Buddha's description of the Diamond Seat, set up two seated, east-facing statues of Avalokiteśvara at the southern and northern boundaries of site. I have heard various elders say that once the statues of the bodhisattva sink down and can no longer be seen, the Buddha-Dharma will disappear. At present, the southern bodhisattva is sunken down to its chest.

The Bodhi Tree above the Diamond Seat is a pipal tree. In the past, when the Buddha was in the world, it was several hundred feet tall. It has since been repeatedly hacked down but it is still forty or fifty feet high. Because the Buddha sat beneath it and attained perfect awakening [*bodhi*], it is called the Bodhi Tree. Its trunk is pale yellow and its branches and leaves are emerald green. In the winter and summer, it does not wither and its luster does not change. Every year on the day of the Tathāgata's nirvāṇa, the leaves all wither and fall but are then quickly restored. On that day, various kings, monks, and laypeople from different places, numbering in the tens of thousands, gather in this place without being summoned. They use fragrant water and fragrant milk to water and bathe the tree. They play music, arrange fragrant flowers, and keep lamps burning throughout the day, competing with each other to make offerings.

CHAPTER 7

Mahābodhi Monastery

from the *Record of the*
Western Regions

While at Bodh Gayā, Xuanzang also visited the large monastic complex located just outside the northern gate of the Bodhi Tree's enclosure. This passage from Xuanzang's *Record* focuses on the history of the monastery. Although archaeological evidence suggests that King Aśoka carried out the first major development at the site in the third century B.C.E., the Mahābodhi Monastery that Xuanzang visited was of relatively recent construction, having been built during the mid-sixth century. According to inscriptions later found at the site, a Sri Lankan monk named Mahānāman donated funds for the construction of the monastery. If Xuanzang's account is accurate, Mahānāman may be the monk dispatched by the king of Siṃhala (Sri Lanka) to establish a monastery near the Bodhi Tree as a residence for monks and envoys from Siṃhala. Foreign monks, according to Xuanzang's account, faced discrimination as they traveled on pilgrimage through India, paying homage at sites associated with the Buddha. The Bodhi Tree, the Diamond Seat, and the Mahābodhi Monastery were major pilgrimage destinations during the mid-seventh century, and Xuanzang concludes with a brief description of the thousands of monks and laypeople who flocked to the area every year at the end of the rains retreat.

———

Outside the northern gate of the Bodhi Tree enclosure is the Mahābodhi Monastery, which a former king of Siṃhala established. There are six compounds with three-storied pavilions, all surrounded by a wall three or four meters high. The craftsmanship is marvelous and it is completely covered in paintings. The Buddha image is cast in gold and silver and adorned with jewels. All the stūpas are broad, lofty, marvelously decorated, and contain relics of the Tathāgata. The bone relics are like finger joints, which are smooth, shiny, and bright white inside and out. The flesh relics are like large pearls, reddish blue in color. Every year on the day of the full moon in the month of the Tathāgata's great supranormal powers, the relics are displayed.[93] (In India, this is on the thirtieth day of the twelfth month; here [in China] it is on the fifteenth day of the first month.) There are fewer than one thousand monks, all of whom study the Mahāyāna and Sthavira teachings, solemnly observe the rules and ceremonies, and faithfully maintain the precepts.

In the past, the king of Siṃhala in the Southern Sea had a genuine, naturally abiding faith in the Buddha-Dharma. He had a younger cousin who became a monk and, seeking the Buddha's traces, he traveled to distant India. In all the monasteries he visited, he was dismissed as a foreigner. When he returned to his native country, the king welcomed him. The monk choked up and it seemed as though he could not speak. The king asked, "What is bothering you? Why so sad?" The monk said, "Relying on the prestige of our kingdom, I traveled to inquire about the Way. I stayed in different places and suffered from heat and cold. My actions were met with insults and humiliation and my speech was viewed with derision. Having endured such shame, how can I be happy?" The king said, "If it is like this, what do you propose?" The monk said, "I sincerely hope that the great king will create a field of merit by building monasteries throughout all India to honor the traces of the Sage and establish your renown. This would generate a store of blessings for our former kings and would be an act of compassion for future generations."

The king said, "Such an act would be most noble. Why I am hearing of it so late?" Thereupon, he donated the kingdom's treasure to the king of India. The king of India received the tribute and, maintaining his honor and cherishing that distant land, said to the envoy, "I now invite you to state your message." The envoy said, "The king of Siṃhala bows to the great propitious king of India! Your power and virtue reverberate through distant lands and your wisdom and benevolence have spread far and wide. A monk of our lowly land, admiring the teachings and yearning for guidance, bravely traveled to your superior kingdom to pay his respects to the Sage's traces. In the various monasteries he visited, he did not see any guesthouses. His hardships were extreme and he returned filled with shame. We have taken the liberty of formulating a plan that we offer as a model for later generations. If you build monasteries throughout India where envoys and wandering monks can stop and rest, our two countries will have good relations and travelers will not be cast out."

The king said, "The Tathāgata has grown remote but his teachings are still present. Among the places with the Sage's traces, you may select one [for this purpose]." The envoy was then dismissed and reported back [to Siṃhala]. Various ministers congratulated him [on his success] and summoned all the monks to discuss the matter. The monks said, "All buddhas have realized awakening under the Bodhi Tree. There can be no objection to this place." Consequently, the treasure donated by the kingdom was used to build a monastery there. Monks from that country maintain and support it. An inscription on a copper tablet reads, "All buddhas teach perfect, selfless giving. The ancient sages clearly taught that the ability to cross the ford of wisdom depends on conditions. Today we humbly receive the king's order and construct this monastery to honor the Sage's traces and bestow blessings on our ancestors and kindness on the people. Only monks from our country can use it freely and other people from our country will be treated the same as monks. This is to be passed on to later generations in perpetuity." Therefore, monks from the kingdom of Siṃhala manage this monastery.

Over ten *li* to the south of the Bodhi Tree, there are so many places with the Sage's traces that they are difficult to describe in full. Every year, when the monks end the rains retreat, tens of thousands of monks and laypeople come from all directions. For seven days and seven nights, they hold incense and flowers, beat drums and play music, and wander through the forest doing obeisance and making offerings. The monks from India rely on the Buddha's teaching and thus all enter the rains retreat on the first day of the first half of the month of Śrāvaṇa, which is the sixteenth day of the fifth month in China. The retreat ends on the fifteenth day during the second half of the month of Aśvayuja, which is the fifteenth day of the eighth month in China.[94] The months in India are established based on stars. They do not change over time and are accepted by all groups. It is surely because of differences in language and errors in translation that the division of times and calculation of months are different here [in China]. This is why we enter the rains retreat on the sixteenth day of the fourth month and end the rains retreat on the fifteenth day of the seventh month.

CHAPTER 8

Vārāṇasī and the Deer Park

from the *Record of the
Western Regions*

The Deer Park at Sarnath is where the Buddha delivered his first teachings seven weeks after awakening under the Bodhi Tree. It is the third of the four main sites of pilgrimage stipulated by the Buddha. The earliest archaeological remains at Sarnath date to the time of Aśoka but the pillar and stūpas probably marked an already functioning place of pilgrimage. When the Chinese Buddhist monk Faxian visited the Deer Park in the early fifth century, he noted the existence of two active Buddhist monasteries. Xuanzang, writing more than two centuries later, describes just one large complex, known now as the Main Shrine, comprising eight subdivisions and housing fifteen hundred monks. He also noted the existence of two Aśokan columns, both of which reportedly exhibited miraculous qualities. Modern excavations have uncovered seven monasteries and multiple stūpas at the site. The last Buddhist monastery built in Sarnath, the Dharmacakra Jina Vihāra, dates to the thirteenth century.

———

The kingdom of Vārāṇasī is over four thousand *li* in circumference.

The great capital of the kingdom, on the west side of the Ganges River, is eighteen or nineteen *li* long and five or six *li* wide. It is densely populated with prosperous residents. Families amass huge profits and fill their storerooms with marvelous goods. The people are warm and respectful and place great weight on intensive study. Many have faith in non-Buddhist traditions and few revere the Buddha-Dharma. The seasons are balanced, the crops are abundant, the branches of the fruit trees interlace, and the luxuriant grasses bend in the wind. There are more than thirty monasteries with more than three thousand monks studying Hīnayāna Saṃmitīya teachings. There are more than a hundred deva temples with more than ten thousand non-Buddhists, all of whom venerate Maheśvara [Great Lord, a title of Śiva]. Some cut off their hair, some wear a top-knot. Some go naked, smearing their bodies with ash. They devote themselves to the practice of austerities, seeking to leave the cycle of birth and death. Within the great city, there are twenty deva temples, built with carved stone and engraved wood on tiered terraces. These are shaded by dense forests and crisscrossed with clear streams. A copper image of the deva rises to less than one hundred feet high. Dignified and solemn, it is awe-inspiring. Northeast of the great city, on the west bank of the Varanā River, there is a stūpa more than one hundred feet tall built by King Aśoka. A stone pillar has been erected in front of this.[95] Its green stone, polished like a mirror, is as smooth as water. Images of the Tathāgata often appear within.

Going more than ten *li* northeast of the Varanā River one reaches the monastery at the Deer Park. The area is divided into eight divisions surrounded by a wall. There are multistoried buildings and pavilions of exceptionally beautiful construction. The fifteen hundred monks all study the Hīnayāna Saṃmitīya teachings. Within the wall sits a monastery that is more than two hundred feet tall. On its top there is a mango made of gold. The foundation and stairs are made of stone, while the multilayered niches are made of brick. There are many hundreds of niches on all four sides. They all enshrine golden Buddha statues. At the center of the monastery is a copper Buddha statue the size of the Tathāgata's body in the posture of turning the Dharma wheel. To the southwest of the monastery there is a stūpa built by King Aśoka. Although the foundation is crumbling, it is still more than one hundred feet tall. A stone pillar more than seventy feet high stands in front.[96] The stone is smooth as jade and shines as bright as a mirror. If a person makes a sincere request, they will see various images in the reflection and signs of good and evil are sometimes seen. This is the place where the Tathāgata turned the Dharma wheel after realizing complete and perfect awakening. Not far to the side there is a stūpa at the spot where Ājñātakauṇḍinya, after seeing the bodhisattva give up his austerities and abandoning him, came to practice meditation on his own. A nearby stūpa marks the place where five hundred pratyekabuddhas entered nirvāṇa together.[97] There are also three stūpas at the spot where three buddhas of the past sat and walked.

CHAPTER 9

Kuśinagara

from the *Record of the Western Regions*

Xuanzang describes Kuśinagara, the site of the Buddha's parinirvāṇa, as isolated and desolate. This is where Śākyamuni, after accepting a tainted meal from a devotee named Cunda, fell ill, lay down between four trees, and made his final exhortation to his disciples: "All conditioned things are subject to decay. Strive on with diligence!" After his death, the Buddha was cremated and his relics were divided among eight different kings. The precise location of Kuśinagara is a matter of debate. It is most often identified with modern Kasia, where archaeologists working in the late nineteenth century unearthed a twenty-foot parinirvāṇa statue of the Buddha carved in the fifth century that may be the image described by Xuanzang below. Other features noted by Xuanzang—two Aśokan stūpas and a pillar—have not been found, leading some scholars to suspect that the real location of the Buddha's last days must lie elsewhere. Although Kuśinagara is one of the four major Buddhist pilgrimage sites, the area does not appear to have been particularly active at the time of Xuanzang's visit. Xuanzang does not mention seeing any shrines or monasteries at the site and, after locating the places where the final events of the Buddha's life, cremation, and relic division occurred, he quickly moves on.

———

To the northeast [of the country of Rāma], I traveled through a great forest. The road was difficult and dangerous and the way was beset with hazards such as mountain oxen, wild elephants, bandits, and hunters that lie in wait and have no compunction about harming travelers. Emerging from the forest, I arrived at Kuśinagara (in central India). The city walls of Kuśinagara are in ruins and the city is desolate. The old wall was made of brick and had a circumference of more than ten *li*. Few people live here and the roads are overgrown with weeds. There is a stūpa built by King Aśoka in the northeastern corner of the city at the site where Cunda (in the past he was erroneously called Chuntuo) lived. Within the house there is the well that was dug at the same time that Cunda made the offering [to the Buddha]. In the months and years since, even if there is a flood, the water remains clear and sweet. Three or four *li* northwest of the city is the Ajitavatī River. (This means "invincible" in Tang China. This is what it is called at present. In the past, it was erroneously called the Aliluobati River. Texts refer to it as the Hiraṇyavatī River, which translates to "containing gold.")

Not far from the western bank, one arrives at the śāla grove. These trees are a type of oak with bluish-gray bark and smooth and glossy leaves. Four particularly tall trees mark the place where the Tathāgata entered stillness and cessation. There is a large brick temple here that contains an image of the Tathāgata's nirvāṇa, [depicting him] lying on his side with his head facing north. A stūpa nearby was built by King Aśoka. Although the foundation has collapsed, it is still more than two hundred feet high. A stone pillar stands in front to record the events of the Tathāgata's entering stillness and cessation. Although there is a written record, it does not record the date. I have heard various elders say that the Buddha lived to be eighty years old and entered parinirvāṇa on the fifteenth day of the latter half of the month of Vaiśākha, which corresponds to the fifteenth day of the third month in China. According to the Sarvāstivāda school, the Buddha entered nirvāṇa on the eighth day of the second half of the month of Kārttika, which corresponds to the eighth day of the ninth month in China. The various schools disagree [about how many years have passed] since the Buddha's nirvāṇa. Some say it has been more than twelve hundred years, some say it has been more than thirteen hundred years, some say it has been fifteen hundred years, while some others say that it has been more than nine hundred but less than one thousand.

CHAPTER 10

Mahākāśyapa

from the *Record of the*
Western Regions

Mahākāśyapa was the leading disciple of the Buddha who, according to tradition, assumed leadership of the sangha following Śākyamuni's death. *The Story of Aśoka* (*Aśokāvadāna*) states that at the end of his life, Mahākāśyapa did not die but entered a state of samādhi that will last until the time that he is called to deliver Śākyamuni's robe to the next buddha, Maitreya. Xuanzang was a devotee of Maitreya. He held that the future buddha currently resides in Tuṣita Heaven, where he had authored several key Mahāyāna texts, most notably the *Discourse on the Stages of Yogic Practice*, the treatise Xuanzang traveled to India to obtain. After returning to China, Xuanzang made one thousand images of Maitreya and, just before his death, he also made a solemn vow to be reborn as a member of Maitreya's inner circle in Tuṣita Heaven. According to the *Lotus Sūtra*, those dwelling in Tuṣita Heaven will be reborn with Maitreya when he finally becomes a buddha and descends to earth. The prophecy of Maitreya's arrival that Xuanzang narrates below was thus one that he hoped to witness someday in the distant future.

Mahākāśyapa was a disciple who heard the teachings directly [from the Buddha] and had obtained the six supranormal powers and eight kinds of liberation.[98] When conditions for the Tathāgata's teaching were coming to an end and he was about to enter nirvāṇa, he said to Mahākāśyapa, "For a long time I have been diligently cultivating ascetic practices in search of the unsurpassed Dharma on behalf of all sentient beings. My past vows are now fulfilled. I want to enter great nirvāṇa, and I entrust the Dharma treasury to you to maintain and promulgate. Do not let it be lost! I leave the robe of golden thread presented by my aunt to be passed on to Maitreya when he becomes a buddha. Those practitioners who follow my bequeathed teachings, such as monks, nuns, *upāsakas* (called *jinshinan* in Tang China; formerly pronounced *yipusai* or also *youposai*, both of which are wrong), *upāsikās* (called *jinshinu* in Tang China; formerly pronounced *youposi* or also *youpoyi*, both of which are wrong) will be the first cross over and exit the flow [of birth and death]. Kāśyapa received this instruction and maintained the correct Dharma.

Twenty years after the [First] Council, [Mahākāśyapa,] tired of the impermanent world, was ready to enter nirvāṇa. He went to Chicken Foot Mountain and ascended its northern slope. Following a winding path, he reached the southwestern ridge. The mountain's peak was precipitous and the path along the cliffs wound through dense undergrowth. Using his metal staff, he cut through it like a knife. The mountain trail opened up and he followed the path, which twisted, turned, and switched back as it ascended the slope. When he arrived at the peak, he went out from the northeastern face and entered the middle of the three peaks. Holding the Buddha's robe, he stood upright and, with the power of his vow, the three peaks closed around him. That is why this mountain has three bulges along the ridgeline.

In the future, the World-Honored One Maitreya will come into the world. After preaching the Dharma at three assemblies, beings filled with boundless pride will climb this mountain to Mahākāśyapa's place. With a wink of Maitreya's eye, the peak will open and everyone will see Mahākāśyapa, which will only increase their pride. At that time, after Mahākāśyapa gives the robe [to Maitreya], says some words, and makes obeisance, he will rise up into the air, display all his supranormal powers, burst into flames, and enter nirvāṇa. Then, the crowd will watch with reverence and their prideful hearts will vanish. Because of this, they will be inspired to awaken and all will realize the fruit of sainthood. That is why a stūpa was built at the top of this mountain. On quiet nights, looking from afar, some see a burning flame. But when they climb the mountain, it cannot be found.

CHAPTER 11

Nālandā

from the *Record of the Western Regions*

Nālandā Monastery, one of the most prestigious sites of Buddhist learning in India, was the ultimate destination of Xuanzang's pilgrimage to India. According to Xuanzang's *Biography*, the monastery dispatched four monks to escort him from Bodh Gayā to Nālandā, a journey of roughly fifty miles. After Xuanzang received permission to enter the monastery, he went to see the Venerable Śīlabhadra, the Yogācāra master he aspired to study under. Crawling on his knees and elbows, Xuanzang approached Śīlabhadra, kissed his feet, and prostrated before him. Śīlabhadra then announced that Xuanzang's arrival had been prophesized by the bodhisattvas Avalokiteśvara, Maitreya, and Mañjuśrī three years earlier. After that, Xuanzang was given a room and generous provisions. In the passage translated here, Xuanzang relates the history of the monastery, which was first established by the king Śakrāditya, a ruler of the Gupta Empire (ca. fourth through sixth centuries), who lived sometime during the fifth century. The precise identity of this king is not known but some scholars have identified him as Kumāragupta I (415–55). Xuanzang goes on to extol the

high standards of scholarship and discipline maintained at
the monastery. He remained at Nālandā for nearly five years,
studying a range of Buddhist and non-Buddhist materials
with Śīlabhadra and other senior monks.

Traveling north more than thirty *li* [from Rajgir], I arrived at
Nālandā (called "Tireless Giver" in Tang China) Monastery. I heard
an elder say that south of this monastery in a mango grove there
is a spring whose resident dragon was named Nālandā. When the
monastery was built nearby, [the dragon's] name was used. The
truth is that in the past when the Tathāgata was carrying out his
bodhisattva practices, he became a king and established his capital here. Out of compassion for his people, he took great pleasure
in universal giving. In praise of his virtue, he was called "Tireless
Giver," and from this the monastery derived its name. The site was
originally a mango grove. Five hundred merchants purchased it
with a billion gold coins and offered it to the Buddha. The Buddha
preached the Dharma here for three months and all the merchants
realized sagehood.

Not long after the Buddha's nirvāṇa, a former king of this country, Śakrāditya (called "Sun Emperor" in Tang China), revered
the One Vehicle and venerated the Three Treasures [the Buddha,
Dharma, and Sangha]. He divined that this place was blessed and
so built a monastery here. When construction commenced, a dragon's body was injured. At that time, a non-Buddhist Nirgrantha
who was skilled at divination saw it and predicted, "A monastery
on this superior ground is sure to prosper and become a model for
the five regions of India.[99] It will flourish for over a thousand years
as a place where generations of students will easily accomplish their
work. However, much blood will be spilt because the dragon has
been wounded." The king's son, Buddhagupta ("Guarding Awak-

ening" in Tang China) succeeded the throne and continued the good work of his father, building another monastery to the south of the original. King Tathāgatagupta (called "Thus Come" in Tang China) earnestly maintained the work of his forebears and built another monastery to the east. He was succeeded by King Bālāditya (called "Child of the Sun" in Tang China), who built yet another monastery in the northeast.

When the work was finally completed, a gathering was convened to celebrate these meritorious deeds. Without distinguishing between the unknown and known, commoners and sages were all invited to attend. At the assembly, monks from the five regions of India came from thousands of miles away and gathered like clouds. Once the assembly was seated and settled, two monks who had arrived late were led up to the third story of a pavilion. Someone asked, "When the king was preparing for this assembly, he first sent out invitations to commoners and sages. Great worthies, where have you come from that you have arrived last?" They said, "We are from China. The senior monk [of our monastery] is suffering from an illness and we had just finished serving him his meal when we received the distant king's invitation. Thereafter we came to attend your gathering." The questioner was shocked and quickly went to report to the king. The king knew in his heart that [these monks] were sages and he personally went to question them. When he arrived later and ascended the pavilion, nobody knew where [the monks] had gone. The king's faith grew even deeper and he gave up his kingdom and left home [to become a monk]. After leaving home, the king occupied the lowest position [in the monastery]. His mind was constantly disturbed and his heart was restless. He said, "In the past when I was a king, I was accorded the highest respect. Now that I have left home, I occupy the lowest position in the community." He went and found another monk and explained the situation. The assembly of monks then had a discussion and decreed that those who had not received the precepts should be ranked according to age. That is why the monastery has this unique system.

When this king's son, Vajra (called "Diamond" in Tang China) succeeded the throne, his faith was steadfast and he built another monastery to the west [of the original monastery]. Following this, a king from central India built another monastery to the north. Thereafter, a towering wall with a single gate was built around the entire complex. Successive generations of kings have continued to build here and the craftsmanship of the various carvings is truly a wonder to behold. In the original monastery built by Śakrāditya there is now a Buddha statue. Each day, forty monks from among the assembly are sent here to eat as a means of repaying the kindness of their benefactor.

There are several thousand monks, all of whom are talented and learned. There are more than several hundred whose virtue is currently held in high regard and whose fame has spread to distant lands. Their practice of the precepts is flawless and their discipline is perfect. The monks are all strictly regulated and the entire assembly is simple and chaste. They are respected in all parts of India. There are not enough hours in the day for them to ask for instruction and discuss the profound teachings. Admonishing each other day and night, younger and older complete one another. Anyone who cannot speak about the deeper meaning of the Tripiṭaka [the three divisions of the Buddhist canon] would be ashamed of himself. For this reason, scholars from different places who want to enhance their reputation come here to resolve their doubts and establish their fame. Those who travel about falsely claiming to have studied here are treated with the utmost respect. If people from distant lands want to enter the monastery to engage in discussion and debate, the gatekeepers interrogate them, causing many to submit [in defeat] and return [to where they came from]. Only those learned in contemporary and ancient works gain entry. Among those guests who are admitted, after an exhaustive discussion [that reveals] their skills and abilities, seven or eight out of ten run away. The assembly then successively questions the two or three broadly learned men that remain and there is no one who does not find their sharpness dulled or their reputation ruined.

With regard to the highly capable and broadly learned teachers here, they have all mastered the many types of knowledge and are wise men of supreme virtue. It is due to their collective brilliance that the path endures. As for Dharmapāla and Candragupta, they earned their fame by upholding the Buddha's teachings. Guṇamati and Sāramati made their name in the present day. Prabhāmitra is known for clear arguments, Viśeṣamitra for lofty discussions. Jñānacandra is brilliant and quick; Śīlabhadra is profound and virtuous.[100] The people know that the virtue of these eminent men surpasses that of previous worthies. They are well versed in the old texts, and they have each produced more than ten commentaries, all of which are in broad circulation and viewed as treasures of our age.

CHAPTER 12

King Kumāra

from the *Record of the Western Regions*

King Kumāra, also known as Bhāskaravarman, was the ruler of Kāmarūpa, a midsized kingdom located in present-day Bangladesh and northeastern India. According to Xuanzang's *Biography*, King Kumāra sought him out after he had returned to Nālandā for a second time and was preparing to leave for China. When King Kumāra's envoy arrived at Nālandā to request that Xuanzang go to Kāmarūpa for an audience with the king, Xuanzang was initially reluctant. King Kumāra was insistent, however, and Xuanzang's teacher Śīlabhadra asked him to make the journey in the hopes of increasing the king's faith in the Dharma—there were not yet any Buddhist monasteries in Kāmarūpa—and avoiding giving any offense. Xuanzang accordingly traveled the nearly five hundred miles to King Kumāra's capital near present-day Guwahati and stayed for more than one month. The passage translated here is one of only two places in the *Record of the Western Regions* that Xuanzang inserts himself into the narrative. In his account of his dialogue with the king, Xuanzang praises the virtue of the Tang emperor and claims that a song composed in China to celebrate the military exploits of Emperor Taizong, "The Tune of the Prince of Qin Breaking Through the Battle Array," had become popular throughout northern India. On learning that Xuanzang is a subject of the emperor depicted in the song, King Kumāra expresses his wish to pay tribute to the ruler of Mahācina, or Great China.

————

The kingdom of Kāmarūpa has a circumference of more than ten thousand *li*. The great capital of the kingdom has a circumference of more than thirty *li*. Springs irrigate the land and crops are planted and harvested in season. Although jackfruit and coconut trees are numerous, [their fruits] remain valuable. Rivers and lakes crisscross the city. The climate is temperate and the customs are simple. The people are short and their skin is slightly dark. Their language is not much different from that of central India. They are rude and aggressive by nature, but they are diligent in their studies. They venerate devas and do not have faith in the Buddha-Dharma. For that reason, from the time of the Buddha to the present, no monastery has been built here and no assembly of monks has been convened. People of pure faith can only study [the teachings] in private. There are hundreds of deva temples and tens of thousands of non-Buddhists.

The current king is a descendent of Nārāyaṇa-deva [Vishnu]. He is of Brahmin caste and is named Bhāskaravarman ("Descendent of the Sun" in Tang China), with the sobriquet of Kumāra ("Child" in Tang China). Ever since this territory was occupied, many generations of monarchs have ruled; the present king is the thousandth generation. The king is fond of study and his people follow his teachings. Talented people travel here from distant lands out of admiration for his righteousness. Although he does not have deep faith in the Buddha-Dharma, he respects monks of high learning. Previously, he had heard that there was a monk from the kingdom of China staying at Nālandā Monastery. [Knowing that I had] come from far away to study the profound Dharma of the Buddha, he cordially sent an emissary three times, but I did not accept his invitation. At that time, Master Śīlabhadra said, "If you want to repay the Buddha's kindness, you should spread the true Dharma. Go, child. Do not be afraid of the long journey. The ancestors of King Kumāra were non-Buddhists, but now he is inviting a monk. This is a good thing. Because of this, he may change course, which would benefit people far and wide. Long ago, you gave rise to the vast mind and made a great vow to travel alone to unknown lands, sacrificing your body in search of the Dharma. Saving all beings—could this be limited to a person's native country? You should forget about gain and loss and have no concern for glory or dishonor. Propagate the Sage's teaching! Guide those who are lost! Put others ahead and yourself behind! Forget about fame and spread the Dharma."

After this [exhortation] I could not avoid [accepting the invitation], so I traveled with the emissary and went to meet [the king]. King Kumāra said, "Although I am incompetent, I have always admired learned scholars. I heard you were a famous monk so I dared to extend an invitation to you." I said, "My abilities are few and my knowledge is narrow. What you have heard is mistaken." King Kumāra said, "Excellent! Yearning for the Dharma and being fond of study, you considered your body like a drifting [cloud] and passed through great danger in your wide-ranging travels through unfamiliar lands. This is due to your king's grace and your kingdom's tradition of learning. Now, the various kingdoms of India all sing a song from the kingdom of Mahācina called "The Tune of the Prince of Qin Breaking Through the Battle Array." It has been a long time since I have heard it. Is this from your native country, great worthy?" I said, "It is. This song is in praise of my lord's virtue." King Kumāra said, "I did not realize the great worthy was from this country. I have always admired their customs and teachings. For a long time I have gazed east, but mountains and rivers block the way and I have been unable to go there." I said, "My great lord's sagely virtue extends far and his humane teachings have reached distant places. Many people from different lands with different customs venerate and submit to His Majesty." King Kumāra said, "Since your emperor's kindness and grace is like that, I would like to pay him tribute.

"Now, King Śīlāditya is in the kingdom of Kajunghira to establish a great almsgiving to propagate blessings and wisdom. Monks from the five parts of India, learned brahmins—everyone is gathering. Today an emissary arrived with an invitation. I would like us to travel there together." And so I went along with him.

CHAPTER 13

King Śīlāditya

from the *Record of the Western Regions*

King Śīlāditya (r. 612–47), also known as Harṣavardhana or Harṣa, controlled all of North India during the first half of the seventh century. King Kumāra, who presided over the much smaller kingdom on Śīlāditya's northeastern border, was a vassal of Śīlāditya. According to Xuanzang's *Biography*, Śīlāditya was initially angry to learn that he had visited Kumāra before having an audience with him, and he demanded that both Xuanzang and Kumāra meet with him at Kajunghira, roughly 350 miles to the southwest of Kāmarūpa. As he had done in his previous meeting with King Kumāra, Xuanzang extoled the virtues of the Tang emperor to King Śīlāditya. Such flattery may have been an attempt to curry favor with the intended audience of the *Record of the Western Regions*—Emperor Taizong and his court—but formal diplomatic relations between the Tang Dynasty and Śīlāditya's Puṣyabhūti Dynasty did begin shortly thereafter. After the audience at Kajunghira, Xuanzang traveled for three months together with both kings and their entourages to reach Śīlāditya's capital at Kānyakubja, where a great festival of almsgiving was taking place. In the following passage, Xuanzang describes the lavish offerings as well as a failed assassination attempt on Śīlāditya that took place amid the festivities. According to Xuanzang, non-Buddhist brahmins, fearing that the king was neglecting them in favor of Buddhist monks, hired an assassin to kill the king. The attempt was thwarted and those brahmins involved in the plot were banished from the kingdom.

———

After receiving King Kumāra's invitation, I traveled from Magadha to Kāmarūpa. At that time, King Śīlāditya was on a tour of inspection in Kajunghira and he commanded King Kumāra, saying, "You and the foreign monk staying at Nālandā should quickly come to attend the assembly." Thereupon, together with King Kumāra, I went to the assembly to see him. King Śīlāditya, who had been hard at work, said, "What country do you come from and what do you want?" I responded, "I come from the kingdom of the Great Tang in search of the Buddha-Dharma." The king said, "In which direction is the kingdom of the Great Tang? Can it be reached by road? Is it far or near?" I replied, "It is tens of thousands of *li* to the northeast of here. In India it is known as Mahācina." The king said, "I once heard that in the kingdom of Mahācina there is a son of Heaven called the Prince of Qin, who was a clever student when he was young and a divine warrior when he was older. During the previous generation, there was death and disorder and the territory was divided and destroyed. Wars broke out and the common people were persecuted. The son of Heaven, Prince of Qin, early on formulated an extensive plan to promote great compassion, save sentient beings, and bring peace to the country. His teachings have spread far, and his virtue extends in every direction to every land. The people all admire and pledge their allegiance to him. People who have been nurtured by him all sing 'The Tune of the Prince of

Qin Breaking Through the Battle Array.' It has been a long time since I have heard this elegant song. Is all the praise of his great virtue true? Could this really be the kingdom of the Great Tang?" I replied, "Yes. 'Cina' is the name of the country used by previous kings. 'Great Tang' is what people call my sovereign's country. In the past, before he assumed the throne, the emperor was known as the 'Prince of Qin.' Now that he has succeeded the throne, he is called 'Son of Heaven.' In the previous generation, the fortunes [of the former dynasty] ended and the people had no ruler. Chaotic wars broke out and people were maimed and killed. The Prince of Qin's heavenly endowment was vast and his heart was filled with compassion and sympathy. Proclaiming his power, he annihilated the murderous mobs. He pacified the eight directions and ten thousand kingdoms paid him tribute. He loves and nurtures the four types of life and reveres the Three Treasures.[101] His taxes are light, his punishments are restrained, and the kingdom has more resources than it can use. There are no rebels and there are more people of virtuous demeanor and great learning than I can describe." King Śīlāditya said, "Magnificent! The people of that place must feel blessed to have such a sagacious ruler."

At that time, King Śīlāditya was about to return to the city of Kānyakubja to hold a Dharma assembly. Together with tens of thousands of his people, he arrived on the southern bank of the Ganges River. King Kumāra, together with tens of thousands of his people, was staying on the northern bank. With the river flowing between them, the two kings proceeded by land and water, leading four divisions of disciplined soldiers. Some rode in boats, some rode on elephants. They were beating drums, blowing conchs, plucking stringed [instruments], and blowing pipes. After traveling for ninety days, they arrived at Kānyakubja and stayed in a great flowering grove west of the Ganges River. At that time, more than twenty kings of various countries, who were the first to receive the summons, gathered for the great assembly with their kingdoms' most talented monks, brahmins, officials, and soldiers. First, the kings built a great monastery to the west of the river. To the east of the monastery, they erected a treasure terrace more than a hundred feet high. At its center was a golden Buddha statue the size of the king's body. South of the terrace, they raised a treasure altar, and this was the place where the Buddha statue was bathed. Fourteen or fifteen *li* to the northeast, a separate temporary palace was constructed. It was the second month of spring, and for the first twenty-one days rare delicacies were fed to all the monks and brahmins. On the road between the temporary palace and the monastery, there were brilliantly adorned pavilions occupied by musicians so that the elegant sound of music was heard all along the route.

The kings emerged from the temporary palace and raised a concealed golden statue into the air. The statue, which was more than three feet tall, was kept [behind] a jeweled curtain on the back of a great elephant. King Śīlāditya, dressed as Indra and holding a jeweled canopy, attended on the left, while King Kumāra, appearing as Brahma holding a white-hair whisk, attended on the right. Each had an army of five hundred elephants completely encased in armor. Behind the Buddha image lumbered another hundred large elephants ridden by musicians beating a rhythm and making music. King Śīlāditya scattered natural pearls, various jewels, gold, silver, and a variety of flowers in all directions as offerings to the Three Treasures. Arriving at the jeweled altar first, the king bathed the image with fragrant water and then carried it on his back up to the western terrace. He then made offerings of various precious jewels and hundreds of thousands of silken garments. At that time, just over twenty monks followed behind and various other kings served as guards. After everyone had eaten, groups gathered to engage in various studies, establishing the truth of the profound teachings and proclaiming the ultimate principle. When the sun began to sink, the kings returned to the temporary palace. In this way, the golden statue was delivered each day from the beginning to the end of the assembly.

[One day,] the great terrace suddenly caught fire and the arch over the monastery's gate was ablaze. The king said, "I have exhausted the kingdom's treasure and built this monastery to honor past kings and illuminate their good works. Because of my trifling virtue and lack of blessings, there has been this strange disaster. If there are such ill omens, what is the use of living?" He then burned incense, made obeisance, and vowed, "Because of my good fortune in past lives, I became king of all India. I vow to use the power of my merit to extinguish this conflagration. If there is no response, I will forfeit my life!" He then raised himself up and jumped through the gate [into the burning monastery] and it was as though he stamped out the flames. The fire was snuffed out and the smoke dissipated. All the kings saw this strange feat and their awe only increased. Later, without a change in his expression and speaking as before, he asked the various kings, "If suddenly this calamity had burned to ashes all that I have accomplished, what do you think it would mean?" The various kings bent down and wept, responding, "Your accomplishments have set a fine example that we hope will be transmitted to later generations. For them to be burned to ashes in a single day, how could we conceive of that? [Only] non-Buddhists would be pleased and congratulate each other." The king said, "Looking at it that way, what the Tathāgata said was true. Non-Buddhists and heterodox schools hold fast to eternalism. Only our great master teaches impermanence. That is why I give my alms universally in accord with my vow. That this could be destroyed only verifies the truth of the Tathāgata's teachings. This is wonderful! We cannot be deeply distressed."

Thereafter he followed the various kings and ascended the great stūpa in the east to survey the area. When they were descending the stairs, a strange man holding a knife confronted the king. The king was in a precarious position but he continued down the stairs, took hold of the man, and handed him over to officials. At the time, the officials had been so frightened that they did not know how to rescue the king. The various kings all requested that the man be put to death, but King Śilāditya was not especially angry. He stopped the order [to execute the man], saying that he should not be killed. The king personally asked him, "How have I wronged you that you would commit such a violent and wicked act?" The man replied, "The great king's selfless virtue and kindness is bestowed on those near and far. I am crazy and stupid and have not given this a great deal of thought. I was encouraged by various non-Buddhists to become an assassin and my initial plan was to murder you." The king said, "For what reason have non-Buddhists produced this wicked thought?" He replied, "The great king has gathered [people from] various kingdoms, exhausting the government storehouses to make offerings to monks and cast Buddha statues. Various non-Buddhists were summoned from far away to gather here. They are not inquired after and so they feel greatly shamed and humiliated. That is why they ordered this crazy and stupid person to boldly attempt your assassination." [The king] then went to question the non-Buddhists. There were five hundred brahmins, all very talented, who had gathered in response to the king's summons. They were jealous that the monks had received the king's obeisance and so shot a flaming arrow to set the jeweled terrace ablaze. They had planned to use the chaos of the crowd trying to escape the fire as a time to assassinate the great king. Having missed that opportunity, they then hired this man to approach and stab the king. At that time, all the kings and high officials requested that the non-Buddhists be put to death. The king only punished the chief culprit, not the other members of the group. The five hundred brahmins were cast out of the territory of India. After this, the king returned to the capital.

CHAPTER 14

Letter from Khotan

from the *Biography of the Trepiṭaka Master*

On his return journey to China, Xuanzang crossed over the formidable Pamir mountain range and then followed a route along the southern rim of the Tarim Basin. The king of Khotan extended a warm welcome and Xuanzang took the opportunity to rest and resupply. Members of his party traveled to the cities of Kucha and Kashgar in search of copies of texts they had lost while crossing the Indus River. During that time, Xuanzang composed the following letter to alert officials in Chang'an that he would soon be returning to the capital. The court's response, which arrived seven or eight months later, must have come as a relief. The emperor eagerly awaited Xuanzang's arrival and he had instructed the governors of the cities ahead to supply him with porters and horses.

———

Monk Xuanzang says: I have heard that Ma Rong was learned and eloquent, so Zheng Xuan went to Fufeng to serve him. Fu Sheng was bright and quick, so Chao Cuo personally went to Jinan to study with him.[102] From this, we know that scholars went where there was expertise and ancients also traveled far in search [of knowledge].

How much more should one, without seeking praise, brave long and dangerous roads in search of the mysterious traces of all the buddhas who benefit beings and the marvelous words of the Tripiṭaka that loosen the bindings.

I went to the Western Regions where the Buddha lived to transmit the bequeathed teachings to the East. Although excellent scriptures had already arrived, the complete teachings were still lacking. I constantly thought of going [to India] to study, disregarding my own well-being. Therefore, in the fourth month of the third year of the Zhenguan era [629], daring to break the law, I secretly went to India. I walked across boundless deserts, ascended lofty snow-capped peaks, passed through the precipitous Iron Gate, and crossed great, roiling waves. I started from the divine capital of Chang'an and ended in Rajgir, traveling more than fifty thousand *li* in between. Although there were thousands of different customs and tens of thousands of different kinds of dangers, relying on the emperor's authority, I arrived unharmed. I received generous gifts, my body did not suffer, and my aspirations were fulfilled. Over the course of seventeen years of travel, I was able to view Gṛdhrakūṭa [Vulture Peak], venerate the Bodhi Tree, see traces I had never seen, hear scriptures I had never heard, study the marvels of the universe, exhaust the transformations of *yin* and *yang*, proclaim the emperor's virtue and benevolence, and come to respect different customs.

Now I have already gone from the kingdom of Prayāga, passed through the territory of Kapisā, traversed the Pamir range, and crossed the Pamir River on my return journey. I have now arrived at Khotan. Because my elephant has drowned and I have many scriptures, I have not been able to arrange transport and have stopped here. I am not able to come quickly to visit the palace but can only gaze toward it from afar. I have entrusted the layman from Gaochang, Ma Xuanzhi, to travel with some merchants and offer this letter to alert you in advance.

CHAPTER 15

Return to the Capital

from the *Biography of the Trepiṭaka Master*

The circumstances of Xuanzang's return to the Chinese capital contrasted starkly with those of his surreptitious depar-
ture more than sixteen years earlier. The very same court that
had denied him permission to travel abroad now gave him a
hero's reception. This passage, excerpted from Xuanzang's
biography, describes the great procession down Vermillion
Bird Street, the central avenue running from the southern
gate of the capital city of Chang'an to the southern gate of
the walled imperial palace. Thousands of people turned out
to watch as Xuanzang, together with the texts, images, and
relics he brought back from India, was escorted through the
capital to Hongfu Monastery. This monastery, built by the
Tang emperor Taizong in memory of his mother just eleven
years earlier, was one of the most opulent monasteries in
the capital. It would be Xuanzang's home in the capital for
the next four years.

———

On the *bingzi* day of the first month of spring in the nineteenth year
of the Zhenguan era (645), the regent of the capital, the left vice

director, the duke of Liang (Fang Xuanling), and others received the scriptures and images presented by the Dharma Master. [The regent] then dispatched the right military marquis general-in-chief Houmochen Shi, the assistant governor of Yongzhou Prefecture Li Shushen, the county magistrate of Chang'an Li Qianyou, and others to welcome [the Master]. He entered [Chang'an] by canal and lodged at a courier station in the capital. His followers amassed like clouds. That day, officials ordered all monasteries to provide curtained sedan chairs, beautiful banners, and other things in preparation for sending the scriptures and images to Hongfu Monastery. The people all enthusiastically competed with one another to make the most splendid displays. The next day, a great assembly was held to the south of Vermillion Bird Street, where the hundreds of items [brought back from India] were put out on display.

These included 150 grains of the Tathāgata's flesh relics that the Dharma Master obtained in the Western Regions; an image of the golden Buddha's shadow from the dragon cave of Mount Prāgbodhi in the kingdom of Magadha, three feet three inches high from base to halo; a replica of the statue of the first turning of the Dharma wheel from Deer Park in the kingdom of Vārāṇasī, made of sandalwood, three feet five inches high from base to halo; a replica of the sandalwood portrait that King Udayana of the kingdom of Kauśāmbī had carved to remember the Buddha, made of sandalwood, two feet nine inches high from base to halo; a replica of the statue from the kingdom of Kapittha depicting the Tathāgata descending the jeweled stairs from the Heavenly Palace, made of silver, four feet high from base to halo; a replica of a statue of the Buddha preaching the *Lotus* and other sūtras on Vulture Peak in Magadha, made of gold, three feet five inches high from base to halo; a replica of the statue of the shadow left [by the Buddha] at the place where the venomous dragon was subdued in the kingdom of Nagarahāra, carved of sandalwood, one foot five inches high from base to halo; a replica of the statue depicting [the Buddha] in the kingdom of Vaiśālī touring the city and preaching, carved of sandalwood; and so forth.

The texts the Dharma Master obtained in the Western Regions were also set out. These included 224 Mahāyanā sūtras; 192 Mahāyāna treatises; fifteen Sthavira sūtras, vinayas, and treatises; fifteen Mahāsāṃghika sūtras, vinayas, and treatises; fifteen Saṃmitīya sūtras, vinayas, and treatises; twenty-two Mahīśāsaka sūtras, vinayas, and treatises; seventeen Kāśyapīya sūtras, vinayas, and treatises; forty-two Dharmagupta sūtras, vinayas, and treatises; sixty-seven Sarvāstivāda sūtras, vinayas, and treatises; thirty-six treatises on logic; and thirteen treatises on grammar. All together, there were 520 bundles containing 657 texts, all of which were carried on the backs of twenty horses.[103]

On that day, the authorities proclaimed that all monasteries with offerings of jeweled canopies, banners, and flags gather on Vermillion Bird Street at dawn on the following day, the twenty-eighth, to prepare to welcome the newly arrived sūtras and images to Hongfu Monastery. For this reason, people redoubled their resolve and competed with one another to make ornaments of the utmost beauty and quality. After different monasteries sent out the banners, canopies, jeweled tables, and jeweled chariots, monks, nuns, and others arranged their robes and followed [the procession]. Refined sages were in front and censers trailed behind. Altogether, there were several hundred items spread out along the street. The sūtras and images were distributed and carried forward amid the clinking of jeweled ornaments and the glimmer of scattered golden flowers. Those in the procession all praised it as a rare event. Overcome by this unusual encounter, they forgot about the dust and overcame their exhaustion. [The procession] began from Vermillion Bird Street and ended at the gate of Hongfu Monastery. For several tens of *li*, residents of the capital, scholars, and officials from within and without [the imperial palace] stood along both sides of the road to watch. It was so crowded that the authorities feared that there would be a stampede. Everyone was ordered not to move but to burn incense and scatter flowers where they were. Every place was thus connected by clouds of smoke and the sounds of homage.

CHAPTER 16

Heart Sūtra

Of the more than thirteen hundred fascicles of texts Xuanzang translated, none has been more influential than the *Heart of the Perfection of Wisdom* (*Prajñāparamitahṛdaya Sūtra*), known in English simply as the *Heart Sūtra*. This short text, framed as an exchange between the bodhisattva Avalokiteśvara and the Buddha's disciple Śāriputra, would be retranslated by later generations of monks, but Xuanzang's rendering has remained the standard version in East Asian Buddhist communities. The *Heart Sūtra* is still recited daily in monasteries and temples throughout China, Korea, Japan, Vietnam, and other parts of the world. According to Xuanzang's biography, before he set off for India, while he was still a young monk living in the southwestern Chinese province of Sichuan, he came across a sick man who was dressed in rags and covered in putrid sores. Xuanzang took the man back to his monastery and gave him food and clothing. The man, wanting to repay Xuanzang's kindness, taught him the *Heart Sūtra*. Decades later, in the summer of 649, Xuanzang made this new translation of the sūtra, which served as an encapsulation of the voluminous *Great Perfection of Wisdom Sūtra*. The *Heart Sūtra* is famous for its succinct presentation of the central Mahāyāna doctrine of emptiness, but, as described in Xuanzang's biography, it also functioned as a powerful talisman for warding off danger.

The bodhisattva Avalokiteśvara, when practicing deeply the perfection of wisdom, saw that all five aggregates are empty and was saved from all suffering.[104] Śāriputra, form is not different from emptiness; emptiness is not different from form. Form is emptiness; emptiness is form. Sensation, perception, volition, and consciousness are also like this. Śāriputra, all dharmas are marked with emptiness, not arising, not ceasing, not stained, not pure, not increasing, not decreasing. Therefore, in emptiness, there is no form, no sensation, perception, volition, consciousness; no eye, ear, nose, tongue, body, or mind; no form, sound, smell, taste, or touch; no realm of sight and no realm of consciousness; no ignorance and also no end of ignorance; [and so on] until no old age and death and also no end of old age and death; no suffering, arising, cessation, path; no wisdom and also no attainment. With nothing to attain, bodhisattvas rely on the perfection of wisdom and their minds are without hindrance. No hindrance thus no fear. Far apart from distortions and delusions, they reach nirvāṇa. All buddhas in the three worlds rely on the perfection of wisdom and thus attain unsurpassed complete perfect awakening. Therefore, know the perfection of wisdom is the great divine mantra, the great bright mantra, the supreme mantra, the unequaled mantra, which can remove all suffering and is true not false. Therefore, say the perfection of wisdom. Say the mantra:

GATE GATE PĀRAGATE PĀRASAMGATE BODHI SVĀHĀ.

CHAPTER 17

Bodhisattva Precepts

While studying at Nālandā, Xuanzang received the bodhisattva precepts from his teacher Śīlabhadra. These precepts, derived from the forty-first fascicle of the *Discourse on the Stages of Yogic Practice*, were slightly different from those already known in China. After his return from India, Xuanzang produced two texts to introduce these new precepts to monks, nuns, and laypeople. The first text, a manual for conferring the bodhisattva precepts, describes in detail the procedure for giving and receiving the vows. The second is a translation of the precepts, beginning with an explanation of the four major offenses (translated here) and ending with a list of forty-five minor precepts (omitted here).[105] Both monastics and laypeople could take the bodhisattva precepts, which were considered supplemental to the more conventional Buddhist precepts, the *prātimokṣa*. Unlike the *prātimokṣa*, whose four grave offenses of sex, theft, murder, and false claims of awakening or supranormal powers constituted an irreversible breach of one's vows, the bodhisattva precepts could be retaken if offenses were properly repented. Xuanzang bestowed these new precepts on several prominent lay officials as well as hundreds of monks and nuns.

If bodhisattvas have already received the pure bodhisattva precepts, they should regularly and carefully consider: Is this what a proper bodhisattva should do? Is this not what a proper bodhisattva should do? Having considered this, they can accomplish their tasks accordingly and diligently attend to their studies. They should also devote themselves to listening to bodhisattva sūtras and treatises. Following what they have heard, they should diligently attend to their studies. For bodhisattvas who abide by the rules and regulations, there are four types of grave offense. What are these four?

If bodhisattvas, out of a desire for profit or praise, extol themselves and denigrate others, this is the first grave offense.

If bodhisattvas have assets but are stingy with their wealth, and if someone who is suffering, impoverished, or has nothing to rely on comes before them in search of money and they do not feel compassion and practice generosity, or if someone comes before them seeking the Dharma and because of their stinginess they do not give freely even though they possess it, this is the second grave offense.

If bodhisattvas continuously nurture various types of anger and, because of causes and conditions, not only use vulgar speech but also, because they are overcome with anger, use their hands, feet, rocks, knives, or staffs to beat and injure sentient beings, their minds filled with fierce resentment, this is a violation. If someone comes seeking forgiveness and they do not accept or tolerate that person, and if they do not abandon their pent-up hatred, this is the third grave offense.

If bodhisattvas slander the bodhisattva treasury, if they take pleasure in expounding and establishing imitations of the true Dharma, whether this imitation Dharma comes from their own understanding or from others, this is the fourth grave offense.

If bodhisattvas commit one of these grave offenses, much less all of them, they are no longer able to receive the accumulated merits of the bodhisattva's vast *bodhi* in their present life. They are also not able to have a pure mind in their present life. They are called counterfeit bodhisattvas, not real bodhisattvas. If bodhisattvas commit minor or middling violations of the four grave offenses, they need not abandon the pure bodhisattva precepts. If they commit a major violation, this is called abandoning [the bodhisattva precepts]. If bodhisattvas violate the four grave offenses repeatedly without shame, and moreover take a deep pleasure in this, seeing it as a virtue, they should know that this is called a major violation.

It is not the case that bodhisattvas who momentarily commit a grave offense must abandon the pure bodhisattva precepts. [It is not] like monastics who must relinquish the precepts of liberation (*prātimokṣa*) when they commit grave offenses. If bodhisattvas commit a violation and relinquish the pure bodhisattva precepts, they may receive them again in the present life. Anyone can do this. If monastics abide in the precepts of liberation but commit a grave offense, they will not be able to receive them again. In this way, it should be ascertained whether bodhisattvas who securely abide in the pure bodhisattva precepts have committed offenses or not, are defiled or not, and whether they are of minor, middling, or superior quality.

CHAPTER 18

Letter to Prajñādeva

from the *Biography of the Trepiṭaka Master*

In the summer of 652, the Indian monk Dharmadīrgha arrived in Chang'an from Bodh Gayā. He carried with him a letter from Xuanzang's friend the monk Prajñādeva, as well as several gifts for Xuanzang. After a stay of nearly two years in the Chinese capital, Dharmadīrgha was preparing to return to India. Before he left, Xuanzang gave him two letters, both presumably written in Sanskrit but now preserved only in Chinese. The first, translated here, was addressed to Prajñādeva, who was then living at Mahābodhi Monastery in Bodh Gayā. Xuanzang refers to him using the honorific "Trepiṭaka": one who has mastered the Buddhist canon (Tripiṭaka). The letter expresses Xuanzang's admiration and respect for the monk but also his disappointment that Prajñādeva, a mainstream Buddhist monk, still refused to accept the teachings of the Mahāyāna. According to a separate passage in Xuanzang's biography, although Prajñādeva was a learned scholar of the Hinayana, "he had not set his mind on the Mahāyāna. Because he persisted in maintaining this prejudiced view, the Dharma Master [Xuanzang] always disparaged him. At the assembly in Kānyakubja, [Xuanzang] soundly defeated him [in debate] and he submitted in shame." Xuanzang alludes to this episode in his letter and once again urges Prajñādeva to see the error in his ways. The undated letter, most likely written in 654, also contains a request for copies of the scriptures Xuanzang lost while crossing the Indus River on his return trip to China.

Bhikṣu Xuanzang of the Great Tang Empire respectfully sends this letter to Dharma Master Trepiṭaka Prajñādeva of the Mahābodhi Monastery.

———

Ever since we parted, I have thought of you with deep admiration. Correspondence being so difficult, there has been no way to satisfy my desire [to speak with you]. Bhikṣu Dharmadīrgha arrived with your wonderful letter, which I respectfully received and read with great delight. I also received two rolls of white [silk] and your volume of verses. Being a person of little virtue, I am ashamed that I am unworthy your generosity. It is distressing! The weather has gradually turned agreeable. I do not know how you have fared since sending your letter. I imagine that your mind is in accord with the treatises of the hundred schools, that you are contemplating the nine divisions of the sūtras, establishing the banner of the true Dharma, guiding people back to the origin, beating the drum of victory, defeating arrogant non-Buddhists, standing undaunted before kings and nobles, and offering praise and censure to eminent men.[106] This would all be good and proper! I am mediocre and worthless and my strength is declining. Moreover, the more I contemplate virtue and esteem humaneness, [the more I realize I must] work harder.

In the past, when I was traveling in your country, I was able to meet your reverence. At the assembly in Kānyakubja, we held a debate so that all the kings and the hundreds of thousands of people in attendance could assess the depth and shallowness [of our arguments]. I established the meaning of the Great Vehicle. You raised the doctrine of the partial teaching [i.e., Hinayana]. Amid the back and forth, our expressions were inevitably high and low. In order to preserve the correct principles, without regard for peoples' feelings, we continually provoked and offended [one another]. However, after the debate, we found each other open and clear. Now the envoy has conveyed the Dharma Master's gratitude and regrets. Why cling to such unnecessary sentiments? The Dharma Master's learning is rich and your words are pure. Your intention is firm and your commitment reaches farther than the waves of the Anavatapta River. The purity of the Māṇi Jewel cannot match the clarity [of your mind]. You are a model for future generations and belong among eminent men. You have vowed to provide a good example by propagating the correct teachings. As for encompassing the truth and speaking about the ultimate, nothing surpasses the Great Vehicle. I regret that the Dharma Master does not have deeper faith in this. This is called focusing on the goat and deer cart but abandoning the white ox cart, or admiring quartz but dismissing crystal.[107] It is clear that you are a person of great virtue. How can you be mired in this confusion? Moreover, our bodies are merely vessels, impermanent and difficult to protect. One should develop the great mind as soon as possible and solemnly adhere to the right view so that one has no regrets at the moment of death!

Now the emissary is returning to your country. I have respectfully asked that he convey my sincerity and the enclosed gifts to express my gratitude for your message. I cannot fully express the depth of my feelings. Please note: on my return journey, I lost a bundle of scriptures while crossing the Indus River. I have recorded the titles in a separate document. Please send the texts listed there. As for other matters, I cannot go into details here.

Respectfully yours, Bhiksu Xuanzang

CHAPTER 19

Letter to Jñānaprabha

from the *Biography of the Trepiṭaka Master*

Xuanzang composed the following letter around the same time he wrote to Prajñādeva. This letter is addressed to the monk Jñānaprabha, the senior disciple and successor of Xuanzang's teacher at Nālandā, Śīlabhadra. The message that Xuanzang received earlier from Prajñādeva conveyed the greetings of Jñānaprabha, whom Xuanzang knew from his years of study at Nālandā. Śīlabhadra selected Xuanzang, Jñānaprabha, and two other monks to represent the Mahayana teachings at a debate organized by the Indian king Śīlāditya. In this correspondence, Xuanzang addresses Jñānaprabha as a friend and an equal. After celebrating their teacher's wisdom and virtue and expressing grief over his death, Xuanzang informs Jñānaprabha of his most recent translation work and repeats his request for copies of the texts he lost while crossing the Indus River.

Bhiksu Xuanzang of the Great Tang has respectfully composed this letter for the senior Dharma Master Trepiṭaka Jñānaprabha of Magadha in Central India.

———

It has now been over ten years since we parted. The distance between us is vast and while I have not heard from you, my feelings of affection have grown ever stronger. When Bhikṣu Dharmadīrgha came to ask after me and report your good health, my eyes suddenly brightened. It was as though I could see your venerable face. My chest heaved; it is difficult to describe in words.

The weather has gradually turned agreeable. I do not know how you have been since sending your letter. Several years ago, a returning emissary informed me that the Great Dharma Master Śīlabhadra had realized impermanence. When I heard this, I was crushed. Ah! This is what is called sinking in the sea of suffering. The eyes of gods and men are extinguished. These painful changes, why do they come so quickly? Śīlabhadra planted the seeds of joy one ancient dawn and that tree of merit has grown through the *kalpas*. Because of this, he obtained the perfect nature that radiates sublime peace and realized the magnificent power that is the mark of great distinction. Heir to the virtue of Āryadeva, continuing the brilliance of Nāgārjuna, he relit the torch of wisdom and reestablished the banner of the Dharma.[108] He extinguished the flames on the mountain of error and stopped the torrent of the sea of confusion. He drove the weary to the land of treasures and showed the lost the great way. Vast! Lofty! He is the ridgepole of the true teachings. Moreover, the works of the three vehicles, the partial and complete teachings, as well as the books of outsiders who espouse nihilism and eternalism, were all carefully studied and stored deeply in the mansion of his mind. He easily understood abstruse literature and could invariably explain obscure principles. He thus inspired insiders and outsiders to take refuge in the Buddha's teaching. He was the leading teacher of India. Moreover, day and night, he never tired of leading people to what is right. His vessel of the Way was overflowing. Though he poured it out, it was never exhausted.

In the past, when I was inquiring about the Way, I was able to receive his teachings. Although I can be called a common fool, I was like the fleabane that relies on hemp to grow straight. When I left to return to China, he exhorted me with words that were exceptionally deep and gracious. It is as though I can still hear them today. I had hoped he would live a long and secure life as an exemplary proponent of the profound teachings. Who knew he would return to eternity so suddenly? It is unbearable to remember what is gone forever.

I humbly presume that the Dharma Master, who long ago inherited the Master's elegant teachings and ascended the hall [as his successor], is reluctant to let him go. It is hard to handle. What to do? What to do? Since this is the nature of things, it must be accepted. I hope you will restrain your emotions. In the past, after the Great Awakened One's radiance faded, Mahākāśyapa carried on the great work. Following Śāṇakavāsin's transformation, Upagupta expounded the excellent path.[109] Now the Dharma General has returned to purity and the Dharma Master has been entrusted with this matter. I only hope that your clear words and subtle arguments will always flow like the four seas and that your merit, wisdom, and dignity will endure like the five mountains.

As for the sūtras and treatises I brought back with me, I have already translated over thirty large and small works, including the *Discourse on the Stages of Yogic Practice*. The *Treasury of Abhidharma with Commentary* (*Abhidharmakośa Bhāṣya*) and the *Treatise on the Abhidharma that Conforms to Correct Principle* (*Abhidharmanyāyānusāra Śāstra*) are not yet complete, but I will certainly finish them this year. Currently, the emperor of the Great Tang is in excellent health and presides over a land at peace. With the compassion of a wheel-turning monarch, he guides as a Dharma king. The sūtras and treatises I have translated have received prefaces from his divine brush, and he has ordered them copied and distributed within our empire and in neighboring kingdoms so that they may be revered and studied. Although we live at the end of the age of the semblance Dharma, the Dharma teachings remain brilliant, harmonious, and profound. It is no different from what transpired at Jetavana in Śrāvasti.[110]

I humbly wish to inform you: back when I was crossing the Indus River, I lost a bundle of scriptures. Now I have recorded their titles as follows. When you send your next letter, please include these texts. I am also sending some gifts. I hope that you will condescend to accept them. The road is long so I could not send more. Please do not be offended by such meager offerings.

Respectfully, Xuanzang

CHAPTER 20

Letter to Emperor Gaozong

from the *Biography of the Trepiṭaka Master*

In the fall of 657, Xuanzang wrote a letter to Emperor Gaozong requesting permission to move from the capital to the
remote Shaolin Monastery in the mountains west of the eastern capital city of Luoyang. Xuanzang had already asked
to live at Shaolin immediately after his return from India
in 645. At that time, Emperor Taizong refused his request
and appointed him to live in Chang'an at Hongfu Monastery instead. After a dozen years of shuttling back and forth
between the two capitals, entertaining officials and patrons,
and overseeing a massive translation project, Xuanzang had
grown weary. Sensing the approach of death, he conveyed
the sense of urgency he felt to put the teachings he had long
studied and translated into practice. At that time, Shaolin
Monastery was famous for its beautiful mountain setting, its
history of translation work, and its conduciveness to meditation. (It is now more famous for its martial arts training.)
In this letter, Xuanzang is appropriately self-deprecating
and writes in the ornate, allusive prose expected of someone
of his aristocratic background. Despite this heartfelt plea
to retire to a more tranquil setting, his request was denied.

Writing that a monk of Xuanzang's stature should be able
to see the marketplace as a hermitage, the emperor warned,
"I hope you will put an end to this talk. Do not ask again."

————

The monk Xuanzang says: I have heard that the road to *bodhi* is long.
Those who seek it require provisions. The river of birth and death
is deep. Those who cross it require a raft. Provisions are the marvelous practices of the three disciplines and the three wisdoms. They
are not things like food. Rafts are the pure activities of the eight
acceptances and eight contemplations.[111] They are not like ordinary
boats. Therefore, all buddhas are equipped to cross to the other
shore, but ordinary people, lacking [provisions], are submerged
in birth and death. Because of this, they are set adrift through the
boundless three realms on the river of seven contaminants. Amid the
vastness of the four kinds of birth, they drown beneath the waves
of the ten fetters.[112] Tossed about in the waves and mist, there is no
one who does not become confused and intoxicated. [This lasts for
as long it takes] an entire *kalpa* stone to be ground down or for an
entire city to be emptied of mustard seeds. [Most people] do not
know that they can ride the three carts to escape the burning house
or that the eightfold path will lead them to the treasure store.[113] It
is truly pitiable! Even the autumn wind cannot add to my sighs. It
is better to consider the sentiments of Confucius. That is why there
has never been someone who attends a meal but refuses to eat or
who goes to sleep but remains alert.[114]

I only have this body that has been provisionally assembled
through myriad conditions and I am constantly reminded that it is
impermanent. Even a tree on a bank or a vine in a well cannot match
this precariousness, and water froth in a dry city cannot compare
with this instability. This is why one cannot expect their days and
nights to last long. Months and years have flown past and sixty years

are already gone. Reflecting on this speed puts one's life in perspective. Moreover, I sought the Dharma and searched for teachers when I was young. There was no country I did not visit. The roads were long and my body was exhausted. Now I am growing increasingly weak. Watching the passing shadows and sunlight, how many more years do I have? My provisions are inadequate and the road ahead is closing in. Every day this pains me. I cannot fully express it in writing. Although my life has little value, I have had the great fortune of meeting brilliant sages. I enjoyed the extraordinary favor of the previous court and the undeserved kindness of Your Majesty. I have been immersed in your generous compassion for many years. My reputation has benefited, my worth has increased, and my fame has spread. Flying without wings and ascending to the sky while remaining seated, receiving offerings of the four necessities and surpassing the glory of peers—I have searched among the ancients and there are none who have achieved this. By what virtue and what merit have I arrived at this place? It all stems from the vast waves of Heaven and the graciousness of the sun and moon. These cause [ordinary] rocks from Mount Yan to be considered treasures and inferior horses to be highly valued.

When I examine myself, I feel only deep shame. Moreover, former sages have correctly pointed out the dangers of conceit and arrogance. To have few desires and know what is enough is also the genuine teaching of all buddhas. Reflecting on myself, my skills and work are inconsequential. My reputation and actions are nothing. It is inappropriate for me to presume that Heaven's compassion and the sage's benevolence will extend indefinitely. I beg to resign and spend my remaining days in the mountains and forests, to worship, recite scriptures, and practice in order to repay all that I have received. Moreover, Your Majesty, with the reverence of a wheel-turning king and the transformative power of a Dharma-spreading monarch, ordered that the scriptures obtained from the

Western Regions be translated. Without good reason, I, a person of no capacity, was appointed to this task. Since receiving this imperial directive, I have worked day and night without rest. I have now translated over six hundred fascicles of the essential teachings of the Tripiṭaka and the four *āgamas*, as well as the pivotal works of the Greater and Lesser Vehicles. In the Western Regions, the forest of practices of commoners and sages and the glimmering sea of the eighty thousand Dharma gates are considered classics and recited for the protection of the kingdom and its territories. Everything one needs can be found within [these texts]. Just like selecting among the larger and smaller trees in a forest, or like gathering angular or round precious stones at the seashore, it is the same with the teachings of scholars. I use these [translations] to repay the kindness of the state. Truly, the debt can never be repaid, but I hope to return one ten-thousandth of what I owe. However, to vanquish afflictions, one must rely on meditation and wisdom. Like the two wheels of a carriage, if one is lacking the carriage cannot function. To study wisdom is to delve into the meaning of sūtras and treatises. To study meditation is to sit quietly in the forest. From a young age, I have concentrated my efforts on the study of doctrine. Only with regard to the four *dhyānas* and nine absorptions have I lacked the time to settle my mind.[115] Now I wish to devote myself to the practice of meditation, to clarify my mind and still its waves, to control the untamed ape of my emotions and restrain the charging elephant of my will. If I do not withdraw to the mountains this cannot be accomplished.

I have heard that in this prefecture Mount Shaoshi in the Song-gao range has overlapping cliffs and ridges and many marvelous peaks and canyons. This place gives birth to wind and clouds and contains stores of benevolence and wisdom. Fruits and medicinal herbs are abundant and the moss and vines hang in the clear air. It is truly one of the famous mountains within the four seas and one of the divine peaks within this country. In this place, there are monasteries such as Shaolin and Xianju. All are nestled among rocks and ravines and surrounded by forests and springs. The Buddhist services here are solemn and dignified and the buildings are remote and uncrowded. This is where the Later Wei Dynasty Tripiṭaka Master Bodhiruci translated scriptures.[116] It is truly a place to take refuge in the practice of meditative contemplation. Moreover, the two court scholars named Shu requested to be released to return to [their native Dong]hai, quitting their glorious [positions]. The laymen Chao Fu and Xu You also knew to dwell in the truth and cultivate simplicity.[117] It is the same with me. I became a monk for the sake of the Dharma. For someone stuck inside city walls, the fresh breeze is compelling. When they consider it, their shame increases. Only Your Majesty's brilliance exceeds that of the seven stars and illuminates the depths of the nine netherworlds. I humbly beg you to shine your light on this ignorant but sincere person. Make an exceptional show of virtue and allow me to quit the common world of dust and noise and sweep away the traces of the human realm. Allow me to go among the deer and follow the flocks of ducks and cranes; to perch myself atop rocks and shelter my shadow in the shade of a tree; to keep watch over the ape of the mind and contemplate the true characteristics of the Dharma; to cause the thieves of the four *māras* and nine bonds to have no point of entry; to simultaneously give rise to the mind of five endurances and ten practices; to make the gradual progression of *bodhi* into the good cause for reaching the other shore; and to, externally, not obstruct the Imperial wind and, internally, augment my work.[118] In this way, I would pay my last regards to Heaven's kindness. If you take pity on me and grant this request, then I would follow the refined conduct of Huiyuan on Mount Lu and continue the lofty work of Daolin on [Mount] Shanxiu.[119] I still hope to continue translating in time spent outside of meditation. I would enjoy that very much.

I have respectfully come to the imperial palace to submit this petition and await a response. Having impudently made contact with the mighty Imperial House, I am profoundly uneasy about my offense.

CHAPTER 21

The Death of Xuanzang

from the *Biography of the Trepiṭaka Master*

Xuanzang finally received permission to leave the capital in the winter of 659. He and some members of his translation team relocated to Yuhua Monastery, a former imperial retreat located in the mountains north of Chang'an. At Yuhua, Xuanzang continued his translation work for five years until, in the spring of 664, he abruptly stopped. Realizing that death was near, he venerated buddha images in the surrounding area and devoted himself to meditation. Confined to bed after a minor injury, Xuanzang had a series of dreams that seemed to presage his impending rebirth as a member of Maitreya's inner circle in Tuṣita Heaven. Three weeks after ending his translation work, Xuanzang assumed the posture of the dying Buddha—lying on his right side with his right hand supporting his head and his left hand on his left thigh—and passed away. He was sixty-two years old.

After the Dharma Master translated the *Great Perfection of Wisdom Sūtra*, he knew that his strength was failing and death was near. He spoke to his disciples saying, "The main reason I came to Yuhua was [to translate] the *Great Perfection of Wisdom Sūtra*. Now my translation work is finished and my life's work is complete. If after I die you want to send me off in an appropriate and frugal way, you can wrap [my body] in woven reeds and leave it in a secluded mountain ravine far from the monastery. Impure bodies must be kept at a distance." When his disciples heard this, they were distraught and choked back tears. Wiping away their tears, they said, "The Master's physical strength is still adequate and his venerable appearance is no different than before. Why is he suddenly saying this?" The Dharma Master said, "I know it myself. How can you understand?"

On the first day of the first month of spring in the first year of the Linde era (664), eminent translators and members of the assembly at Yuhua Monastery respectfully requested that the Master translate the *Great Sūtra of Accumulated Treasures*. The Dharma Master, seeing the assembly's sincerity, bowed his head and accepted [their request]. After translating a few lines, he gathered up the Sanskrit text and stopped, saying to the assembly, "The [number of] scrolls in this sūtra are similar to those in the *Great Perfection of Wisdom Sūtra*. I no longer have the strength to manage this. The time of my death is already approaching. It is not far off. Now I want to go to Lanzhi and other valleys to pay my last respects to the many buddha images." Thereafter, he went out together with his disciples. The remaining monks looked at one another; everyone was crying.

After paying his respects [to the buddha images], the Master returned to the monastery and devoted himself completely to practicing the Way, putting an end to all translation work. On the eighth day, his disciple, the Gaochang monk Xuanjue, dreamed that he saw an imposing and lofty stūpa suddenly collapse. Seeing this, he was startled and told the Master. The Dharma Master said, "It is not about you. It is a sign of my cessation." On the evening of the ninth day, while crossing a ditch behind his room, [the Master] fell and injured his shin slightly. For that reason, he was confined to bed and his breathing gradually grew faint. On the sixteenth day, as though awakening from a dream, he said, "There is a white lotus flower before my eyes. It is bigger than a basin, lovely, fresh and pure."

On the seventeenth day, he had another dream in which he saw hundreds of thousands of people of great size, all wearing brocade robes. They first decorated the Dharma Master's bedroom with embroidered silks, beautiful flowers, and jewels. They then adorned the inside and outside of the sūtra translation cloister. In the mountains and forests behind the cloister, they erected banners of various colors and played music. Outside the gate [the Master] also saw innumerable jeweled chariots. Inside the chariots were hundreds of thousands of different types of fragrant foods and fine fruits. These were not of the human realm. One after the other, the [spirits] presented these things to the Dharma Master as offerings. The Dharma Master declined, saying, "These kinds of rare delicacies can only be eaten by those who have obtained supranormal powers. I have not reached this stage. How could I dare accept?" Even though he declined, [the spirits] continued to bring him food. When one of his attendants coughed softly, the Master opened his eyes and related the aforementioned events to the abbot Huide.

The Dharma Master also said, "My whole life I have cultivated merit and wisdom. Based on the appearance [of these spirits], it seems that my efforts have not been in vain. I believe and know that the Buddha's teaching of cause and effect is not false." Thereafter he asked Dharma Master Jiashang to record all the sūtras and treatises that he had translated. There were a total of 74 volumes in 1,338 fascicles. The many images that he had made were also recorded. [These included] one thousand images of Maitreya and ten koṭīs of clay images.[120] He had copied the *Diamond Sūtra*, *Original Vows of the Medicine Master Tathāgata of Lapis Light*, *Dhāraṇī of the Six Gates*, and other sūtras ten times each. He had made offerings to more than ten thousand members of the two merit fields—those pitiable and poor and those worthy of respect. He had lit hundreds of thousands of lamps and redeemed countless beings. After the record was complete, [the Master] asked Jiashang to read it aloud. Having heard it, he put his palms together in joyful celebration. He also told his disciples, "The time of my death is approaching. I would like to make my confession. It is appropriate for all those with whom I have an affinity to gather together." Thereupon, he gave away his clothing and other possessions. He then requested that an image be made and exhorted the monks to practice the Way.

On the twenty-third day, there was a vegetarian feast and a distribution of alms. On this day, [the Master] also requested that the sculptor Song Fazhi erect an image of [Maitreya realizing] *bodhi* in the Jiashou Hall.[121] Once the frame was finished, he joyfully said farewell to members of the monastic community, eminent translators, his disciples, and others, saying, "I have a deep aversion to this noxious body. My work is finished and it is not appropriate to remain any longer. I vow that the blessings and wisdom I have cultivated will be transferred to all beings. May all beings be born together in Tuṣita Heaven within Maitreya's inner circle to serve the Compassionate Sage. When the [next] Buddha descends to be born, I vow to follow him down to fully carry out the Buddha's work until I reach supreme *bodhi*."

After saying goodbye, quieting and concentrating his mind, he again chanted: "The aggregate of form does not exist; sensation, perception, volition, consciousness also do not exist. The realm of eyes does not exist [and so on up to] the realm of mind, which also does not exist. The realm of eye consciousness does not exist [and so on up to] the realm of mind consciousness, which also does not exist. Ignorance does not exist [and so on up to] old age and death, which also do not exist. *Bodhi* does not exist. Nonexistence also does not exist." He also spoke a verse to instruct those around him: "Homage to Maitreya Tathāgata, worthy, perfectly awakened. I vow, together with all beings, to swiftly behold your compassionate face. Homage to the inner circle that dwells with Maitreya Tathāgata. I vow to relinquish my life to be born among them." At that time, the monastery's abbot Huide also had a dream in which he saw a thousand golden bodies coming from the east. They entered the Sūtra Translation Hall and the scent of fragrant flowers filled the air.

In the middle of the night on the fourth day of the second month, the monk in charge of tending the sick, Chan Master Mingzang, saw two people, each of whom were about ten feet tall. They carried a white lotus flower the size of a cart wheel. The flower had three layers of petals, each over a foot long, that were bright, pure, and lovely. As they were bringing it before the Dharma Master, the people holding the flower said, "All the master's beginningless bad karma that has harmed sentient beings is now completely eradicated because of this minor illness. This is a cause for joy and celebration." When the Dharma Master saw this, he held his palms together for a long time. Then he supported his head with his right hand and placed his left hand on his left thigh. Reclining on his right side, he positioned one foot on top of the other. Until the time of his death, [the Master] did not turn over and did not drink or eat.

In the middle of the night on the fifth day, his disciple Guang-deng asked, "Has the master decided to obtain rebirth in Maitreya's inner cloister or not?" The Dharma Master responded, "I will obtain rebirth." After speaking, his breathing gradually grew faint. A little while later, his spirit departed. His attendant did not realize [at first], but by holding a thread of silk [before his nose] it was confirmed. Starting from his feet, he gradually grew cold until just the crown of his head was warm. His face was pink and looked happier than usual. After forty-nine days, there was no change [in his appearance] and no unusual smell.[122] If not for the dignity of his meditation and wisdom and the endowment of his pervasive discipline, how could this be?

Legacy

CHAPTER 22

Xuanzang's Teachings

Yogācāra in East Asia

XUANZANG was laid to rest in the spring of 664. According to his disciples, more than a million people attended his funeral procession with thirty thousand staying on to spend the night near his grave. It was a remarkable expression of mourning for one of the empire's most celebrated monks, yet there were some conspicuous absences. Although Emperor Gaozong formally expressed his sorrow at Xuanzang's passing and ordered all funeral expenses covered by the court, there is no record of the emperor or any other high official attending the services. Contrary to custom, no member of the court composed a eulogy or a funerary inscription for Xuanzang, nor was he awarded any titles or other posthumous honors. There was no stone stele detailing his accomplishments erected at his grave, and no memorial halls were established at any of the monasteries where he had lived. These were conventional honors accorded to other prominent clerics of his generation, but they were not bestowed on Xuanzang. Immediately after learning of Xuanzang's death, Emperor Gaozong abruptly terminated the translation work that Xuanzang had overseen for so long. The team of translators he assembled was disbanded and dispersed. Rather than preserve Xuanzang's memory and legacy, it was as though the emperor and the court were seeking to distance themselves from the monk they had once kept so close. Just five years after his death,

Xuanzang's body, which had been buried ten kilometers southeast of the city at a place known as White Deer Plateau, was disinterred and moved farther from the capital. "This was because," his disciple reported, "the original tomb was too near the capital. It was visible from the imperial palace, and the emperor was distressed whenever he saw it."[123]

It may be that Emperor Gaozong could not bear to be reminded of the loss of his friend and mentor, but some modern scholars have suggested another, less charitable reading: Xuanzang had fallen out of favor in the years before his death and members of both the court and the sangha were leaving him behind.[124] Politically, Xuanzang had unavoidably become entangled in the purges of Emperor Gaozong's and Wu Zetian's political opponents, several of whom had been early students and supporters. For many clerics in the capital, however, the problem was not Xuanzang's political allegiances but his teachings. During Xuanzang's life, his "new" interpretation of Yogācāra doctrine had been elevated to orthodoxy, but the popularity of these teachings seemed to derive more from his charisma and the imperial support it garnered than from any consensus of its superiority. In fact, some elements of Xuanzang's teachings were so at odds with mainstream Chinese Buddhist Mahāyāna that the smoldering controversies they provoked during his life flared into open rejection after his death.

The central point of contention was whether all beings had the capacity for awakening. Xuanzang championed the position of the Indian Yogācāra master Dharmapāla (530–61), who identified five distinct lineages of sentient beings. There were those who were destined to be buddhas, those who would be *pratyeka* (solitary) buddhas, and those who would become voice hearers, or *arhats*. The destinies of a fourth lineage of beings were classified as "undetermined"; they had the capacity to move from one lineage to another, based on the teachings they received and the practices they carried out. Those belonging to the fifth lineage, most controversially, had no capacity for awakening at all. These unfortunate beings were "without lineage." Also known as *icchantikas*, they were doomed to wander in saṃsāra forever. The premise that there were distinct classes of beings with predetermined, unalterable spiritual destinies ran counter to the broadly accepted notion of the *ekayāna*, or one vehicle.

According to influential Mahāyāna scriptures like the *Lotus Sūtra* and the *Nirvāṇa Sūtra*, there are different levels of teachings and various speeds for advancing along the path to awakening. There is, however, only one unified Dharma that eventually leads all beings to the singular destination of nirvāṇa. The Yogācāra teachings promoted by Xuanzang not only appeared to contradict the conviction that diverse Buddhist teachings were expressions of a single truth, but it also asserted that the potential for buddhahood was not universal but restricted to particular kinds of beings. For the majority of Chinese Buddhists, all sentient beings, no matter their status or condition, held within them the "seed" of awakening. Buddhahood, in other words, was not something external that a person could acquire but was something innate that only needed to be realized. This latent potential was nondiscriminatory; it was the same in the sage as it was in the sinner. There was, therefore, no ultimate distinction between qualities like wisdom and ignorance, purity and defilement, nirvāṇa and saṃsāra. These states were merely different expressions of the same unified buddha nature. This teaching was so central to many popular sūtras and treatises that Xuanzang's version of Yogācāra, critics argued, could only be understood as a rudimentary form of the Mahāyāna.[125] The doctrines that he and his disciples referred to as "Consciousness Only" (Weishi), were thus disparaged as "Dharma Characteristics" (Faxiang), implying that they dealt only with superficial forms of the Dharma. This was in contrast to the more advanced, perfect form of the Mahāyāna, which proponents called "Dharma Nature" (Faxing) because, they held, it represented the true nature or essence of the teachings. The fact that Xuanzang's new Yogācāra translations and commentaries came to be known by the initially pejorative title of "Dharma Characteristics" gives a good indication of how the tradition was received by later generations.

The work of Xuanzang's immediate disciples played a decisive role in clarifying and popularizing their master's doctrinal positions and exegetical methods. In the immediate aftermath of Xuanzang's death, two of his students in particular rose to become preeminent authorities on the new Yogācāra translations. The first was Ji (aka Kuiji; 632–82). Orphaned at the age of nine, Ji became a monk at seventeen and joined Xuanzang's translation team at Ci'en Monastery shortly thereafter. For the remainder of Xuanzang's life, Ji remained by his side, serving as his amanuensis and composing influential commentaries on several key Yogācāra works. He is credited with helping Xuanzang compile the *Treatise Establishing Consciousness Only* (*Cheng weishi lun*), an influential work that foregrounds Dharmapāla's teachings. Two of Ji's commentaries on this text—the *Commentary on the Treatise Establishing Consciousness Only* (*Chengweishi lun shuji*) and the *Essentials for Grasping the Treatise Establishing Consciousness Only* (*Chengweishi lun zhangzhong shuyao*)—became foundational works for later generations of Dharma Characteristics adherents in China, Japan, and Korea. Ji's long tutelage under Xuanzang culminated in his elevation as Xuanzang's successor at Ci'en Monastery. For this reason, he is honored as the first patriarch of the so-called Ci'en branch of the Dharma Characteristics tradition.

The Dharma Characteristics sect in Japan (known as Hossō, the Japanese pronunciation of the Chinese Faxiang) still venerates Ji as a founding figure in its lineage, but the monk responsible for first introducing Xuanzang's teachings to Japan was the Japanese cleric Dōshō (629–700). After arriving at Ci'en Monastery in 653, according to later Japanese accounts, "Dōshō stayed with Tripitika Master Xuanzang, living with him in the same room and studying under him together with Kuiji for many years. The Tripiṭaka Master secretly transmitted the outline of the Dharma Characteristics school to him, particularly the gate of meditation."[126] After a seven-year apprenticeship, Dōshō returned to the Japanese capital of Nara to propagate the new teachings at Gangōji Temple. Other Japanese monks, eager to learn more about the new texts and teachings Xuanzang had brought back from India, followed in Dōshō's footsteps. The clerics Chitsū (fl. 658–72) and Chidatsu (fl. 658), both of whom traveled to China in 658 to study under Xuanzang, returned to Japan with additional translations and treatises. The second transmission of the Dharma Characteristics sect to Japan is traced to these two monks. Although the influence of these new Yogācāra teachings would later subside in favor of other China-derived traditions like Tendai, Shingon, Pure Land, and Zen, the Hossō sect maintained a distinctive identity in Japan. Unlike in China and Korea, where the Dharma Characteristics tradition soon became obsolete, the study and practice of Xuanzang and Ji's teachings has continued in Japan for well over thirteen hundred years.[127]

Xuanzang features prominently in the ritual paintings of Yogācāra patriarchs displayed at the headquarters of the Japanese Hossō school. These works conventionally show Xuanzang together with his five Indian predecessors and his three Chinese successors: Ji, the first Chinese patriarch; Huizhao (650–714), the second; and Zhizhou (668–723), the third and, it seems, the last (p. 193). This seemingly straightforward line of succession implies an uncomplicated transmission of Xuanzang's teachings from master to disciple over the course of several generations. In fact, conventional lineage schemes simplify the more complicated, competing interpretations of Yogācāra doctrines that divided some of Xuanzang's immediate disciples. While Ji was overseeing operations at Ci'en Monastery, for example, eight blocks away at Ximing Monastery, another of Xuanzang's disciples was preaching a divergent form of Yogācāra, one in which all beings, even *icchantikas*, had the capacity for awakening. That disciple, Wŏnch'ŭk (613–99), had arrived in China from his native Korea in 627 at the age of fifteen. At that time, Xuanzang was still preparing to leave for India, and, like Xuanzang, Wŏnch'ŭk first studied Yogācāra through the "old" translations of Paramārtha. After Xuanzang's return, Wŏnch'ŭk joined his translation team as a "verifier"—a task entrusted to someone so conversant with Indian Buddhist doctrine that they could identify infelicities in Chinese translations. After Xuanzang's death, Wŏnch'ŭk's attempted to reconcile the translations of Paramārtha he had studied in his youth with the new translations he helped Xuanzang produce later in life. These ecumenical efforts earned him the scorn of some of Xuanzang's disciples and a rivalry appears to have developed between factions loyal to Ji and those devoted to Wŏnch'ŭk. Some went so far as to accuse Wŏnch'ŭk of bribing monastic gatekeepers so that he could surreptitiously listen to Xuanzang's lectures and then present them as his own, disingenuously building a reputation as Xuanzang's brightest student. The story is almost certainly baseless but it is indicative of Wŏnch'ŭk's controversial legacy in China, which some scholars have attributed to his "heterodox" doctrinal

OPPOSITE: Mandala of the Dharma Characteristics Lineage. The sixteen patriarchs surrounding the bodhisattva Maitreya include five Indian masters (Asaṅga, Vasubandhu, Dharmapāla, Dignāga, and Śīlabhadra) at the top; four Chinese masters (Xuanzang, Ji, Huizhao, and Zhizhou) in the middle; and eight Japanese masters, beginning with Zenju Sōjō (723–97) and ending with Senkō Sōzu (934–1104), at the bottom. Kōfukuji, Nara, 15th c. Source: *Saiyūki no shiruku rōdo*.

positions and others have suggested stemmed from anti-Korean discrimination. Whatever the cause, Wŏnch'ŭk's influence in China and Japan was relatively muted despite the fact that his learned commentaries were studied in both places.

His legacy in Korea is, unsurprisingly, rather different. There, Wŏnch'ŭk is revered as the first patriarch of Ximing Branch of the Pŏpsong (the Korean pronunciation of Faxiang) lineage. Although Wŏnch'ŭk died in China and never returned to Korea, tradition holds that the monk Tojŭng (fl. 692) transmitted Dharma Characteristics texts and teachings back to his native Silla after a period of study under Wŏnch'ŭk at Ximing Monastery in the Chinese capital. As in China, other Buddhist schools in Korea eventually absorbed the once distinctive Yogācāra teachings. Wŏnch'ŭk's writings nonetheless continued to inspire later generations of monks and nuns, spreading as far as Tibet, where his famous *Commentary on the Sūtra That Explicates the Profound Meaning* (*Jieshenmi jing shu*), known paradoxically as the "Great Chinese Commentary," played a formative role in the teachings of Tsongkhapa (1357–1419) and the Gelugpa tradition.

In the centuries following Xuanzang's death, Buddhism in China underwent a gradual shift away from Indic models toward more distinctively "Chinese" forms of practice. These new approaches, which emphasized meditation, recitation, and visualization, had less use for the detailed exegeses on scholarly Indian treatises that Xuanzang and his disciples had mastered. For some monks, all scriptures and commentaries were mere expedients, if not outright impediments, to realization. Chan clerics, for example, famously claimed to possess a special mind-to-mind transmission that occurred "outside the scriptures and did not rely on words and letters." Authority and authenticity, for later generations of Chinese Buddhists, became less a matter of identifying and aligning with Indian notions of orthodoxy and more about developing immediate, personal relationships with buddhas, bodhisattvas, and patriarchs.

Interest in Xuanzang's teachings on Yogācāra consequently faded rather quickly. Tradition holds that the Dharma Characteristics school petered out in China after the death of the third patriarch, Zhizhou (668–723), but this is misleading. While its time in the spotlight was brief, and while other monks roundly rejected its more controversial doctrines, many of the teachings that Xuanzang championed during his life had a profound influence on the later development of Buddhism in East Asia. Other Buddhist traditions accepted and adopted fundamental Yogācāra doctrines concerning the structure and function of consciousness and the methods for cultivating the body and mind. Even Chan monks, who dismissed the text-based, scholastic approach epitomized by Xuanzang and his disciples, took the existence of the storehouse consciousness (*ālayavijñāna*) for granted. Yogācāra teachings, having become part of the fabric of Buddhism in China, were no longer exclusively associated with Dharma Characteristics tradition. The very success of their doctrines rendered the Yogācāra tradition redundant.

As interest in Yogācāra waned, many of the commentaries produced by Xuanzang's disciples were neglected and eventually lost to fire, insects, and mold. Very few of these works were ever printed, existing instead as laboriously hand-copied manuscripts that, if not widely distributed and regularly reproduced, were at constant risk of being lost. At least some of these texts survived into the tenth century, when Chan monks quoted from them, but by the Ming Dynasty (1368–1644) most had disappeared. Anyone wanting to study Yogācāra doctrines at that time could still turn to Xuanzang's translations, which were included in various editions of the Buddhist canon, but they could no longer access the influential commentaries authored by Ji and other Tang Dynasty exegetes. During the sixteenth century, when some monks attempted to resurrect Yogācāra teachings after a lull of nearly five hundred years, they were hobbled by a lack of material. The impetus for the sudden revival appears to have been self-defense. At that time, Neo-Confucian thought (Daoxue), reinvigorated through the work of Wang Yangming (1472–1529), offered compelling accounts of human experience and moral responsibility. Many of these teachings drew liberally from Buddhist doctrines, but they were framed in part as correctives to the allegedly anti-intellectual and self-centered practices of Buddhists and Daoists who, Wang Yangming argued, were "lost in vagaries, illusions, emptiness, and stillness and had nothing to do with the family, state or world."[128] In the midst of this Neo-Confucian renaissance, the Buddhist cleric Xuelang Hong'en (1545–1608) assembled an anthology of eight "essential" Yogācāra works to showcase Buddhist methods for analyzing the nature and processes of consciousness, the relationship between knowledge and action, and the ethical implications of karma.[129] The collection included several of Xuanzang's translations of Indian treatises on Yogācāra doctrine and logic as well as his *Verses on the Structure of the Eight Consciousnesses*. These works, which inspired dozens of new commentaries, were meant to demonstrate that the Buddhist tradition could not be dismissed as simplistic faith or solipsistic contemplation and should be taken seriously as a system of epistemological, ethical, logical analysis every bit as efficacious as Neo-Confucian theories.

Around the same time that monks were responding to challenges from Neo-Confucian critics, they were also confronted with an entirely new, unprecedented adversary: Christian missionaries. Arriving in China in the late sixteenth century, Jesuit clerics found common cause with Neo-Confucian scholars but were unimpressed with Buddhist monks, whom they dismissed as superstitious adherents of a nihilistic religion. In response, Xuanzang's translations of Yogācāra texts were cited as evidence that Buddhists were not only perfectly rational but also that their system of logic confirmed the inherent superiority of Buddhist epistemology over Christian theology. Deploying the classic Buddhist syllogism developed by Dignāga and introduced to China by Xuanzang, some monks claimed to prove definitively the premise that the world was comprised of consciousness only, thereby belying the Christian assertion that an omnipotent God created and sustained the world. The Buddhists, not surprisingly, declared themselves the victors in this one-sided debate and wondered if the Jesuits should not observe the conventional protocol of Indian debates, where the losers voluntarily surrendered under the banner of the winners, reversed their robes and left through the side door, or submitted to beheading.[130] The Jesuits, all evidence suggests, remained unconvinced, unrepentant, and in full possession of their heads.

Interest in Christianity only continued to grow in China while enthusiasm for Yogācāra-based apologetics dwindled. It was another four centuries before the teachings of the Dharma Characteristics tradition returned again to relevance. This second revival was, like the first, spurred by criticism. But now, rather than relying on a limited selection of translated Indic texts, modern proponents of Yogācāra finally had access to the long-lost commentaries of Ji and other Tang Dynasty scholars. The rediscovery of these important works was the result of an extraordinary collaboration between European scholars, Japanese monks, and Chinese intellectuals. The modern Yogācāra resurgence set in motion by these men—and they were all men, as the discipline of Buddhist studies remained segregated along both gender and ethnic lines—won Xuanzang and his teachings a new modern, global audience.

Over the course of the nineteenth century, British and French colonial officers and scholars in India were engaged in an unprecedented search for the historical origins of Buddhism. The identification and excavation of early Buddhist archaeological sites (many of which were located using Xuanzang's *Record of the Western Regions*) and the translation and study of Buddhist Sanskrit texts by European scholars were part of a broad effort to reconstruct a tradition that was all but forgotten in India and was still poorly understood in Europe. Texts and artifacts discovered in northern India and Central Asia were regularly sent back to England, France, and Germany, and European universities consequently developed into major centers for the emerging academic discipline of Indology. One of the leading figures in this new field was Max Müller (1823–1900), a German-born Orientalist named the first professor of comparative philology at Oxford's Corpus Christi College in 1868. Müller and his pioneering work on early Buddhist manuscripts attracted the interest of a small but influential group of Japanese Buddhist clerics eager to explore the origins of their own tradition. Among these, one of the most prominent was Nanjō Bunyū (1849–1927), who traveled from the Higashi Honganji Temple in Kyoto to London in 1876 to begin several years of study under Müller. Like Xuanzang, Nanjō worried that the Chinese translations of Indian Buddhist texts available in his country contained errors and discrepancies that perpetuated serious misunderstandings among Japanese Buddhists. Vowing to devote his life to rectifying these errors, he subsequently became an important member of Müller's team, translating and editing Sanskrit texts preserved in Japanese monastic libraries.

After five years in England, Nanjō and Müller completed work on their coedited volume *Buddhist Texts from Japan*. That same year, a Chinese diplomat named Yang Wenhui (1837–1911) arrived in London. Yang, a pious Buddhist layman who had established a Buddhist printing house in Nanjing decades earlier, was intrigued by the work being done by European Indologists. Through Nanjō he learned that not only did some Chinese versions of Sanskrit Buddhist texts differ significantly from the originals but also that many lost Chinese commentaries could still be found in Japan. Yang continued to correspond with Nanjō after they had both returned to their respective countries, and over the course of several years, from 1891 to 1896, Nanjō sent Yang 235 Buddhist texts gathered from monastic libraries in Japan. Included among these works were the lost Yogācāra commentaries of Xuanzang's disciples, which Yang immediately began printing and distributing. After an absence of nearly one thousand years, the definitive works of the Dharma Characteristics tradition were once again available in China.

The timing was fortuitous. Buddhists in China were still recovering from the destruction wrought by the Taiping Rebellion (1850–64), led by a man who, claiming to be the younger brother of Jesus Christ, initiated a violent campaign to destroy Buddhist monasteries and libraries. Monks and nuns were also under increasing pressure from intellectuals and officials who accused them of promoting outmoded traditions that hampered economic development and undercut social stability. In response to competition from Christian missionaries and the influx of new philosophical and scientific ideas imported from Japan, Europe, and North America, some Buddhist clerics and laypeople felt compelled to justify their tradition not only as a modern, rational religion but also as a system thoroughly grounded in logic and thus aligned with the scientific method. Inspired in part by the example of Japanese Buddhists, who had turned to Yogācāra to assert their relevance in the face of critiques during the Meiji Restoration (1868–1912), a network of monks and laypeople in China championed Yogācāra teachings as emblematic of Buddhists' past accomplishments and future potential. The Dharma Characteristics commentaries reintroduced from Japan were touted as inherently superior to the prevailing Chinese Buddhist traditions of Chan, Tiantai, and Pure Land, which many intellectuals criticized as naïve, simplistic, and ethically bankrupt. Most Chinese Buddhists, detractors argued, hid behind the doctrine of inherent awakening to obviate the need for self-improvement. If everyone is already awakened, why should they bother with changing their behavior or beliefs? Buddhists were thus accused of using "dirty tricks to justify the status quo" and intentionally obstructing progress and reform.[131] Yogācāra, in contrast, rejected the doctrine of universal, latent buddhahood and demanded the kind of arduous, transformative effort that many people believed the Chinese nation and its citizens desperately needed. So it was that the very theory that led to the rejection of the Dharma Characteristics teachings in the premodern period was singled out as its most important contribution in the modern era.

As a result, dozens of new works on Yogācāra were published during the turbulent Republican era (1912–49). In addition to the social and political theories some people divined in Yogācāra treatises, Xuanzang's translations and his disciples' commentaries were also mined for medieval Buddhist responses to modern China's problems. In the realm of philosophy, Yogācāra was heralded as a form of idealism that not only countered Western materialism but also anticipated Immanuel Kant and G. W. F. Hegel. Critically, because logic was seen as a precondition for philosophy, China required an indigenous system of logic if it were to claim a philosophical tradition on par with the West. Xuanzang's translation and Ji's commentary on the *Introduction to Logic* (*Nyāyapraveśa*) were presented as proof that such a tradition had a long history in China, and no fewer than thirty new works on Buddhist logic were published over the course of as many years. Given its close association with logic and rationality, Yogācāra was also promoted as the Buddhist tradition most compatible with modern science. The mental disciplines prescribed in Yogācāra texts, some argued, even allowed individuals to enhance their ordinary observational powers. A mind so attuned could not only validate current scientific findings, but it could also observe phenomena that modern instruments were incapable of measuring. In the emerging discipline of psychology then known as "mind science," moreover, Yogācāra theories of consciousness, particularly the workings of the "storehouse consciousness," generated insights into the origins of instinct and the mechanics of memory. Even the physical structure and biological functions of the brain were supposedly accurately described in Yogācāra texts.[132] Whatever the question, Yogācāra seemed to have the answer.

Around the same time that this renaissance was taking place in China, European scholars also began reading and writing about Xuanzang's translations. When Japanese monks traveled to Europe to learn the languages and history of early Indian Buddhism, they alerted their hosts to the value of Chinese translations of Sanskrit texts. Louis de la Vallée Poussin (1869–1938), a Belgian Indologist based at the University of Ghent, was the first to take Xuanzang seriously as a translator rather than a traveler. La Vallée Poussin's mentor at the Sorbonne in Paris, Sylvain Lévi (1863–1935), had introduced the Western world to the teachings of Yogācāra through his translation of two works by Vasubandhu.[133] La Vallée Poussin followed suit with a monumental translation of Vasubandhu's *Abhidharmakośa Bhāṣya*. At that time, the Sanskrit version of this text was presumed lost, so La Vallée Poussin based his French translation largely on Xuanzang's Chinese rendering. When a copy of the Sanskrit text was later discovered in a Tibetan monastery, Xuanzang's translation was found to be so faithful to the original that there was little need to amend La Vallée Poussin's work. La Vallée Poussin went on to publish *Vijñaptimātratāsiddhi: La Siddhi de Hiuan-Tsang*, a two-volume translation and study of Xuanzang's *Treatise Establishing Consciousness Only*. The pioneering works of Lévi and La Vallée Poussin marked the beginning of Yogācāra studies in the West and demonstrated that Xuanzang was not only a source of archaeological information but also an erudite scholar of Indian Buddhist doctrine.

Back in China, the newfound enthusiasm for Yogācāra teachings was short-lived. The various centers established for Yogācāra learning in the early decades of the twentieth century—the China Institute for Inner Studies, the Three Times Study Society, the Yogācāra Study Association—had all closed their doors by the early 1950s, shortly after the Communist Party came to power. Today, most Buddhist monastics and laypeople in China either adhere to the doctrines and practices that prevailed during the premodern period—Chan, Pure Land, Vinaya, Tiantai—or have gravitated toward the newer "humanistic Buddhism" that developed during the Republican era. Many of the Chinese intellectual traditions that once looked to Yogācāra as an invaluable native resource to rival Western learning have now mostly abandoned Xuanzang's teachings as irrelevant to their concerns. Yogācāra, they reason, was an Indian tradition transplanted to Chinese soil. The teachings of Confucius and his intellectual heirs make for better representatives of native Chinese thought. The so-called New Confucians, as the self-appointed standard-bearers of the ancient Chinese philosophical tradition, seek dialogue with their counterparts in the modern West rather than with medieval Indian Buddhist monastics and pandits.[134] Given recent nationalistic attempts to promote the uniqueness of China's history and culture, Yogācāra as a viable system of thought and practice has once again receded into the background.

Xuanzang, by contrast, is more influential than ever. His iconic status, however, has little to do with his translations and teachings. In the modern era, it is Xuanzang's travels that have become a seemingly inexhaustible source of value and meaning.

CHAPTER 23

Xuanzang's Travels

The *Record of the Western Regions* and
the Birth of Buddhist Studies

IN THE OPENING SCENE of Rudyard Kipling's *Kim*, a Tibetan Buddhist monk walks through a museum in Lahore filled with Indian Buddhist antiquities recently excavated by British archaeologists. "Delighted as a child," the monk is particularly impressed with the wise, white-bearded English curator (modeled on Kipling's father) who knows so much about the history of Buddhism.

> [The Tibetan] had heard of the travels of the Chinese pilgrims, Fu-Hiouen [Faxian] and Hwen-Tsiang [Xuanzang], and was anxious to know if there was any translation of their record. He drew in his breath as he turned helplessly over the pages of Beal and Stanislas Julien. "'Tis all here. A treasure locked." Then he composed himself reverently to listen to fragments hastily rendered into Urdu. For the first time he heard of the labours of European scholars, who by the help of these and a hundred other documents have identified the Holy Places of Buddhism.[135]

So it was that readers of the best-selling, critically acclaimed novel learned how an old English curator taught a Tibetan monk about the European scholars who had finally revealed the treasures of the Buddhist tradition.

During the nineteenth century, British explorers discovered long-lost Buddhist monasteries and stūpas using modern French and English translations of medieval Chinese Buddhist texts. These men surveyed and excavated the buried monuments and then sent their contents to museums for the edification of a curious public. Xuanzang's *Record of the Western Regions* played a central role in these new discoveries. In a strange twist of fate, the book Xuanzang wrote to document the history and culture of the Buddhist heartland later became an indispensable guide for Europeans attempting to locate a vanished tradition. It was, to use Kipling's metaphor, the key that opened the lock.

Xuanzang wrote his *Record* in the seventh century as a report on the cultural, political, military, and economic conditions of Central Asia and India. By the nineteenth century, however, the information the *Record* contained was of little value in Qing Dynasty China, a struggling empire more concerned with the soldiers, merchants, and missionaries of modern Europe, America, and Japan than it was with the trade routes, capitals, and monasteries of ancient India. Although a cult of sorts had developed around the mythical version of Xuanzang portrayed in the epic sixteenth-century novel *The Journey to the West* (*Xiyou ji*), there was scant interest in the historical details of his biography. Xuanzang was a figure from the distant past in a country that was preoccupied with its immediate future.

The route by which Xuanzang's *Record* returned to India was longer and more circuitous than his original pilgrimage. It began in Paris with the pioneering Sinologist Jean-Pierre Abel-Rémusat (1788–1832). Abel-Rémusat, for whom the first chair of Chinese at the Collège de France was created in 1814, initially became aware of Xuanzang and his work after he was commissioned to compile an inventory of Chinese texts in the Bibliothèque Royale. In the library, he discovered the account of Xuanzang's early predecessor, the Chinese Buddhist monk Faxian (337–442). After Abel-Rémusat's untimely death from cholera in 1832, his efforts to translate Faxian's *Record of Buddhist Kingdoms* were continued first by Julius Heinrich Klaproth (1783–1835) and then, after Klaproth's death, by Ernest-Augustin Xavier Cerc de Landresse (1800–1862). The completed translation was finally published in 1836 and was heralded as "remarquable pour le époque" by a later occupant of Abel-Rémusat's chair of Chinese at the Collège de France, the renowned Sinologist Henri Maspero (1883–1945). Not only did Faxian's account contain a wealth of information regarding the history and geography of Central Asia and India, it also demonstrated that Buddhism had originated and flourished in northern India, a fact that was still disputed in Europe at the time. Prior to the publication of Faxian's *Record*, the history of India before the Muslim conquests in the thirteenth century was virtually unknown. The early history of the subcontinent was of particular interest to British and French officials tasked with governing colonial India. Accurate accounts of ancient cities and trade routes were also valuable to the European treasure hunters, surveyors, and spies who were covertly exploring and mapping Central Asia during the late nineteenth and early twentieth centuries.

The appendix to Abel-Rémusat's translation of Faxian's record contained a brief summary of Xuanzang's *Record of the Western Regions* stating that Xuanzang's account covered a far greater geographical area in much more detail than Faxian's work. Abel-Rémusat's summary, "Itinéraire de Hiuan Thsang," was not based on Xuanzang's *Record of the Western Regions*, which was not yet available in Europe, but on summaries of the text contained in two eighteenth-century Chinese encyclopedias in the collection of the Bibliothèque Royale. Despite Abel-Rémusat's efforts to acquire a copy of Xuanzang's *Record*, it was more than a decade before his successor, Stanislas Julien, was able to secure a copy from the Imperial Library in Nanjing. Julien spent more than twenty years translating works by and about Xuanzang into French. He completed his translation of Xuanzang's biography in 1853; his two-volume translation of the *Record of the Western Regions* was published several years later, in 1857 and 1858.[136]

In the twenty-year gap between Abel-Rémusat's brief summary of Xuanzang's *Record* and Julien's complete translation of the text, there was heated disagreement among some British officials in India regarding the historical veracity of the account. Some, like Major William Anderson of the Bengal Artillery, thought it was a worthless forgery of relatively recent provenance. Others, like Captain Alexander Cunningham (1814–93) of the Bengal Engineers, were convinced that the work was an authentic and accurate guide to the history and geography of ancient India. The publication of Julien's translation of the *Record* effectively ended any debate about the authenticity of Xuanzang's account, and efforts were swiftly undertaken to correlate the descriptions recorded in the *Record* with contemporary sites in India and Central Asia. The first attempt, *Mémoire analytique* by the French geographer Vivien de Saint-Martin (1802–96), was largely speculative, relying as it did on maps produced by German and British scholars during the first half of the nineteenth century.[137] It was not until Alexander Cunningham, armed with Julien's complete translation, began to triangulate between Xuanzang's *Record*, newer European maps, and his own fieldwork in northern India that portions of Xuanzang's route were first retraced on the ground.

For nineteenth-century European scholars and explorers, particularly those active in India and Central Asia, Xuanzang seemed a kindred spirit. He was the archetypical explorer: courageous and learned, selfless in his pursuit of knowledge, and willing to leave the comforts of home to embark on long and arduous journeys through uncharted, often dangerous territories. Max Müller, in a review of

Julien's translation of the *Record of Western Regions*, grouped Xuanzang together with the heroes of Greece, the martyrs of Rome, the
knights of the Crusades, and the explorers of the Arctic. Xuanzang's
only shortcoming, it seemed, was that he was born in China and
ordained as a Buddhist monk. Müller lamented that Xuanzang
"deserved to have lived in better times, and we almost grudge so
high and noble a character to a country not our own, and to a religion so unworthy of such a man."[138]

While some Western Orientalists imagined Xuanzang as a precur-
sor to modern, European, Christian colonizers, Alexander Cunningham was convinced that the accounts of medieval Chinese Buddhist
pilgrims could be instrumental in shoring up British control in India
and in converting the people to Christianity. In a letter to William
Henry Sykes (1790–1872), a former lieutenant-colonel in the British Army then serving as the director of the East India Company,
Cunningham argued that the travelogue of Faxian demonstrated
that, historically, India only maintained sovereignty when it was
unified under a single monarch—an observation that could be used
in support of British rule. Moreover, Faxian's account, he believed,
showed that Brahmanism was only of relatively recent origin and
existed in a state of instability. These facts, Cunningham concluded,
proved that "the establishment of the Christian religion in India
must ultimately succeed."[139] In the interests of the British government and the Christian church, Cunningham hoped that he might
be afforded the opportunity to retrace the routes taken by Faxian in
India. In addition to the political and religious benefits of uncov-
ering India's past, Cunningham also hinted at rich rewards to be
reaped in the present. There were, he said, "invaluable treasures"
still buried in Buddhist ruins.

Cunningham was appointed director-general of the newly established Archaeological Survey of India in 1861. By that time, he had
turned his attention to Julien's translation of Xuanzang's *Record*

of the Western Regions, declaring that Faxian's account, which Cunningham's predecessors used with mixed results, was too concise and overly concerned with sacred sites and Buddhist objects. Xuanzang's *Record* and *Biography* were much richer in terms of geographical coverage and more accurate in their descriptions of ancient cities and trade routes. In this way, Cunningham, a British official, came to rely on a French translation of a seventh-century Chinese account to locate, survey, and excavate archaeological sites in India. Over the next several decades, Xuanzang's *Record* led Cunningham, his colleagues, and his successors to the temples and stūpas (also called by the cognate name "topes") at Bodh Gayā, the cities of Śrāvastī and Kauśāmbī, the monasteries and stūpas at Nālandā and Taxila, and a host of other long-forgotten sites. Xuanzang had gone to India twelve hundred years earlier in an attempt to reinvigorate Chinese Buddhism. He never could have imagined his records would one day be used to locate the relics and ruins of a tradition lost in its own heartland.

During his years in the field, Cunningham made a series of extraordinary discoveries and produced several detailed surveys of excavated sites. Like many men of his generation and station, he saw himself as a savior of India's past and a steward of its future. Reflecting on his accomplishments in verse, he once wrote,

> Nought but the Topes themselves remain to mock
> Time's ceaseless efforts; yet they proudly stand
> Silent and lasting up their parent rock,
> And still as cities under magic's wand;
> Till curious Saxons, from a distant land,
> Unlock'd the treasures of two thousand years.[140]

The treasures of ancient India had long been "locked" away, but Cunningham and other Europeans now possessed the key. For all of

Alexander Cunningham with some of the Buddhist artifacts he collected during his time as the director of the Archaeological Survey of India. Source: E. W. C. Sandes, *The Military Engineer in India*, vol. 2.

Cunningham's good intentions, the mixture of pride and paternalism he expressed was part of an ethos of ownership and extraction that resulted in the loss of countless Indian antiquities. Many of the sculptures, wall panels, reliquaries, coins, and other artifacts discovered by Cunningham were subsequently removed, shipped off, and sold to collectors in England. The British Museum, Cunningham's biggest buyer, currently lists 2,377 of his antiquities in its collection. A peculiar congruence is evident in the work, if not the motives, of Cunningham and Xuanzang. Both were foreigners who traveled to India in search of Buddhist sites; both collected texts, statues, and relics to bring back to their own countries; and both hoped to salvage and preserve the treasures of Buddhist India. The legacies of the nineteenth-century British Christian archaeologist and the seventh-century Chinese Buddhist monk who unwittingly served as Cunningham's guide have come to be unexpectedly intertwined. Without Xuanzang, Cunningham's work would not have been nearly as successful as it was. And without men like Cunningham, Xuanzang's life might never have achieved the international renown he currently enjoys.

In addition to facilitating the discovery of important archaeological sites in northern India, Xuanzang and his *Record of the Western Regions* also played a key role in one the most consequential and controversial acquisitions of Buddhist texts and paintings of the modern era. The man at the center of this remarkable story was Aurel Stein (1862–1943), a self-styled "archaeologist explorer" who was born in Hungary but naturalized as a British citizen in 1904. As a student in Germany, Stein had read Julien's translation of the *Record of the Western Regions*, which, since 1884, was also available in Samuel Beal's English translation. Stein, who had studied Persian and Sanskrit, was eager to continue the work begun a generation earlier by men like Alexander Cunningham. He got his chance at the age of twenty-five, when he received his first post in northern India as principal of Oriental College, Lahore, and registrar of Punjab University. From this home base, he began to explore India with his three guides: Alexander the Great, Marco Polo, and Xuanzang. But it was only after accepting a new post as the principal of Calcutta Madrasa, which afforded him longer vacation time, that Stein was finally able to embark on extended archaeological expeditions. In the summer of 1900, he turned his attention away from the Buddhist centers of northern India, which had already been intensively surveyed and excavated, toward the largely unexplored mountains and deserts of Central Asia. Stein's first expedition took him into the southern reaches of the Tarim Basin for nearly a year and earned him some renown back in Europe, but it was his second trip into the region, which lasted from 1906 to 1908, that led to his most momentous acquisition.

The government of India and the British Museum jointly funded Stein's second expedition. His lofty (and misleading) title of "prime minister of education of Great Britain" commanded the respect of Chinese officials and allowed him access to sites that might otherwise have been off limits. Although Stein had no interest in Buddhist doctrines or practices, he was inspired by the determination and daring of early Buddhist pilgrims "who, simple in mind but strong in faith and in superstition, had made their way to India, braving all difficulties and risks."[141] Like Cunningham before him, whose work he had studied closely, Stein used translations of Xuanzang's *Record* and *Biography* to guide his explorations. Xuanzang, Stein liked to tell people, was his patron saint.

After arriving in the town of Dunhuang in the spring of 1907, Stein began hearing "vague rumors" about a cache of ancient manuscripts hidden in the nearby Mogao complex of caves. A Daoist caretaker of the site, Wang Yuanlu (d. 1931), had discovered a hidden chamber in one of the caves seven years earlier. Behind the wall lay a secret chamber filled with thousands of manuscripts and paintings. Most of the texts were Buddhist, but Daoist, Nestorian Christian, Jewish, and Manichean manuscripts, as well as local administrative documents, were also preserved there. These works were written in an array of different languages; in addition to the predominant Chinese, there were also texts in Sogdian, Uighur, Khotanese, and Tibetan. The cave appears to have served as the storehouse of a nearby Buddhist monastery until it was finally sealed sometime in the early eleventh century, most likely in an effort to protect its contents from approaching Muslim armies. The contents remained undisturbed for the next thousand years until Wang Yuanlu broke through the false wall.

After discovering the cache, Wang initially tried to interest Chinese scholars and officials in the materials, hoping to sell some of the items to finance restorations at his temple. The extraordinary nature of Wang's find was not immediately apparent, however, and the governor of Gansu ordered the cave and its contents resealed in 1904. By that time, word of the find, together with some of the original texts and paintings, had begun to spread. Stein saw one of the manuscripts in the possession of a local Tibetan monk shortly after his arrival in Dunhuang. The prospect of a horde of ancient manuscripts attracted Stein "with the strength of a hidden magnet," yet he proceeded with caution. He knew his greatest obstacle would be Wang Yuanlu himself. Stein and his Chinese assistant Jiang Xiaowan predicted that Wang, who appeared ignorant yet clever, "would be a difficult person to handle." Realizing that money alone might not be enough to convince Wang to part with the manuscripts in his care, Stein prepared himself for a "long and arduous siege."[142]

To win Wang's trust, Stein presented himself, as he often did, as a pilgrim in the tradition of Xuanzang, traveling across dangerous mountains and deserts in order to transmit the Buddhist teachings to his homeland in Europe. Hearing this, Wang excitedly took Stein to the exterior gallery of the temple he was restoring and showed him the murals he had commissioned depicting scenes from *The Journey to the West*. Stein, who was not familiar with the novel, was bemused by Wang's fantastical understanding of Xuanzang's life,

Wang Yuanlu photographed by Aurel Stein in the gallery of his temple
beside murals depicting scenes from *The Journey to the West*.
Source: Stein, *Ruins of Desert Cathay*, vol. 2.

but he was also delighted to learn that this "credulous cicerone"
was a devotee of Xuanzang. Stein had finally found his opening.
"I emphatically called his attention to the panel which showed
Hsüan-tsang [Xuanzang] returning from India as he leads his horse

heavily laden with sacred manuscripts. It was the most effective parable in support of my plea to be allowed to render accessible to Western students as much as possible of the relics which Wang Tao-shih [Wang Yuanlu] had discovered, and yet was keeping from daylight."[143] It would be an act of real religious merit, Stein explained, for Wang to part with the manuscripts.

Wang Yuanlu was visibly uneasy about the prospect of selling off ancient manuscripts entrusted to his care. Local officials had also become suspicious about Stein's intentions, and a small contingent of soldiers was assigned to accompany Stein on his explorations of the caves and to ensure that he did not surreptitiously remove any artifacts. One afternoon when his escorts had fallen asleep after smoking opium, Stein went to the library cave to see its contents for the first time. "The sight of the small room disclosed was one to make my eyes open wide," he reported. "Heaped in layers, but without any order, there appeared in the dim light of the priest's little lamp a solid mass of manuscript bundles rising to a height of nearly ten feet, and filling... close on 500 cubic feet."[144] Stein was eager to examine the contents of the cave, but Wang Yuanlu would only permit small numbers of texts to be taken out at a time, and then only for closer inspection and only under cover of darkness. As luck would have it, the first texts that Wang selected were copies of scriptures that had been translated by Xuanzang. This seemed an auspicious omen. "Surely it was 'T'ang-seng' [Xuanzang] himself," Stein would later recall his assistant declaring, "who at the opportune moment had revealed the hiding-place of all those manuscripts to an ignorant priest in order that I, his admirer and disciple from distant India, might find a fitting antiquarian reward awaiting me on the westernmost confines of China."[145]

Over the next seven nights, Wang Yuanlu continued to provide bundles of texts and paintings to Jiang Xiaowan, who then quietly conveyed them to Stein's tent. The pretense that Stein, who could not read Chinese, was merely examining the texts out of scholarly interest quickly gave way to negotiations over quantities and price. Stein did his best to reassure Wang that these transactions were motivated by piety, not profit. Their mutual admiration for Xuanzang was once again raised to quell Wang's misgivings. "In order to assuage his spiritual scruples as well as I could, and to give visible proof of grateful attachment to my 'patron saint's' memory, I had previously arranged through the priest to have one of the abandoned smaller shrines in the southern group of grottoes redecorated with a new clay image of Hsüan-tsang [Xuanzang]. The Tun-huang sculptor's work in due time produced an artistic eyesore, but widely advertised by the Tao-shih it helped to dispel suspicions about my long visit."[146]

In the end, Wang Yuanlu agreed to sell Stein well over a thousand manuscripts—significantly less than what Stein had hoped for but still an extraordinary haul. Both men knew that this purchase, if discovered, would spark outrage. Wang's one condition, Stein wrote, was that nobody else have "the slightest inkling of what was being transacted, and that as long as I kept on Chinese soil the origin of these 'finds' was not to be revealed to any living being."[147] Stein left the Mogao caves with manuscripts and paintings hidden in his baggage. In addition to his initial acquisition of seventeen cases of material, Stein, through an emissary, bought another three thousand manuscripts from Wang just a few months later. For these priceless works, he paid a total of 220 pounds sterling.[148]

The Stein Collection at the British Library is now estimated to contain more than twenty-eight thousand manuscripts collected over the course of three major expeditions, with the lion's share coming from the Mogao caves. Stein portrayed his work at Dunhuang as an effort to salvage and preserve the abandoned cultural heritages of China and Central Asia. He would later describe himself as "a *confrère* who has done as much as any one to throw light on the great and beneficent part played by ancient China in the history of Central Asia."[149] He was reportedly stunned, therefore, to learn that many people in China viewed him as a liar and a thief. When an expedition from Harvard University's Fogg Art Museum arrived at the Mogao caves in 1925, they were met by an angry mob and forced to retreat without so much as a photograph of the site. The leader of the expedition, Langdon Warner, attributed the backlash to past work of Stein and Paul Pelliot (1878–1945), the French Sinologist who arrived at the Mogao caves in 1908 and left with more than ten thousand texts. Neither Stein nor Pelliot, according to Warner, "could ever come back [to Dunhuang] and live."[150]

In 1930, China's recently established National Commission for the Preservation of Antiquities issued a scathing statement condemning Stein's role in what it viewed as the wholesale looting of the Mogao manuscripts:

> Sir Aurel Stein, taking advantage of the ignorance and cupidity of the priest in charge, persuaded the latter to sell to him at a pittance what he considered the pick of the collection which, needless to say, did not in any way belong to the seller. It would be the same if some Chinese traveler pretending to be merely a student of religious history went to Canterbury and bought valuable relics from the cathedral caretaker. But Sir Aurel Stein, not knowing a word of Chinese, took away what he considered the most valuable, separating many manuscripts which really belonged together, thus destroying the value of the manuscripts themselves. Soon afterwards French and Japanese travelers followed his trail with the result that the unique collection is now divided up and scattered in London, Paris, and Tokyo. In the first two cities at least, the manuscripts lie unstudied for the last twenty years, and their rightful owners, the Chinese, who are the most competent

scholars for their study, are deprived of their opportunity as well as their ownership.[151]

The Mogao cave where the manuscripts and paintings were once stored now lies empty. Its contents reside in the British Library and the Bibliothèque Nationale de France, with smaller collections kept in Japan, Russia, and China.

It is a testament to Xuanzang's legacy that he and his work played such pivotal roles in the transmission, translation, and study of Buddhist texts in the modern era. Men like Cunningham and Stein used his *Record* and *Biography* to locate lost Buddhist sites and uncover buried Buddhist art, architecture, and texts. The monasteries and stūpas excavated by Cunningham and the manuscripts collected by Stein helped ignite an interest in Buddhism among the people of Europe and, soon thereafter, in North America. When he was alive, Xuanzang spent more than sixteen years in Central Asia and India with the goal of acquiring texts and teachings that would reinvigorate the Buddhist traditions of China. Twelve hundred years later, his work played a crucial role in introducing those same teachings and traditions to the West. And yet, for all that is known about Xuanzang's life and work, the ways in which he is portrayed often bear uncanny resemblances to those painting the portraits. For Alexander Cunningham, Xuanzang was a historian and surveyor, methodically traveling to important sites and meticulously recording what he saw. For Aurel Stein, the monk was a bold adventurer who braved dangerous mountain and desert crossings in search of new experiences and old treasures. For the Daoist Wang Yuanlu, Xuanzang was a kind of immortal who, together with a monkey, a pig, and a dragon horse, battled hordes of demons on his way to Heaven. Other people have taken other liberties with Xuanzang and his *Record*. When Xuanzang's physical remains were accidentally unearthed in the 1940s, the old monk was once again reconceived in the image of his handlers. In those politically fractious times, Xuanzang emerged as an emissary of peace and diplomacy.

CHAPTER 24

Xuanzang's Relics

Discoveries, Distributions, and Diplomacy

ON DECEMBER 23, 1942, Captain Takamori Takasuke (d. 1954), the commanding officer of Japanese soldiers stationed in occupied Nanjing, was overseeing the construction of a Shinto shrine just outside the city's southern gate. While excavating the shrine's foundation, his men discovered the crypt of an old Buddhist stūpa. Inside a stone sarcophagus they found two nested boxes, the outer of bronze, the inner of silver. The inner box contained one small gold Buddha statue, several bronze and ceramic implements, hundreds of coins, and an offering of wheat grain. A separate copper box enclosed a small shard of bone, grayish brown in color and roughly rectangular in shape. Two inscriptions carved into the walls of the sarcophagus identified the bone as a fragment of Xuanzang's skull.[152]

It was a remarkable discovery. Just a few decades after Xuanzang's translations and commentaries were brought back from obscurity, his long-lost physical remains were also unearthed. Because Xuanzang's life and literary legacy left such a deep imprint on the Buddhist cultures of Asia, his remains were sought by various groups—religious and secular, national and transnational—in the service of starkly different agendas. In the years since its discovery, Xuanzang's parietal bone has been broken and divided more than a dozen times. Fragments of what is believed to be the original relic now reside in mainland China, India, Japan, and Taiwan. In each of these countries, Xuanzang's remains are memorialized in ways that often have less to do with what he accomplished in the past than with what various modern nations aspire to achieve in the present.

Xuanzang, the consummate traveler, has remained on the move. Following his funeral in 664, his body was first buried in the eastern suburbs of Chang'an at the White Deer Plateau. As noted previously, the Tang emperor Gaozong (r. 649–83) later had Xuanzang's remains disinterred and relocated to a site several miles south of the city. According to the inscriptions carved on the side of the sarcophagus discovered in Nanjing, Xuanzang's bones were surreptitiously moved to a small complex deep in the Zhongnan Mountains during a rebellion that laid waste to the capital in the late ninth century. There they remained until the eleventh century, when a wandering monk salvaged a piece of Xuanzang's skull from its crumbling reliquary, brought it to Nanjing, and interred it in a stūpa on a hill to the east of Changgan Monastery.

This monastery was one of the most prominent Buddhist sites in Nanjing, famous for its towering stūpa that purportedly contained a portion of the Buddha's relics distributed by the great Indian king Aśoka. With the exception of a single building, the entire temple complex was razed in the middle of the nineteenth century, when Nanjing served as the headquarters of the iconoclastic Taiping Rebellion. The old monastery lay forgotten in ruins until Japanese troops started their excavations in the winter of 1942.

Once the relic was unearthed, word of its discovery spread quickly and government dignitaries and clergy from both China and Japan held a grand procession to escort the bone through the center of Nanjing to Jiming Monastery, a prominent Buddhist monastery located just inside the city's northern wall. After the ceremony, the relic was sent to Nanjing's Department of Cultural

Relics, where, newspapers report, one hundred thousand people prostrated themselves before it.

The initial plan was to re-inter the relic at a site on the grounds of one of Nanjing's flagship Buddhist institutions, Pilu Monastery. The Chinese government would pay for the construction of a new stūpa, while the Japanese authorities would fund the construction of a Xuanzang memorial hall. Foreseeing Japan's imminent victory in the war, the complex was also slated to include a memorial stūpa for the casualties of the "Great East Asian War"—the first of what would be many attempts to enlist the salvific powers of Xuanzang's relic for the benefit of fallen soldiers and civilians. Although fundraising for the complex was carried out in Tokyo, in those financially strained times the Japanese delegation was unable to secure the necessary funds and plans for the construction of the monument were put on hold until the conclusion of the war. The memorial, not surprisingly, was never built, but a stūpa modeled on Xuanzang's original reliquary at Xingjiao Monastery was constructed in late February 1944, on the summit of Little Jiuhua Mountain, on the outskirts of Nanjing. The stūpa still stands, but its crypt contains only a small portion of Xuanzang's original relic.

After so many centuries underground, the relic appears to have grown restless. According to the original inscription for the Little Jiuhua stūpa, on December 28, 1943, nearly one month before the bone was to be enshrined in the new stūpa, a relic division ceremony was held in Nanjing and the shard was broken. Two portions remained in Nanjing and a third was sent to Beijing so that "the radiance of the numinous bone could illuminate both the north and the south."[153] What may at first appear sacrilegious—the violation of sacred remains—was in fact neither unorthodox nor uncommon. The holographic quality of Buddhist relics ensures that even the smallest portion retains the undiminished efficacy of the original. Division only increased the relic's reach.

Of the two relics in Nanjing, one was interred as planned in the stūpa at Little Jiuhua, but the other was shuttled around to various institutions in the city over the course of the next thirty years. The reason for withholding a portion of Xuanzang's relic from the stūpa in Nanjing was never made public, but it likely stemmed from competing conceptions of the status of relics in China at the time. Both the Nationalist and the Communist governments engaged in protracted campaigns to eradicate "superstitious" practices, and Buddhist relics—the remains of the dead, venerated as if alive—were seen, at best, as inert cultural artifacts of a bygone era, which belonged in a museum if they belonged anywhere. Many monastics and laypersons, however, continued to venerate relics as sacred objects, imbued with miraculous life force, which should only be enshrined in a traditional Buddhist context. To split Xuanzang's relic was to split the difference; one piece was interred in a reliquary and the other was sent back to Nanjing's Department of Cultural Relics. The former has remained in its reliquary, but the latter has lived an unsettled existence.

In 1949—the year that Mao Zedong (1893–1976) marched into Beijing and inaugurated the People's Republic of China (PRC)—the uninterred relic was moved from the Department of Cultural Relics to the Nanjing Museum, where it was put on display together with ancient bronzes, paintings, depictions of the evolution of mankind, and the ascent of Communism. In 1953, the local Buddhist association relocated the bone to Pilu Monastery, which the Chinese Communist Party maintained as a showcase monastery for visiting foreign dignitaries. This move coincided with the founding of the Chinese Buddhist Association (CBA) earlier that year, with its mission of organizing all Buddhists to participate in "movements for the welfare of the motherland." Ten years later, in 1963, during the relative calm between the Great Leap Forward and the Cultural Revolution, the relic was transferred yet again, this time to Qixia

Monastery, a historic monastic complex situated in the hills to the northeast of Nanjing. At that time, Qixia Monastery, along with other sites in China, Taiwan, and Japan, was preparing to host an international event commemorating the thirteen hundredth anniversary of Xuanzang's death. Events in China were staged in part to demonstrate the continued vitality of Buddhism in the PRC; the government was eager to discredit rumors that the regime was hostile toward religion and to highlight the Buddhist culture China shared with its political and economic allies. International concerns about religious repression in China, however, were well founded. Mao Zedong launched the Cultural Revolution in 1966 and the local Buddhist association, fearing that the relic would be seized or destroyed during the virulent attacks on Buddhist monasteries, had the bone moved to Nanjing's Cultural Management Board for safekeeping.

The Cultural Revolution lasted until 1976, but in 1973, Xuanzang's relic was taken out of government storage and enshrined at Nanjing's newly restored Linggu Monastery, a modest though politically significant temple situated near Xuanzang's stūpa on Little Jiuhua Mountain. With the onset of the Cultural Revolution, Linggu had ceased to function as a Buddhist monastery; the monks were sent to labor camps, many of the temple's buildings and icons were destroyed, and the local branch of the Revolutionary Committee occupied the structures that remained. In May 1973, however, just seven months after the normalization of Sino-Japanese relations, the Japan-China Buddhist Exchange Group was scheduled to tour Buddhist sites in several Chinese cities. Shortly before their arrival in Nanjing, government officials sprang into action and, in the span of fifteen days, restored Linggu to its former status. The Revolutionary Committee was removed and monks were reinstalled. A Memorial Hall for Jianzhen (J. Ganjin, 688–763)—the Chinese monk credited with introducing the Vinaya tradition to Japan—was hastily established, and Xuanzang's relic was installed in a new Xuanzang Memorial Hall. Linggu was thus quickly transformed from a headquarters of the Communist Revolutionary Committee into a kind of Buddhist museum with exhibits showcasing the cultural and diplomatic ties between Japan, China, and India.

During the same period that Xuanzang's relic was traveling around Nanjing, the fragment of his skull that had been sent to Beijing years earlier was spilt into three more portions. The only pieces of this relic known to still exist in China were sent to Sichuan in 1949 and are currently enshrined at Wenshu Monastery in the city of Chengdu. A second portion was lost during the Cultural Revolution. The third fragment was initially taken to the city of Tianjin but then, in 1957, it was sent to India.

The PRC's gift of Xuanzang's relic to the government of India was part of a long process of political courtship. Throughout the 1950s, the two countries had been working to strengthen diplomatic and economic ties, and in June 1954 Premier Zhou Enlai (1898–1976) visited India for the first time to promote the newly agreed upon Five Principles of Peaceful Coexistence. In October of that year, a Sino-Indian trade agreement was signed in Beijing and Sino-Indian Friendship Associations were established in both countries. In addition to demonstrating their respect for India's heritage, officials in Beijing were eager to emphasize the historical roots of the two countries' friendship. Xuanzang served as a ready-made symbol of China's indebtedness to Indian culture while also exemplifying China's native ingenuity and initiative. The propaganda potential was obvious, and in November 1955, the *Times of India* announced that China, India, and the USSR were jointly planning to produce a film based on Xuanzang's life.

Xuanzang was emerging as an effective figurehead for Sino-Indian cooperation. Temples associated with his life were some of

The Dalai Lama presenting Xuanzang's relic to Jawaharlal Nehru at Nālandā
in January 1957. Source: Nava Nālandā Mahā Vihara Archives.

the first Buddhist institutions to be restored by the PRC and were
regularly shown to visiting Indian dignitaries. In the fall of 1956,
an eleven-person delegation of Buddhist monks from India visited
China and requested permission to enshrine a portion of Xuanzang's remains at Nālandā—the long-defunct Buddhist monastery
in northern India where Xuanzang had studied. Zhou Enlai offered
the portion of the Beijing relics then kept in the city of Tianjin
and asked the young fourteenth Dalai Lama, whom Indian officials
had invited to Bodh Gayā to attend the celebrations marking the
2,500th anniversary of the Buddha's nirvāṇa, to deliver a piece of
Xuanzang's skull to Nālandā. Along with the relic, Zhou Enlai
sent copies of Xuanzang's translations and a copy of the Buddhist
canon, as well as three hundred thousand *yuan* and blueprints to
be used for the construction of a Xuanzang Memorial Hall in traditional Chinese style. The relic was presented to Prime Minister
Jawaharlal Nehru on January 12, 1957, in a ceremony at Nālandā's
Mahā Vihara (see above).

Disputes over shared border regions stalled construction of the memorial until 2006, "India-China Friendship Year," when, along with several other highly publicized demonstrations of mutual goodwill, efforts to complete the hall were revived. A group of ten Chinese and Taiwanese monks, carrying a statue of Xuanzang sculpted from Chinese and Taiwanese clay, spent four months retracing Xuanzang's journey to India. Their arrival at Nālandā was scheduled to coincide with that of another delegation of "experts, scholars, media people, entrepreneurs, and celebrated personages from all walks of life" assembled by the state-run China Central Television Station.[154] Both groups toured the Memorial Hall and admired the life-size statue of Xuanzang that stood near its entrance. The plaque on the statue's pedestal clarified Xuanzang's global significance: "Xuan Zang belongs to a galaxy of world Citizens whose great mission was to interpret, for the good of mankind, sublime volumes of human civilization." Xuanzang, in this description, was not necessarily Chinese and not necessarily Buddhist; he was simply one of the world's greatest intellectuals. Assertions of universality notwithstanding, the symbolism of these events conveyed a clear political message. The traditional Chinese hall built in India and the image molded from Chinese and Taiwanese clay unequivocally identified Xuanzang with China and China with Taiwan.

Despite excellent credentials, Xuanzang's career as a lobbyist for cross-straits unity got off to a rocky start. During the mid-1950s, another portion of Xuanzang's relics was at the center of a diplomatic fallout between mainland China, Japan, and Taiwan. Japan's possession and distribution of Xuanzang's relics remains a sensitive and controversial issue in mainland China. A new plaque, affixed to the base of Nanjing's Little Jiuhua stūpa in 2003, is one of many indications that old wounds have been slow to heal:

During the Republican period, Japanese invaders occupied China, Nanjing fell into enemy hands, and the skull of the great master was plundered. Patriots and disciples of the Buddha, sacrificing their lives to protect the Dharma, resisted the Japanese and rescued the bone. In the end, it was returned to Jiuhua. A stūpa was built and offerings were made. Immediately, great crowds gathered to venerate the sage's bone in a display of the nation's patriotism.

Extolling the fortitude of Nanjing's residents, the plaque recounts how they risked their lives to rescue one of the nation's great treasures from the clutches of Japan. This oft-repeated claim, while not exactly inaccurate, is misleading. Monastic and civil authorities in Nanjing did manage to prevent the entire relic from being taken to Japan. But on October 10, 1944, just before it was interred in the newly built stūpa on Little Jiuhua, the minister of foreign affairs for the Japan-installed collaborationist government in Nanjing divided that fragment into several more pieces. One was sealed inside the stūpa; the rest were given to the Japanese missionary monk Mizuno Baigyō (1878–1949) as an "expression of gratitude." Shortly thereafter, Mizuno carried a portion of Xuanzang's remains from China to Japan.

Construction later commenced on a thirteen-level granite stūpa to house Xuanzang's relics in Saitama Prefecture, Japan, on the grounds of Jionji—whose name, "Compassionate Kindness," is the same as the monastery in the Chinese capital where Xuanzang had carried out his translation work. While the stūpa was under construction, Mizuno Baigyō brought the bones to the city of Nagoya to commemorate the fiftieth anniversary of a gift of a piece of Śakyamuni Buddha's skull from the Thai king Chulalongkorn (1853–1910) to Japan in 1900. On October 22, 1949, a procession of two elephants (the only two to survive the war) carried Xuanzang's relics through the city of Nagoya to Nittaiji (Japan-Thailand Temple), where the Buddha relic was enshrined. Xuanzang had venerated a shard of Śākyamuni's skull in Hilo, Afghanistan, thirteen hundred years earlier. Now his own skull was reunited with the Buddha's.

Xuanzang's remains were ceremonially interred at Jionji in 1950, and they rested in their crypt for several decades until they were, once again, summoned back to the surface. The request to dig up and further divide the relics came from the director of Yakushiji Monastery, the headquarters of the Hossō, or Yogācāra, sect in Japan. In the late 1970s, the monastery was in the midst of major renovations that included plans to build a new hall to memorialize Xuanzang as the founding patriarch of their tradition. It would be fitting, they reasoned, for some of Xuanzang's relics to be enshrined in the new building.

Excavation at Jionji began in 1980, and the painter Hirayama Ikuo (1930–2009), known for his depictions of the scenes along the Silk Road, attended the relic division ceremony later that year. He subsequently recalled:

> One day, a proposal of dividing the skull and enshrining it in the Genjo Sanzo-in [Xuanzang Trepiṭaka Cloister] was made by the priests of Yakushi-ji Monastery and it was conducted... I was able to see the chief priest placing my much-admired Xuanzang's skull, the real skull, which was at least 1,300 years old, into a pot with chopsticks. I was so moved by the fact that I was participating in the ceremony that was so important in Japanese history. The chief priest Kōin Takada carried the bone to various places, which are closely related to Xuanzang, as a service in memory of Xuanzang's spirit.[155]

The complex built to house Xuanzang's relic at Yakushiji was completed eleven years later, in 1991. While construction was under

Takada Kōin chanting before Xuanzang's relic along the Silk Road. Source:
Takada, *Gandāra Daitō Seiikiki no tabi.*

way, Yakushiji's abbot, Takada Kōin (1924–98), took the relic on
tour, revisiting places associated with Xuanzang's life. In 1984, on
the 1,320th anniversary of Xuanzang's death, Takata, along with
an entourage of thirty Japanese monks and laypeople, followed
Xuanzang's original route along the Silk Road. Throughout the
pilgrimage, Takada carried a copy of Xuanzang's *Record of the Western Regions* along with a brocade box that hung from a cord around
his neck. At significant sites along the route, the group would erect
an altar, unfurl a scroll with Xuanzang's image, open the box to
remove a glass reliquary containing Xuanzang's relic, and chant
Xuanzang's translation of the *Heart Sūtra* (see above).[156] In this
way, Xuanzang's *Record*, translations, and bodily remains retraced
the journey he had taken while alive.

The memorials built for Xuanzang's relics at Jionji and Yakushiji
monasteries are well known. At least four other locations in Japan
also inter a portion of Xuanzang's remains.[157] These sites are more
obscure and the provenance of their relics is murky, often intentionally so. The detailed detective work of the Japanese scholar

Sakaida Yukiko, however, has revealed that both Takamori Taka-suke (the military officer who first discovered the relic in Nanjing) and Mizuno Baigyō (the monk who brought the relic from China to Japan) secretly retained some grains of Xuanzang's original relic in their private possessions. Several of these—it is not clear how many ever existed—were later given as gifts to friends and associates. As least two pieces of Xuanzang's skull ended up inside memorials honoring the Japanese soldiers who died during World War II. It can seem ironic that the remains of a medieval Chinese monk were enshrined inside memorials for soldiers responsible for the deaths of some twenty million Chinese during the war. And yet, it is precisely because Xuanzang is a Chinese monk that he is uniquely placed to placate the spirits of Japanese soldiers, an estimated 447,000 of whom died in China between 1937 and 1945. There seemed to be a special affinity between Xuanzang and the people of Japan—Japanese Buddhists had revered him for hundreds of years, Jap-anese soldiers had discovered his relics, and the people of Japan were now the caretakers of those relics. If any Chinese could bring solace to the spirits of the war dead, it was Xuanzang. Many people hoped that he would come to the aid of the millions of Japanese left stranded in China after Japan's sudden surrender and withdrawal in 1945. In recent years, during the annual Xuanzang festival held at Jionji every spring, the families of those who never returned from China have gathered before Xuanzang's reliquary to pray for the lost souls of their loved ones.[158]

Most of the relics that were brought to Japan at the end of the war have remained there, but one has not. In 1952, Japan hosted the second meeting of the World Fellowship of Buddhists in Tokyo. Five hundred and forty delegates representing nineteen countries attended, and Taiwan sent a delegation of prominent monks and laymen under the leadership of the Zhangjia Living Buddha (1891–

1957), a Mongolian tulku then serving as the head of the Buddhist Association of the Republic of China (ROC). In Tokyo, Zhangjia and the members of his party met with Takamori Takasuke, who informed them that a portion of Xuanzang's relic was enshrined in the new stūpa at Jionji. The Taiwanese delegation immediately enlisted Takamori's help in securing some or all of Japan's relic for Taiwan. One year later, the Japan Buddhist Federation voted to grant Taiwan's request.

The news was celebrated throughout Taiwan, but the representatives of the mainland's Chinese Buddhist Association, along with some Japanese Buddhist and political organizations, were outraged. If the relic was to be moved, the CBA contended that the only logical destination was mainland China, its place of origin. By no means should it be sent to the "renegade" government on the island of Taiwan. Zhao Puchu (1907–2000), serving as the secretary-general of the CBA, circulated an open letter requesting that all plans to transfer the relic to Taiwan be abandoned and warning that such a move would seriously damage the fragile trust that had been building between Chinese and Japanese Buddhists since the end of the war. In response, the Japan Buddhist Federation offered three justifications for approving the transfer: the relic had been freely given to Japan; the gift of the relic to Taiwan was purely a religious matter and should have no bearing on the friendly relations between Japanese and Chinese Buddhists; and, finally, China already had a portion of Xuanzang's relics while Taiwan did not. The director of the Japan Buddhist Federation informed Zhao Puchu that, although they took the concerns of the mainland Chinese Buddhists seriously, the relic would proceed to Taiwan as planned.

One problem remained. Since the completion of the Xuanzang stūpa at Jionji, the relic lay buried under several tons of granite. Fortunately and incredibly, it was revealed that during the interment process participants discovered that the relic was too big to fit into the crystal reliquary that had been prepared for it. Part of the relic was therefore broken off, placed in a wooden box, and stored in the temple. It was this piece that was then conveniently available to be sent to Taiwan. That, at least, was the official story. In fact, it appears that Takamori Takasuke provided relics from his private collection to the Taiwanese delegation.[159] A ceremony for "dividing" the relic was nonetheless held at Jionji on November 24, 1955. A Japanese delegation left Japan the next day and arrived in Taipei amid a throng of onlookers waving Republic of China and Buddhist flags. The event was widely reported in the Taiwanese press with headlines proclaiming that the entire relic had been "returned" or "given back" to "China."

Japanese Buddhists, of course, retained most of their relics. Xuanzang, moreover, had never been to Taiwan, so his remains could not be returned there. But since neither the ROC nor Japan recognized the authority of the PRC, politically speaking, Taiwan was China. So, on November 26, a "reinstatement" ceremony took place at Shandao Monastery in Taipei. Addressing those who had gathered to welcome the relic, the leader of the Japanese delegation expressed his hope that the return of Xuanzang's relic would strengthen the friendship and trust between the peoples of China and Japan. He also understood the exchange as a step toward reconciliation and forgiveness: "Regarding the past wrongs committed by the Japanese in mainland China during the Second Great War, President Chiang [Kai-shek] has announced that he will requite enmity with virtue. This demonstrates the Buddhist spirit of compassion and for this the people of Japan are deeply grateful."[160]

The relic was eventually enshrined in the newly built Xuanzang Temple on the shore of Sun Moon Lake in central Taiwan, where it remains today. After so much travel and so much intrigue, Xuanzang's relic must have been exhausted, but its travels were not yet over. Following the warming of cross-straits relations in the late 1980s and 1990s, the Taiwanese cleric Liaozhong (b. 1932) wrote to Zhao Puchu requesting a portion of Xuanzang's relics for his recently opened Xuanzang University in the city of Hsinchu in northwestern Taiwan. Zhao Puchu was receptive to the idea, noting that although Taiwan already possessed one of Xuanzang's relics, that fragment had come from Japan. For mainland China to freely make a gift of the relic to Taiwan was seen as a much more significant exchange, one that could help to strengthen the political and cultural ties between the divided PRC and ROC.

The relic, broken off from the ever-shrinking piece kept at Linggu Monastery in Nanjing, arrived in Taipei on October 2, 1998. A public ceremony complete with a marching band in miniskirts was held the following day at Xuanzang University and attended by a host of dignitaries, including Taiwan's premier. If Taiwanese Buddhists thought Xuanzang's relic would draw attention to the new university and to the Buddhist foray into higher education in general, officials in Beijing clearly hoped this gesture of goodwill would speed the process of political reunification. In his speech, Zhao Puchu's representative expressed his wish that the gift of the relic would "help advance the friendly cooperation between Buddhists on both sides of the strait, safeguard world peace, and encourage the writing of model theses on the peaceful reunification of the motherland."[161] Thus, in a peculiar way, the division of Xuanzang's relic was heralded as a harbinger of unity.

With his travels between China and India and his influence on the Buddhist traditions of East Asia, Xuanzang has become a potent symbol of the shared identities and entwined histories of modern Asian nations. His popular appeal among the people of China and Japan is also inextricably bound up with the fantastical legends that have long circulated about his life. When Xuanzang's relic arrived in Taiwan from China, for example, it was accompanied by a man dressed as a monkey and another wearing the snout of a pig. These were Xuanzang's divine companions from the famous *Journey to the West*, a wildly influential novel that may be Xuanzang's most enduring and most unexpected legacy.

CHAPTER 25

Xuanzang's Legend

Deification and Fictionalization

NOBODY REALLY KNOWS what Xuanzang looked like. None of the portraits that were made during his life have survived. His direct disciples described him as standing seven feet tall, with pink skin and striking facial features, "solemn as a spirit, handsome as a painting."[162] We tend to think of him now as a monk with a flywhisk in his right hand, a scroll in his left, carrying a towering bamboo backpack overloaded with texts. But there are other, stranger renderings. In the British Museum, for example, there is painting that shows Xuanzang with his palms pressed together in a gesture of supplication. He wears a bright red and gold robe, a matching hat, and is flanked by three other figures: a monkey dressed and standing like a man, a pig similarly arrayed, and a balding monk with a non-Chinese appearance. The group is facing the Buddha, who is holding a text and descending, haloed and barefoot, on a cloud. A short inscription written on the painting describes the scene: "Trepiṭaka [Xuanzang] went to Western Heaven to obtain the scriptures, traveling thousands of miles and [visiting] hundreds of thousands of courts. He obtained the *Heart Sūtra* in a single scroll, and this has been transmitted to the world for the salvation of the dead" (p. 237). The painting, created in Taiwan in 1940, is part of a set of fifteen hanging scrolls—the others depict the gruesome tortures of hell and the benevolent buddhas and bodhisattvas of the pure lands—that mourners traditionally display during funerals. Although many people know the *Heart Sūtra* as a brief but compelling encapsulation of the Buddhist doctrine of emptiness, it is also commonly chanted during mortuary rites to help the dead escape from hell and attain rebirth in the pure land. In the same way, while many people consider Xuanzang to have been an eminent medieval Buddhist pilgrim, scholar, and translator, still others see him as a divine cleric who, together with an entourage of human-animal hybrids, works to protect the living and liberate the dead.

These contrasting images—Xuanzang as pilgrim walking under the weight of hundreds of scrolls and as magical monk meeting the Buddha—are both products of the elaborate mythologies that developed around Xuanzang in the centuries after his death. The former derives from ritual paintings produced in Japan that honor Xuanzang as the monk most closely associated with the *Great Perfection of Wisdom Sūtra*. The latter is part of a long tradition in China of venerating Xuanzang and his fellow pilgrims as exorcists and spirit guides. Later generations of admirers and devotees have never tired of reimagining Xuanzang and retelling his life story, and the colorful legends that have grown up around him now eclipse his early biographies. Just about everyone in East Asia is familiar with tales of Xuanzang—often known simply as the "Tang Monk"—confronting ghosts and demons together with a martial monkey, a lazy pig, a demonic monk, and a dragon horse along the route to "Western Heaven." Historically accurate accounts of Xuanzang mastering Sanskrit grammar and expounding on the various functions of the storehouse consciousness have been decidedly less popular.

An otherworldly aura clung to Xuanzang even during his own

OPPOSITE: Funerary scroll featuring Xuanzang and his companions from *The Journey to the West*. Qingmei, Taiwan, 1940. Source: British Museum, copyright Stephan Feuchtwang. © The Trustees of the British Museum.

lifetime. In his *Record of the Western Regions*, he documents the cities and landscapes he passed through, but he also describes the bizarre places he only heard about. There was, for example, the island of Nārikela, where dwarfish people used their bird-like beaks to dine on coconuts. There was also the Iron City on the island of Siṃhala. Sailors who passed this place were summoned ashore by beautiful maidens. Once the women lured the men inside the city, they reverted to their true form as demons, locked the sailors in an iron prison, and fed on their flesh.[163] In the seventh century, long before the globe was explored and mapped, the people of China, like people everywhere, assumed that strange, dangerous, and magical beings dwelled beyond the borders of civilization. Xuanzang's earwitness accounts of quasi-human realms were remarkable but not unreasonable. He never personally encountered any beaked dwarves or murderous demonesses, of course, and his *Record* does not dwell on the strange places and creatures he heard about or the many real dangers he surely faced. Xuanzang describes some mountain and river crossings as particularly fraught. In some of the more isolated regions, travelers were vulnerable to thieves, and many people followed religious practices that were antithetical, perhaps even hostile, to Buddhist monks like himself. There were inevitably difficult people to be endured and unsavory places to be passed quickly through, but Xuanzang wrote his *Record* to document the histories, cultures, and conditions of the Western Regions, not to narrate his own struggles or extol his accomplishments.

For Xuanzang's disciples and supporters, however, it was a different story. They had no qualms about embellishing their master's biography with dramatic descriptions of near-death experiences, merciless attacks by bandits and heretics, divine apparitions and interventions, and heroic victories. Even Emperor Gaozong rhapsodized about how Xuanzang "sailed beyond the Milky Way and shook the rings of his staff above the smoke and mist. On the towering swells of the vast ocean, he forged ahead across the frightening waves. Over the heavy frost of the broad earth, he battled the cold and passed alone."[164] In the effusive praise showered on a venerable teacher, Xuanzang's life takes on a cosmic quality as he rises up to the heavens above and passes unscathed through earthly dangers below. The qualities of fearlessness and invincibility are echoed by Xuanzang's disciple Huili, who recounted how his teacher traveled alone across lands with "dark and frozen mountains, swift and turbulent rivers, black and poisonous winds, and packs of fearsome, predatory beasts."[165] Deities in the desert reportedly protected Xuanzang, and he used the power of meditation to ward off bloodthirsty Durgā pirates. These hagiographical flourishes, written by devoted disciples and patrons, are not unusual and they represent only the earliest phase in what would become a long, imaginative process of mythmaking. In later retellings of Xuanzang's life, bandits and wild animals evolve into ever more terrifying monsters and demons. The appearance of guardian spirits and Buddhist deities grow more and more frequent. Seemingly insurmountable obstacles and moments of impossible peril drive the story, while Xuanzang's long years of undramatic study and translation fade until they finally vanish altogether.

The transformation from medieval scholar to mythic traveler advanced in increments. For hundreds of years after his death, people were content to revere Xuanzang as a pious cleric, a courageous pilgrim, a prolific translator, and a learned exegete. Early paintings depicted him together with other historically prominent monks famous for their service to the imperial family and the empire, their transmission of Buddhist traditions from India to China, and their translation of Buddhist texts from Sanskrit into Chinese. During the Ming Dynasty (1368–1644), Xuanzang was sometimes venerated as the monk responsible for transmitting *all* Buddhist texts from India to China, but during earlier periods, he was more modestly portrayed as one of the most consequential translators China had ever known.

In premodern East Asia, learned monks and lay scholars carefully studied the kinds of Buddhist texts Xuanzang translated, but for the average person—who could not read basic Chinese characters let alone technical Buddhist hybrid Chinese—Buddhist sūtras and commentaries were valued not as repositories of doctrinal treatises, ritual procedures, monastic regulations, and historical information; they were sacred objects and sources of divine power. One did not necessarily need to understand them or put them into practice; one merely needed to be in their presence. The extraordinary powers attributed to Buddhist sūtras extended to those monks and nuns who read, memorized, and embodied them, and no monk was more closely associated with the Buddhist canon than Xuanzang. He was responsible for translating seventy-five texts in 1,335 fascicles, more than one quarter of the entire Chinese Buddhist canon. One of Xuanzang's titles is "Sanzang," or Trepiṭaka (Master of the Tripartite Canon). If the texts in the canon were endowed with miraculous qualities, it stood to reason that those same attributes adhered to the monk who retrieved, transmitted, and translated them.

This conflation between text and teaching is notable in the shrines to Xuanzang set up in or near monastic libraries in China and in the many rituals that summon his spirit to transmit talismanic, apotropaic texts. It is also evident in Japan, where Xuanzang has long been venerated both as a founding father of the Yogācāra (Hossō) tradition and as the transmitter and guardian of the *Great Perfection of Wisdom Sūtra* (*Mahāprajñāpāramitā Sūtra*). Xuanzang translated this massive sūtra just before his death, and it has become one of his most influential works. According to tradition, Śākyamuni delivered the teachings recorded in the sūtra in four places to sixteen assemblies. At each of these assemblies, the Buddha preached one of the sixteen sūtras that together make up the larger work. (With six hundred chapters and fifty million Chinese characters, it is the longest text in the Buddhist canon.) These smaller sūtras include famous works such as the *Diamond Sūtra* and the *Perfection of Wisdom in One Hundred Thousand Lines*; the brief *Heart Sūtra* is held to be a condensation of the entire collection. The "perfection of wisdom" that the sūtra celebrates is the wisdom of all buddhas, insight into the truth of emptiness.

As an encapsulation of the most advanced and efficacious Mahayana Buddhist teachings, the *Great Perfection of Wisdom Sūtra* was an object of reverence and ritualized recitation in India, Tibet, China, Korea, and Japan. It would take a single person roughly one month to recite the entire sūtra from beginning to end, so recitations often involved large groups of monks simultaneously intoning individual portions of the text. In Tang Dynasty China, government officials—or, more rarely, the imperial court—sponsored these large recitation assemblies for the purpose of safeguarding their territories. In one example dating from the tenth century, the merits of staging a recitation of the sūtra are announced: participants will be protected by devas and they will be neither harmed by weapons nor molested by demons or ghosts. The power of the sūtra is likened to *māghī*, a plant considered a cure for all manner of poisons in ancient India. As the *Great Perfection of Wisdom Sūtra* itself declares, "Worldly evils will dissipate in front of the *Perfection of Wisdom* just like a serpent recoils from the mere smell of *māghī*."[166]

The *Great Perfection of Wisdom Sūtra* was transmitted to Japan from China shortly after it was translated into Chinese by Xuanzang, and it soon developed a reputation as a panacea. It not only warded off natural calamities, ghosts, malevolent spirits, and military incursions, but it also ensured that the realm was at peace, families were safe and harmonious, rains were timely, harvests were bountiful, and the dead were reborn in heavenly pure lands. Ritual readings of the sūtra in Japan, known as "Great Perfection Assemblies" have continued from the ninth century until today. These "readings," which are held by all Japanese Buddhist sects, often take the abbreviated form of dramatically fanning the accordion-style texts while reciting select passages from the sūtra. The content of the work is not meant to be heard or understood; its powers are made manifest through the mere act of "turning" its pages.

Sixteen "good spirits" are responsible for protecting the *Great Perfection of Wisdom Sūtra* and its devotees. In ritual paintings hung above the altar during Great Perfection Assemblies and on the frontispieces of the sūtra printed in Japan, these fierce-looking martial deities typically cluster around Śākyamuni Buddha, who, as the source of the sūtra, sits on a lotus throne at the center of the scene. Xuanzang stands among the spirits holding a flywhisk and a scroll and wearing a string of skulls around his neck and a pack full of texts on his back. (This iconography is the origin of the famous image of Xuanzang carrying a bamboo backpack shown on the frontispiece of this book.) Next to Xuanzang stands a red-skinned, bare-chested figure, with a child's face peering out from his stomach. The demon has wild long hair, white fangs, a necklace of skulls, and a snake coiled around his wrist. This is the Great General of Deep Sands, the spirit that appeared to Xuanzang when he was lost and close to death in the Gashun Gobi. As the savior of Xuanzang, Deep Sands is honored as a guardian of the sūtra. In some versions of this painting, dating back as far as the fourteenth century, Xuanzang displaces the central figure of Śākyamuni, as though he rather than the Buddha was the human embodiment of the Perfection of Wisdom.[167]

The transformation of a long-dead Chinese monk into a living member of the Japanese Buddhist pantheon is an honor rarely

OPPOSITE: Xuanzang and Sixteen Protective Deities, Daruma-ji, 14th c. Source: *Tenjiku e.*

accorded historical clerics. Xuanzang was venerated not just as a great pilgrim and translator but also as a deity endowed with extraordinary powers. The mythology that grew up around his life— his association with the Buddha, his ability to subjugate demonic forces, and his retinue of divine escorts and guardians—was not unique to Japan. A similar apotheosis took place in China during roughly the same period, but legends of Xuanzang's life on the continent were far more elaborate, colorful, and widespread.

During his life, Xuanzang leveraged his standing as a venerable court cleric to strengthen the position of monastic institutions at court and throughout the empire, and later generations remembered those accomplishments and venerated Xuanzang as an eminent patriarch of China's Buddhist tradition. For roughly four hundred years after his death, written accounts and artistic renderings placed Xuanzang in the context of other clerics renowned for their contributions to the sangha and the state. By the early twelfth century, however, something had shifted. Xuanzang began to be associated not only with historical patriarchs but also with buddhas, bodhisattvas, dragons, and demons. His travels took him not merely to India but to the purgatories and pure lands of Buddhist cosmology, and the divine scriptures he received came not from seventh-century South Asian monks and scholars but issued directly from buddhas and bodhisattvas. Xuanzang had passed beyond mundane landscapes of the human realm and into the boundless worlds of Mahāyāna mythology.

This vision of a superhuman Xuanzang first emerged in conventional Buddhist contexts. His epic, otherworldly pilgrimage was depicted in cave temples, on stūpas, in commemorations of monastic libraries, and in narrative accounts used for preaching and proselytizing. His life story was told as an episode in the broader history of Buddhism—a history already densely populated with divine and demonic beings. Images carved and painted on the walls

of Buddhist caves throughout China in the early twelfth century
show Xuanzang accompanied by an attendant—sometimes depicted
as a human, sometimes as a monkey—and a horse carrying a bundle of texts radiating light. This triad occupies the peripheries of
larger iconographic motifs that usually center on the bodhisattva
Avalokiteśvara. Xuanzang is never the main subject of these works,
but he is the primary figure in the small band of pilgrims venerating
the bodhisattva; his special status is indicated by his position in the
lead, his large size, and often by the presence of a halo around his
head—a sign of sainthood.

In early Chinese narrative accounts, elements of Xuanzang's
conventional, "historical" biography—his desire for more efficacious texts, his long, challenging journey, his visions and legends
of demons and bodhisattvas, his acquisition of precious texts, and
his triumphant return—were transformed into archetypical accounts
that established the divine origins of Buddhist scriptures, described
the sacrifices involved in their acquisition and transmission, and
testified to their efficacy. The most detailed of these early narratives,
first printed sometime around the late twelfth century, resemble a
genre of popular Buddhist literature known as "scripts for narrating
sūtras," which present Buddhist teachings to lay audiences through
the medium of engaging storytelling. Such scripts were often accompanied by images and were intended to be dramatic and entertaining
to attract largely illiterate audiences. Xuanzang's story, variously
titled *The Poetic Tale of the Great Tang Trepiṭaka Master's Acquiring the
Scriptures* or *The Newly Arranged Record of the Great Tang Trepiṭaka
Dharma Master's Acquiring the Scriptures*, describes how he departed
the human world and ventured into a strange, uncivilized territory.
Beset by ghosts and demons, he is guided and protected by powerful
spirit-animals—most prominently a monkey novice—and Buddhist
deities. After enduring severe hardship, Xuanzang and his companions eventually arrive in a heavenly realm, populated by spirit monks,

immortals, bodhisattvas, and buddhas. From Śākyamuni Buddha, they receive a collection of apotropaic texts with the power to safeguard the living and liberate the dead. Xuanzang then transmits these divine revelations back to the human realm before he and his entourage ascend to Heaven on the fifteenth day of the seventh lunar month—the date of the Ghost Festival, an annual ritual for delivering the damned out of purgatory. The story maps the landscape of a postmortem shadow world and identifies the scriptures that guard against demonic molestation and ensure a beneficial rebirth: the Buddhist canon in general and the *Heart Sūtra* in particular.

Xuanzang's ability to access buddhas and bodhisattvas, transmit their teachings, and lead others into their presence made him and his companions the objects of adulation and invocation. In some areas of China, versions of Xuanzang's mythic pilgrimage have long been recited or performed during funerals to help the dead cross from the earthly to the heavenly realm. In rural villages, masked ritual specialists still dress as Xuanzang, a monkey, and a pig to perform exorcistic dances to drive demons and ghosts away from homes and fields. In small temples scattered across mainland China, Taiwan, Singapore, and Malaysia, Xuanzang's monkey companion, known as Sun Wukong or Great Sage Equal to Heaven, descends into the bodies of spirit mediums and speaks through their mouths. Scenes from the pilgrimage are painted on monastery walls and carved on temple pillars. Entire temples and shrines are devoted to Xuanzang's companions—the monkey (confidant of gamblers, healer of children) and the pig (patron saint of prostitutes)—and the spirits of his fellow travelers are regularly summoned to observe and participate in a range of communal and private rituals.[168]

These ceremonial re-creations of Xuanzang's fantastical pilgrimage have a long history in China but they are not well known today. In the realm of popular culture, they have been eclipsed by a literary version of the same story. In the late sixteenth century, an anonymous author assembled and elaborated on the many myths and legends associated with Xuanzang and his otherworldly travels to create one of China's best-known novels: *The Journey to the West.* The novel, like the oral, theatrical, liturgical, and illustrated versions that preceded it, is loosely based on Xuanzang's biography, incorporating, at some points, actual historical documents into the narrative. Its cast of characters, however—the Buddhist bodhisattvas, Daoist immortals, shape-shifting demons, ferocious monsters, and talking animals—is far more extensive than anything that had existed before. Over the course of one hundred chapters—more than fifteen hundred pages in Anthony Yu's authoritative English translation—the story tells how Xuanzang and his companions made a perilous journey from the capital of China to India, the land of the Buddha.[169] The pilgrimage is set in motion when the Tang Dynasty emperor Taizong prepares to hold a Grand Mass of Land and Water—an elaborate mortuary ritual for liberating sentient beings—so that those "orphaned souls in the Region of Darkness might find salvation." Xuanzang, serving as the lead officiant of the ritual, is interrupted midway through the ceremony by the bodhisattva Avalokiteśvara, who mocks him, shouting "Hey, Monk! You only know how to talk about the teachings of the Little Vehicle. Don't you know anything about the Great Vehicle?" The texts of the Great Vehicle, she explains, are able to "send the lost to Heaven, to deliver the afflicted from their sufferings, to fashion ageless bodies, and to break the cycle of comings and goings." After Avalokiteśvara reveals that the most efficacious mortuary texts can be found in India, Emperor Taizong provides Xuanzang with an imperial travel rescript granting permission to travel west to the land of the Buddha in order to obtain the miraculous, salvational sūtras.

Xuanzang is the ostensible leader of the mission, but the true hero of the novel is his monkey attendant, Sun Wukong. Like many of the other main characters in the book, Sun Wukong is a divine being that has been banished to earth for his mischievous misdeeds in Heaven. To atone for his transgressions, he must escort and protect Xuanzang on his journey to India. With his shape shifting, his astounding martial prowess, and his unvarnished disdain for authority, Sun Wukong serves as the indispensable if unruly guide for Xuanzang as he traverses treacherous, demon-infested terrain. The slothful but formidable pig Zhu Bajie, the demon-monk Sha, and a dragon-horse round out the escort. The bulk of the novel recounts the group's passage through haunted landscapes, their harrowing battles with predatory demons and ghosts, and their narrow escapes. All manner of monsters attempt to capture Xuanzang. Male demons want to eat his flesh, which, being so pure, can bestow magical powers. Female demons scheme to sleep with Xuanzang because his semen, which has never been dissipated, can confer immortality. All told, the pilgrims persevere through eighty-one trials. After a succession of cunning abductions, dramatic battles, and heroic rescues, Xuanzang and his companions finally encounter the Buddha, receive the sacred scriptures, and duly deliver them back to China. Their arduous task complete, at the conclusion of the novel, all five pilgrims ascend to Heaven, apotheosized as buddhas or bodhisattvas.

Prior representations of Xuanzang portrayed him as fearless, brilliant, and decisive. In the novel *The Journey to the West*, however, he comes across as feeble and skittish. Devout yet credulous, principled yet cripplingly timid, he is unable to defend himself and constantly in need of rescue. When overwhelmed, he folds in on himself, breaking down in tears. ("Pity me! How can I walk through those thousands hills and ten thousand waters?") The monkey Sun Wukong takes charge, chastising Xuanzang for being so "thin-skinned" and acting like a "namby-pamby." It is an unflattering portrayal of such a historically significant cleric, and one can only imagine that the author of the novel was not especially enamored of Buddhist monks. And yet, *The Journey to the West* has been so consistently influential that most people are more familiar with the faltering, fictional "Tang Monk" than they are with the historical figure who inspired the character.

After its publication in 1592, *The Journey to the West* circulated throughout China, Korea, and Japan, inspiring commentaries, abridgments, sequels, spin-offs, puppet shows, and plays. As new mediums for storytelling developed, *The Journey to the West* was one of the first works in China to be adapted. From 1926 to 1928, for example, as the film industry was gaining momentum in China, no fewer than fourteen movies based on scenes from *The Journey to the West* were produced. The very first animated feature produced in China, *Princess Iron Fan*, released in 1941, was stylistically modeled on Walt Disney's *Snow White and the Seven Dwarves* but its content was derived from *The Journey to the West*. Cinematic retellings of the mythic pilgrimage have only proliferated in the years since. The same is true for television series, children's books, and video games. The figure of the "Tang Monk" continues to evolve in tandem with the interests of authors and audiences. Ever since the 1970s, for example, it has become conventional to cast a woman in the role of Xuanzang in television and film adaptations. The novelty of a young woman portraying a celibate monk pales in comparison to more recent, more radical reimaginings of Xuanzang in Japan. In the 126 manga versions of *The Journey to the West* that have been produced so far, Xuanzang is variously portrayed as a yakuza, a hypersexualized woman dominated by a sadistic monkey, and a submissive partner in a queer male relationship. Every generation finds the Xuanzang it is looking for.

It was only a matter of time before *The Journey to the West* made its own inevitable journey to the West. M. Théodore Pavie (1811–96) made the first French translation of three chapters of the novel in 1857. Several more partial translations followed, with the first English rendering of chapter ten made by Rev. Dyer Ball in 1884. Many of these initial attempts to introduce and interpret the novel for Western audiences were wildly speculative. The Welsh Baptist minister Timothy Richard (1845–1919), for example, concluded that *The Journey to the West* was originally a biblical text, with Xuanzang as Jesus Christ and the monkey Sun Wukong as an apostle. In the introduction to another English translation, the American scholar and translator Helen Hayes described Xuanzang as "that Principle inherent in man which understands its oneness with all life and is willing in its devoted love to spend and be spent."[170] The translations of Pavie, Ball, Richard, Hayes, and a dozen others have now been largely forgotten. Most readers in Europe and North America know the novel from just one work: *Monkey: Folk Novel of China*, Arthur Waley's abridged English translation. In that widely celebrated 1942 work, Waley presented the pilgrimage as an allegory of the human condition. The character of Xuanzang, for instance, represented "the ordinary man, blundering anxiously through the difficulties of life."[171] In the United States, the book was promoted as a lighthearted, amusing classic of Chinese literature. A review in the *Nation* described it approvingly as "a combination of picaresque novel, fairy tale, fabliau, Mickey Mouse, Davy Crockett, and *Pilgrim's Progress*." Waley's translation has stood the test of time. *Monkey* has remained in print for more than seventy years and is a staple of Chinese literature courses in Anglophone universities. Generations of college students and casual readers have enjoyed the book as an imaginative comic fantasy, the Chinese equivalent of *Don Quixote*.

The success of *Monkey* prompted Waley to publish a follow-up essay titled "The Real Tripitaka" to distinguish between the historical cleric and the mythical monk of the novel. That clarification notwithstanding, it is the fictional character that has taken root in American popular culture. There have been multiple English

Xuanzang as a character in the Joycity online game
FreeStyle Street Basketball.

rewrites of the tale, including comics drawn for children, super-
hero variations ("If you think Superman or Spiderman has been
around a long time, think about Monkey," suggests the sales copy),
graphic novels for adults, award-winning literary adaptations, Net-
flix series, cartoons, puppet shows, operas, plays (reviewed in the
Chicago Sun-Times as "part vaudeville, part mystical dreamscape and
Eastern-inflected ballet"), and high school world literature lessons.
Monkey, once described by the puppeteer Caroll Spinney as the
"Bugs Bunny of China," has even made guest appearances on *Sesame
Street*. It is an extraordinary legacy for a seventh-century Chinese
scholar of Yogācāra doctrine. Even with all the bizarre creatures
Xuanzang heard about on his long pilgrimage—the beaked dwarves
and cannibalistic women—he surely never could have imagined the
likes of Big Bird and Mr. Snuffleupagus.

CHAPTER 26

Xuanzang's Future

Politics, Profit, and Piety

WHEN XUANZANG met the Indian king Kumāra, he praised the benevolence of the reigning Chinese emperor, Taizong: "My great lord's sagely virtue extends far and his humane teachings have reached distant places. Many people from different lands with different customs venerate and submit to His Majesty." King Kumāra, according the *Record of the Western Regions*, was duly impressed. "Since the emperor's kindness and grace is like that," he said, "I would like to pay him tribute." At the Chinese court after his return from India, Xuanzang explained that he had been serving the emperor's interests abroad, educating the people of Central and South Asia about the deep learning, formidable strength, and benign intentions of "Mahācina." He also informed Chinese officials of the wisdom and honor of the North Indian rulers he encountered. Thanks in part to Xuanzang's diplomacy, the two empires began exchanging envoys and gifts. The engagement was short-lived but it set a precedent for cooperation that modern Buddhist monks and government officials have strived to emulate. When the Chinese Buddhist cleric Taixu (1890–1947) embarked on a "good-will mission" in India in 1940, he cast himself as a modern-day Xuanzang. "The day is not far distant," he predicted, "when the cultural relations existing between India and China in the days of Xuanzang will be re-established between these two countries."[172]

Indeed, the political and economic interests of India and China are now more entwined than ever. Annual trade between the two countries approaches $100 billion. In their regular bilateral talks, India's prime minster Narendra Modi and China's president Xi Jinping both invoke Xuanzang as a symbol of their peoples' shared history and abiding friendship. Some 1,350 years after his death, Xuanzang's work as a cultural ambassador continues.

In 2015, the state-owned China Film Corporation launched a joint venture with Eros International, a prominent Indian film production and distribution company. Together they produced *Xuanzang*—a lavishly funded blockbuster featuring a star-studded cast of Chinese and Indian actors. The mainstream Chinese film industry dutifully nominated the movie for a slate of awards and submitted it as the country's entry for Best Foreign Language Film at the 2017 Academy Awards. *Xuanzang* was not selected and did poorly at the box office but it was only one part of a larger effort to repackage and popularize Xuanzang's story as a tale of Chinese perseverance, ambition, and outreach. As the PRC continues to extend its regional influence through the Belt and Road Initiative—a massive program of development and investment, known as the "New Silk Road"—Buddhism in general and Xuanzang in particular have become increasingly important elements of China's soft-power strategy. According to the state-run media, "Religion is becoming the glue that can help bond the region under the Chinese dream."[173]

To make this dream a reality, the Chinese government has mobilized a range of resources. The Chinese Buddhist Association, which is overseen by the United Front Work Department of the Chinese Communist Party, has been assigned the task of exploring how the "spirit of Xuanzang" can best support the Belt and Road Initiative. Societies for the "promotion of Xuanzang culture" and Xuanzang research centers are now organizing major international conferences on Xuanzang's life and legacy. The China National Traditional Orchestra, whose mission is to implement the Belt and Road Initiative, developed *Xuanzang's Pilgrimage* to showcase "the diverse yet connected cultures found along the legendary Silk Road, combining music from China's Han, Uygur, Kazak, Tajik and other ethnic groups."[174] The massive production—with an eighty-piece orchestra and twenty-four performers—has performed in London and Washington, DC.

In the international sphere, Xuanzang, like Confucius, has become the bearer of China's best intentions. In recent retellings of Xuanzang's story in China, he not only endures hardship for the greater good of the nation and works tirelessly to enrich the intellectual and spiritual life of China, but he also nurtures international partnerships based on cultural exchange, mutual respect, and mutual enrichment—just as the PRC seeks to do today. His role as transmitter of Indian Buddhist traditions to China is often downplayed, while his efforts to introduce Chinese culture to India (through his purported translation into Sanskrit of the *Daode jing*) and the rest of Asia are highlighted. Xuanzang is depicted not just as a student during his time in India but, more significantly, as an ambassador and a teacher; he had bested Indian monks in debate and even the elders at Nālandā and regional kings pleaded with him to remain in India. After Xuanzang returned to China, these narratives continue, the translations and commentaries he produced led to great revivals of Buddhism in Korea, Japan, and Southeast Asia. Xuanzang bestowed the gift of understanding on all Asia. In the present age of rampant materialism and social alienation, China and Chinese Buddhists are now called to a similar mission—to bring the wisdom of the East to the disenchanted West.

In India, local and national governments are similarly attuned to the potential diplomatic and economic value of its Buddhist heritage. Nālandā is being revived as a "secular Buddhist" university, part of a broader initiative to unleash India's "soft power on

Asia and the world." The numbers have been crunched and the potential tourist dollars calculated. A new Xuanzang pilgrimage route through Bihar is in the works. These and other developments are explicitly aimed at reasserting India's position as the cradle of Buddhist civilization. As the Belt and Road Initiative extends into Pakistan, Nepal, Bangladesh, and Sri Lanka, India, virtually surrounded, is determined to "use Buddhism to neutralize any Chinese soft-power advantage."[175] Xuanzang has become an unwitting foot soldier in this cultural cold war.

Nationalistic deployments of Xuanzang's legacy stand in an uneasy relationship with attempts to mold him into a paradigmatic symbol of a unified, pan-Asian Buddhist culture in contrast to the Christian West. As a founding patriarch of a transregional Buddhist tradition, Xuanzang belongs to a select pantheon of Buddhist saints whose influence extends well beyond their empire of origin. As a transmitter of Buddhist texts and teachings, he is part of an elite group of clerics revered for their courage, insight, and contribution to spreading the Dharma throughout Asia. Since the end of World War II, several medieval monks have been made modern exemplars of Asian solidarity. They have been apotheosized in elaborate public memorials and commemorations designed to highlight points of past cultural unity and generate positive models for future cooperation in Asia.

During Xuanzang's travels, several regional rulers tried to coerce him to abandon his quest and embrace the power and prestige they said were his due. He always declined. After his return to China, the emperor twice asked Xuanzang to return to lay life so that he might serve as an official and channel his considerable talents into serving the state. Both times, he refused, reminding the emperor that he had become a monk to study and spread the Buddhist teachings. "If you order me to return to lay life," Xuanzang is said to have explained, "it would be like dragging a boat out of water and onto dry land. Such a vessel would not only be useless, but it would also rot and decay."[176] Xuanzang eventually moved to the mountains, where he hoped to be left in peace. But the emperors, it seems, are not done with him yet.

Notes

1. Huili et al., *Da Tang da Ci'en si Sanzang fashi zhuan* (hereafter *Zhuan*), 261a1–15. Unless otherwise noted, all translations are my own. Several other translations of Xuanzang's biography have been published. For ease of reference, I provide the corresponding page numbers in Li Rongxi's translation, *A Biography of the Tripiṭaka Master of the Great Ci'en Monastery of the Great Tang Dynasty* (hereafter *Biography*), 227–28.

2. Both passages translated in this paragraph come from Xuanzang, *Da Tang xiyu ji* (hereafter *Xiyu ji*), 945c15–22. The best annotated edition of this text is Mizutani Shinjō, *Daitō Seiikiki*. Cf. Li Rongxi's translation, *The Great Tang Dynasty Record of the Western Regions* (hereafter *Record*), 388.

3. On the reliability and textual history of Xuanzang's biography, see Saito Tatuya, "Features of the Kongō-ji version of the Further Biographies of Eminent Monks"; and Jeffrey Kotyk, "Chinese State and Buddhist Historical Sources on Xuanzang." It is worth noting that most of the documents included in the *Biography*—Xuanzang's correspondences and his memorials to the throne—appear to be genuine. They circulated independently in China and Japan; in the *Biography* itself, letters that once existed but are now lost are also noted.

4. These examples are drawn from Mishi Saran, *Chasing the Monk's Shadow*; Richard Bernstein, *Ultimate Journey*; and Sun Shuyun, *Ten Thousand Miles without a Cloud*. Other accounts include Kōin Takata, *Gandāra Daitō Seiikiki no tabi*; Zhihong Wang, *Dust in the Wind*; and, most recently, Deepak Anand, "Retracing Bodhisattva Xuanzang Project."

5. *Zhuan*, 224b19–20; *Biography*, 27. This account, though extraordinary, is not beyond reason. In 1896, the Swedish explorer Sven Anders Hedin (1865–1952) survived six days without water in this same region. Aurel Stein, whose horse spent four days in the Taklamakan desert without water, thought the account in Xuanzang's biography was accurate.

6. There is no scholarly consensus regarding the precise date that Xuanzang departed from the capital. Étienne de La Vaissière ("Note sur la chronologie") has argued for 629, Kuwayama Shōshin ("How Xuanzang Learned about Nālandā") believes it was 628, and Yoshimura Makoto ("Genjō no nenji mondai ni tsuite") claims it was 627.

7. Xuanzang was most likely reading Paramārtha's translation of the *Compendium of the Great Vehicle* (*Mahāyānasaṃgraha Śāstra*). See the English translation by John Keenan, *The Summary of the Great Vehicle*.

8. *Zhuan*, 221a8–10; *Biography*, 7.

9. Xuanzang probably learned about Nālandā and Śīlabhadra from the Indian monk Prabhākaramitra, who had studied under Śīlabhadra at Nālandā before arriving in Chang'an in 626 or 627. Kuwayama, "How Xuanzang Learned about Nālandā."

10. Hansen, *The Silk Road*, 141.

11. *Zhuan*, 225b5–7; *Biography*, 31–32. The unflattering portrayal of Qu Wentai in Xuanzang's biography should be read in relation to the political context of the time. The Tang army conquered Gaochang in 640 and Qu Wentai died during the campaign. Overthrown rulers are typically portrayed as villains in official Chinese historical sources, and this would be particularly true for accounts like Xuanzang's biography, which discussed individuals and events closely associated with China's imperial court.

12. The name "Silk Road" is a relatively recent invention, coined in 1877 by the German explorer and geographer Baron Ferdinand von Richthofen in *Ergebnisse eigener Reisen*. For excellent maps of the principle trade routes and political boundaries of Central Asia during the sixth and seventh centuries, see Yuri Bregel, *An Historical Atlas of Central Asia*.

13. Song Yun, together with his companion Hui Sheng, spent three years traveling as far as northwestern India and returned to China with 170 Mahāyāna texts. Their accounts are no longer extant but a summary of their journey is preserved in Yang Xuanzhi's sixth-century *Record of Buddhist Monasteries in Lo-Yang*. For a study of Song Yun's travels, see Édouard Chavannes, "Voyage de Song Yun dans l'Udyāna et le Gandhāra." Faxian's *Record* has been translated by James Legge as *A Record of the Buddhistic Kingdoms*.

14. Local residents farmed rice and various fruits; mined gold, copper, iron, lead, and tin; raised horses and cattle; and produced luxury items like felt wall coverings, makeup, and incense. Hansen, *The Silk Road*, 116.

15. *Zhuan*, 227a16–22; *Biography*, 41. The exact route of Xuanzang's traverse is not known, but he likely went over Bedel Pass (14,060 ft.). From there he presumably would have proceeded to Suyak Pass (13,220 ft.) and then Barskoon Pass (12,530 ft.) before descending to Issyk Kul. Some scholars have suggested that Xuanzang took the route that is now followed by National Highway 217, but this does not accord with the description in his *Record*.

16. La Vaissière ("Note sur la chronologie") argues that Xuanzang actually met Tong Yabghu's son, Si Yabghu.

17. *Zhuan*, 227b8–9; *Biography*, 42.

18. On Sogdian history, culture, and trade, see La Vaissiére, "Sogdians in China" and *Sogdian Traders*; Frantz Grenet, "The 7th-century A.D. 'Ambassadors' Painting'"; Frantz Grenet and Zhang Guangda, "The Last Refuge of the Sogdian Religion"; and Patrick Wertmann, *Sogdians in China*.

19. *Xiyu ji*, 871a16–17; *Record*, 27.

20. *Zhuan*, 227c20–21; *Biography*, 45.

21. The king's conversion is described in the Buddhist text *Milinda's Questions* (see I. B. Horner, trans.), though scholars have questioned the veracity of this conversion. See Richard Salomon, *The Buddhist Literature of Ancient Gandhāra*, 24–28.

22. According to the Indian Buddhist monk and translator Paramārtha (499–569), the Mahāsāṃghika school was divided over the validity of Mahāyāna texts. Whereas some sects rejected Mahāyāna sūtras as fabrications, the Lokottaravādins were among those that accepted the texts as *buddhavacana*, or the words of the Buddha.

23. For historical accounts of Bamiyan, see Kuwayama, "Chinese Records on Bamiyan." On the early archaeological work in this region, see Elizabeth J. Errington et al., *Charles Masson and the Buddhist Sites of Afghanistan*. One of the monasteries Xuanzang visited in Bamiyan was excavated in 1993–95. The birch-bark and palm-leaf manuscripts of texts found at the site are now in the Schøyen Collection in Norway. The recently discovered monumental parinirvāṇa Buddha was excavated by the Délégation Archéologique Française en Afghanistan.

24. *Zhuan*, 229a28–29; *Biography*, 52.

25. *Xiyu ji*, 879c2–4; *Record*, 70. Xuanzang refers to non-Buddhist temples, what we might call "Hindu" temples, as "deva shrines" (*tianci*).

26. *Xiyu ji*, 888c5–6; *Record*, 114.

27. The Mahāsāṃghikas split from the Sarvāstivādins and others over the observance of arcane Vinaya rules, such as whether or not monks could carry salt in an animal horn or possess mats with fringe.

28. *Xiyu ji*, 894 b27–29; *Record*, 143–44. This passage, relating how the king converted an entire continent to vegetarianism and had hunters and butchers put to death, reminds us that Xuanzang is not always a reliable reporter. It is true that Harṣa controlled a large swath of northern India, stretching from Kashmir in the west to the Bay of Bengal in the east. His domain reached into Nepal in the north but it ended around the Narmada River in the south. Harṣa thus had no authority in southern India, and it took him much longer than six years to consolidate his territory in the north.

29. *Zhuan*, 245a24–b4; *Biography*, 132–33.

30. Mark L. Blum, trans., *The Nirvana Sutra*, 219.

31. Two of the three plays attributed to Harṣa are dedicated to Śiva, while the third invokes the Buddha. Wendy Doniger and Harṣavardhana, *Lady of the Jewel Necklace*, 15.

32. Sister Vajirā and Francis Story, trans. *Last Days of the Buddha: The Mahāparinibbāna Sutta*, pp. 62–63.

33. *Zhuan*, 236c24–237a14; *Biography*, 91–92.

34. Monastic complexes at Nālandā had twin sets of double ovens in the middle of their courtyards, presumably used to cook communal and individual meals.

35. *Zhuan*, 238c28–239a4; *Biography*, 101.

36. *Xiyu ji*, 923c22–23; *Record*, 283.

37. Yijing, *A Record of the Inner Law*, 112–13.

38. According to the Indian translator Divākara, Śilabhadra followed the divisions given in the *SaṃdhinirmocanaSūtra*. On this text, see John Powers, *Hermeneutics and Tradition in the Saṃdhinirmocana-sūtra*, and John Keenan's translation of *The Scripture on the Explication of the Underlying Meaning*. Only one of Śilabhadra's texts survives (in Tibetan translation), the *Buddhabhūmivyākhyāna*. See Nishio Kyōo and J. Rahder's translation, *The Buddhabhūmi Sūtra and the Buddhabhūmivyākhyāna of Çīlabhadra*, and John Keenan, *A Study of the Buddhabhūmyupadeśa*.

39. *Zhuan*, 244c1–3; *Biography*, 129.

40. On the philosophical distinctions between Yogācāra and Madhyamaka, see Jay L. Garfield and Jan Westerhoff, *Madhyamaka and Yogācāra*. On

Xuanzang's assessment of the two traditions, see Dan Lusthaus, "Xuan-zang and Kuiji and Madhyamaka."

41. See Lambert Schmithausen, *Ālayavijñana* and *On the Problem of the External World in the "Ch'eng wei shi lun."*

42. The Sthavira school was one of the earliest schools of Indian Buddhism, claiming to trace its tenets back to the elder disciples of Śakyamuni. About a hundred years after the death of the Buddha, the Sthavira split from the majority of the monastic sangha (the Mahāsāṃghika, or "Great Congregation") over a disagreement about whether or not ten specific Vinaya rules, which the rest of the assembly viewed as dispensable, should continue to be upheld. Several later "schools," notably the Saṃmitīya (School of Correct Logic), the Sarvāstivāda (Teaching that All Exists), and Vibhajyavāda (Teaching of Differentiation) were offshoots of the Sthavira.

43. The precise location of Parvata is not known but it may have been in the ancient region of Harrapa. On possible locations, see Mizutani, *Daitō Seiikiki*, vol. 3, 338–39. The Saṃmitīya school was, according to Xuan-zang, the largest Buddhist school in India during the mid-seventh century. An offshoot of the Sthavira, it is best known for its controversial teaching that there is an "inexpressible person" (*pudgala*) neither the same nor different from the aggregates (*skandhas*). Some Buddhists (most famously, Vasubandhu) thought this teaching contradicted the fundamental doc-trine of no-self (*anātman*). For that reason, the Saṃmitīya school is also known as the "Pudgalavāda" (Proponents of the Person).

44. On Jayasena's teachings and their reception in East Asia, see Moro Shigeki, "Jayasena's Proof."

45. By the time Huili recorded this episode in 688, King Harṣa had been dead for more than forty years and reports of the ensuing wars in North India were well known in China.

46. *Zhuan*, 245a2–7; *Biography*, 131.

47. *Zhuan*, 245a17–18; *Biography*, 132.

48. *Zhuan*, 246b26–c1; *Biography*, 141.

49. *Xiyu ji*, 927b11–13; *Record*, 299.

50. *Xiyu ji*, 895a20–25; *Record*, 146–47.

51. *Zhuan*, 248b29–c4; *Biography*, 151–52.

52. *Zhuan*, 246a12–1; *Biography*, 137–38.

53. *Zhuan*, 249c21–250a8; *Biography*, 157–58.

54. *Xiyu ji*, 941b21–24; *Record*, 367.

55. *Xiyu ji*, 943a8–10; *Record*, 374.

56. Kotyk, "Chinese State and Buddhist Historical Sources on Xuanzang."

57. On diplomatic exchanges between India and China during the seventh century, see Tansen Sen, *Buddhism, Diplomacy, and Trade*, 34–44.

58. *Zhuan*, 252a6–11; *Biography*, 169. The Jumo River is now known as the Qarqan River.

59. *Xiyu ji*, 945c9–11; *Record*, 387–88.

60. *Zhuan*, 253c9–12; *Biography*, 179–80.

61. On the political ramifications of the *Record of the Western Regions*, see Max Deeg, "Has Xuanzang Really Been in Mathurā?" and "Show Me the Land Where the Buddha Dwelled."

62. *Zhuan*, 260a18–23; *Biography*, 222.

63. *Zhuan*, 256a9–11; *Biography*, 194.

64. *Zhuan*, 256c14–16; *Biography*, 199.

65. Cen Shen's (715–70) poem is translated in Stephen Owen, *The Great Age of Chinese Poetry*, 178.

66. *Zhuan*, 277b22; *Biography*, 335.

67. *Zhuan*, 260b28–29; *Biography*, 224. Xuanzang's set of instructions, the *Pusa jie jiemo wen*, has been translated by Chanju Mun and Ronald S. Green, "Xuanzang's Manual for Conferring the Bodhisattva Precepts."

68. *Zhuan*, 271a23–24; *Biography*, 297.

69. *Zhuan*, 271c19–21; *Biography*, 301.

70. Marc S. Abramson, *Ethnic Identity in Tang China*, 59–60.

71. Paul Pelliot (1912). There is no record of the translation ever being made. For more on Daoism during this period, see Timothy Barrett, *Taoism under the T'ang*.

72. Friederike Assandri, "Yinming Logic."

73. This text has been translated into English by Giuseppe Tucci, *The Nyāyamukha of Dignāga*.

74. *Zhuan*, 263a26–28; *Biography*, 243.

75. *Zhuan*, 265b1; *Biography*, 257.

76. For a detailed discussion of the challenges faced by Xuanzang during the last decade of his life, see Liu Shufen, "Xuanzang de zuihou shinian."

77. Daoxuan, *Ji gujin fodao lunheng*, 388c24–389a1.

78. On Empress Wu and her relationship to Buddhism, see Antonino Forte,

Political Propaganda and Ideology in China, and Timothy H. Barrett, *The Woman Who Discovered Printing*.

79. The *Treatise Establishing Consciousness Only* differed from most of Xuanzang's work because, in addition to containing translations of Dharmapāla's commentary on Vasubandhu's *Thirty Verses on Consciousness Only*, it also provides selections of other masters' commentaries, often arranged to demonstrate the superiority of Dharmapāla's interpretation. The *Treatise Establishing Consciousness Only* is therefore not a straight translation but a compilation composed by Xuanzang and his disciples.

80. *Zhuan*, 279b24–25; *Biography*, 346.

81. Daoxuan, *Xu gaoseng zhuan*, 458b15–17.

82. The three standard garments of a monk are the outer robe (*saṃghāti*), the upper robe (*uttarāsaṅga*), and the lower robe (*antarvāsa*).

83. The five vehicles are those of humans, gods, voice hearers, pratyekabuddhas, and bodhisattvas.

84. The four Vedas are more conventionally titled the *Ṛg-veda*, a collection of hymns and verses to deities, considered the oldest extant Indic text; the *Yajur-veda*, a collection of mantras for recitation during rituals; the *Sāmaveda*, which consists of stanzas from the *Ṛg-veda* that are set to melodies for use in ritual; and the *Atharva-veda*, a collection of incantations, philosophical speculations, and ritual explication written in verse and prose.

85. One *li* is the equivalent of roughly one-fifth of one mile or one-third of one kilometer. Xuanzang is alluding to a classic description of the selfless pursuit of knowledge. According to the Confucian classic *Mencius*, when Mencius visited Emperor Hui of Liang, the emperor praised him saying, "Even a thousand li wasn't too great a journey to for you. You must come bringing something of great profit to my nation." *Mencius* 1a.1, translated in David Hinton, *Mencius*, 3.

86. A "pure person" refers to someone who lives within the monastery but has not taken monastic vows.

87. Uttarāṣāḍhā names the constellation through which the moon passes during the second half of the fourth lunar month. This, according to many Buddhist traditions, is the period during which the Buddha was conceived.

88. *Last Days of the Buddha*, 63.

89. *Zhuan*, 236c1–2; *Biography*, 89–90.

90. The Auspicious Kalpa (Skt. *bhadrakalpa*) refers to the present eon, slated to last roughly 236 million years. According to traditional Buddhist cosmology, the Auspicious Kalpa follows the previous "Glorious Kalpa" and will in turn be succeeded by the "Kalpa of Constellations." The present *kalpa* is auspicious because it is when buddhas manifest in the world. Xuanzang notes that one thousand buddhas will appear during the present auspicious *kalpa*. Śākyamuni, usually identified as the fourth buddha of the current *kalpa*, will be followed by Maitreya, who will in turn be succeeded by 995 other buddhas.

91. The trichiliocosm represents the total extent of the Buddhist universe. According to some accounts, this includes a billion world systems similar to our own. Each of these systems has its own succession of buddhas, all of whom will become awakened while sitting on the Diamond Seat. Buddhist cosmological accounts describe the Diamond Seat as rooted in a wheel of metal, which rests on top of a wheel of water, itself above the lowermost wheel of wind. Together, these three wheels support the earth.

92. The diamond *samādhi*, or admantine absorption, is the final, consummate stage of Buddhist training, whereby the practitioner destroys all defilements and becomes a buddha.

93. The months of supernatural powers—the first, fifth, and ninth months of the year—were believed to be a time when buddhas and devas tour the world taking note of people's good and bad deeds. In this context, however, it refers to the day of the Buddha's nirvāṇa, which, according to Xuanzang, occurred on the fifteenth day of the first month of the Chinese lunar calendar.

94. Śrāvaṇa was typically the hottest month of the summer while Aśvayuja marks the first month of autumn.

95. This likely refers to the pillar that stood at Lat Bhairo until it was destroyed during riots in 1908.

96. The stūpa is now known as the Dharmarājika Stūpa. The Aśokan pillar remains today in its original position. The pillar's capital, which depicts four lions, was adopted as the official emblem of India in 1950. It is currently kept in the Sarnath Museum.

97. The stūpa mentioned here presumably refers to the Dhamekh Stūpa. Ājñātakauṇḍinya was the first of the Buddha's former five ascetic companions to receive the Buddha's teachings and become an arhat. According to tradition, five hundred pratyekabuddhas, after learning that the Bud-

dha was about to be born, self-immolated because there cannot be more than one buddha living at a time. The stūpa where this event supposedly took place may have been Chaukhandi, which was later converted into a watchtower.

98. The six supranormal powers possessed by buddhas and advanced arhats are (1) an unimpeded bodily action (the ability to fly through space, become invisible, etc.); (2) divine vision; (3) divine hearing; (4) the ability to know the minds of others; (5) knowledge of past lives; and (6) the ability to eradicate contaminants. The eight liberations are (1) in the realm of form, one sees external forms; (2) without form, one sees external forms; (3) the ability to develop determination by contemplating the beautiful; (4) the realm of infinite space; (5) the realm of infinite consciousness; (6) the realm of nothingness; (7) the realm of neither perception or nonperception; and (8) the extinction of perception and sensation.

99. Nirgrantha, literally "one without ties," often refers to monks of the Jain tradition but it is also used more generally to indicate non-Buddhist mendicants who go without clothes.

100. Dharmapāla (530–61), a renowned master of Yogācāra, succeeded his teacher Dignāga (ca. 480–540) at Nālandā. Candragupta was a contemporary of Dharmapāla. Most of what we know of Guṇamati comes from Xuanzang's *Record of the Western Regions*, which states that he was a monk from South India who took up his post at Nālandā after defeating a series of learned brahmins in debate. Sāramati was a contemporary of Guṇamati. Originally a kṣatriya from central India, he went on to write important Mahāyāna treatises after becoming a monk. The identity of the monk Xuanzang calls "Illuminated Friend," rendered here with the Sanskrit "Prabhāmitra," is not entirely clear. He may have been Prabhākaramitra (565–633), a monk from central India who became a disciple of Śīlabhadra at Nālandā. In 626, he arrived in Chang'an, where he worked as a translator and a tutor to the imperial family. Xuanzang was living in Chang'an at this time and he may have learned about Śīlabhadra and Nālandā from Prabhākaramitra. Viśeṣamitra, according to Xuanzang's disciple Ji, was a disciple of Dharmapāla. Both Viśeṣamitra and Dharmapāla appear on Ji's list of the ten great masters of the Yogācāra. Viśeṣamitra authored a summary of the Sarvāstivāda Vinaya, the *Sarvāstivādavinaya Saṃgraha*. The biographical details of Jñānacandra (dates unknown), another figure on Kuiji's list, are not known.

101. The "four types of life" refer to the various ways beings were thought to be born in ancient India: by egg, by womb, by moisture, and by spontaneous transformation.

102. Ma Rong (79–166) was a prominent scholar of the Confucian classics who served as an official in the court of the Later Han Dynasty (25–220). Ma Rong's reputation was such that the younger scholar Zheng Xuan (127–200) sought him out and became his disciple. Zheng Xuan went on to become one of the most celebrated scholars of his generation. Fu Sheng (dates unknown), an expert in the *Book of Documents* (*Shang shu*), lived during the early years of the Former Han Dynasty (206 B.C.E.–8 C.E.). The high minister Chao Cuo (d. 154 B.C.E.) visited the aging Fu Sheng at the behest of the emperor and eventually carried on his studies of the *Book of Documents*.

103. The number of texts listed in this passage totals 658, but the number given here, 657, is probably correct. The one additional text comes from a mistake in the total number of Sthavira texts. In the *Record of the Western Regions*, Xuanzang gives the total Sthavira texts at fourteen rather than the fifteen listed here.

104. The five *skandhas*, or aggregates, that constitute a person are form, sensation, perception, volition, and consciousness.

105. Tsongkhapa's commentary on this section of *Yogācārabhūmi* has been translated by Mark Tatz in *Asanga's "Chapter on Ethics."*

106. The phrase translated here as "arrogant non-Buddhists" is literally one who "wears metal plating on his belly." It refers to a story from the *āgamas* in which a non-Buddhist attempts to protect his wisdom, stored in his belly, with metal armor. The Buddha ultimately defeated him in debate, whereupon the non-Buddhist became his disciple.

107. The various carts listed here refer to the famous parable of the burning house from the *Lotus Sūtra*. The goat cart represents the voice-hearer vehicle while the deer cart stands for the pratyekabuddha vehicle. The cart pulled by the white ox represents the bodhisattva vehicle of the Mahayana, which, according to the *Lotus Sūtra* and Xuanzang, is the most efficacious vehicle.

108. Āryadeva (ca. 170–270) was a direct disciple of the famous Madhyamaka master Nāgārjuna. Both monks are traditionally associated with Nālandā Monastery, though it is not at all certain that Nālandā existed in the third century.

109. According to the Sarvāstivāda tradition, Mahākāśyapa and Ānanda were the first and second leaders of the Buddhist community after the Buddha. Śāṇakavāsin and Upagupta were the third and fourth.

110. Jetavana Park in the city of Śrāvasti was one of the main residences of the Buddha.

111. The three disciplines are *śila* (morality), *samādhi* (meditative absorption), and *prajñā* (wisdom). There are different descriptions of the three wisdoms. According to Xuanzang's *Treatise Establishing Consciousness Only*, they are the wisdom of those who are free, the wisdom generated through contemplative investigation, and the wisdom stemming from nondiscrimination. The eight acceptances are aligned with the four noble truths: acceptance of the dharma of suffering, acceptance of suffering, acceptance of the dharma that suffering has a cause, acceptance of the cause of suffering, acceptance of the dharma of cessation, acceptance of cessation, acceptance of the dharma of the path, acceptance of the path. The meaning of the eight contemplations is not clear. Xuanzang may have been referring to the so-called eight knowledges that result from the eight acceptances. The eight knowledges follow the same structure: knowledge of the dharma of suffering, knowledge of suffering, and so on. Together, the eight acceptances and eight knowledges make up the sixteen mental states that put an end to all delusion.

112. The three realms are the realms of desire, form, and formlessness. The seven contaminants are those of (wrong) view, action (motivated by greed, hatred, and ignorance), sense organs, bad karma, sensations, and (deluded) memory. The ten fetters that bind beings to saṃsāra are lack of conscience, shamelessness, jealousy, stinginess, regret, sleepiness, restlessness, dullness, anger, and deceit.

113. By some accounts, a *kalpa* lasts as long as it takes a rock more than three thousand miles high to be worn away by being brushed with a soft cloth once every hundred years. Another example explains that if there were a large city filled with mustard seeds, it would take one *kalpa* to empty the city if one seed was carried out once every hundred years. The three carts refer to the parable of the burning house in chapter 3 of the *Lotus Sūtra* (see note 107).

114. The translation here is tentative. Xuanzang may be referencing a line from the *Analects*: "The Master said, 'I once spent an entire day without

eating and an entire night without sleeping in order to think. There was no benefit. [Thinking] cannot compare with studying'" (*Analects* 15.31).

115. The four *dhyānas* are stages of meditation that progress from the desire realm to the heavenly realm. The first four of the nine absorptions, also known as the nine graduated absorptions, correlate with the four *dhyānas*. The second four in this series refer to states of absorption in the formless realm. The ninth and final absorption is characterized by the cessation of perception and sensation.

116. Bodhiruci (fl. sixth century), originally from northern India, was an important translator of Mahāyāna texts in China during the early sixth century. Initially based in the capital of Luoyang, he later continued his translation work at Shaolin Monastery.

117. Shu Guang and his nephew Shu Shou were prominent scholar officials during the Former Han Dynasty. Having reached the pinnacle of success, they then retired, with Shu Guang citing the *Daode jing*: "He who knows what is enough will not be shamed; he who knows where to stop will not be in danger." According to the third-century text the *Biographies of Eminent Scholars* (*Gaoshi zhuan*), when the scholar Xu You was asked by Emperor Yao to assume control of the empire, he hid himself in the mountains. When Emperor Yao then offered him the governorship of nine different regions, Xu You went to wash out his ears in the river. It was there that Chao Fu, looking for a place to water his ox, came across Xu You and asked what he was doing. After Xu You explained what had happened and how he was cleansing his ears of such dirty talk, Chao Fu took his ox upstream to avoid its drinking the water that had been contaminated by Xu You's ears.

118. The four *māras* are the demons of afflictions, aggregates, death, and devas. The nine bonds are love, hate, pride, ignorance, (wrong) views, attachment, doubt, jealousy, and stinginess. The five acceptances are submission, faith, compliance, birthlessness, and extinction. The ten practices of a bodhisattva are compassion, having few desires, not misusing sexuality, truthful speech, wisdom, safeguarding the Dharma, eliminating bad behavior and promoting good behavior, generosity, forbearance, and praising the three treasures.

119. Huiyuan (334–416) was an eminent Chinese Buddhist monk who spent his later years at a monastery on remote Mount Lu in the Jiangxi region. Daolin (314–66), also known as Zhi Dun, likewise retired from a promi-

nent career under imperial patronage to practice in the Shan mountains in southeastern China.

120. A *koṭi* refers to a very large number, anywhere from one hundred thousand to one hundred million.

121. The artist Song Fazhi traveled to India in 644 together with the envoy Wang Xuance. One of Song's most famous images was a painting he made of Maitreya under the Bodhi Tree. This painting was used as a model for a series of sculptures in the capitals of Luoyang and Chang'an. Sen, *Buddhism, Diplomacy, and Trade*, 38.

122. These were all signs that Xuanzang would be reborn in a heavenly realm. His consciousness left from his head (the last part of his body to turn cold) rather than his feet, which would indicate a lower rebirth. His body, moreover, did not decay during the traditional forty-nine-day period during which a person transitions to a new birth. An incorruptible body was taken as evidence of high spiritual attainment.

123. *Zhuan*, 278b10–11; *Biography*, 339.

124. Liu Shufen, "Xuanzang de zuihou shinian (655–664).

125. Yoshimura, "The Weishi School and the Buddha-Nature Debate."

126. Translation slightly modified from Green and Mun, *Gyōnen's "Transmission of the Buddha Dharma,"* 125–26.

127. The monasteries of Kōfukuji and Yakushiji, both located in the old capital of Nara, are the headquarters of the school. The current abbot of Kōfukuji, Tagawa Shun'ei, has been instrumental in spreading Yogācāra thought in modern Japan and, through his translated work, in Europe and North America. For an accessible introduction to Yogācāra, see his *Living Yogācāra*.

128. Justin Tiwald and Bryan W. Van Norden, *Readings in Later Chinese Philosophy*, 244.

129. William Chu, "The Timing of Yogācāra Resurgence."

130. Jiang Wu, "Buddhist Logic and Apologetics in 17th Century China."

131. Chen-Kuo Lin, "The Uncompromising Quest for Genuine Buddhism," 360.

132. On new interpretations of Buddhism in China during the late nineteenth and early twentieth centuries, see Sin-Wai Chan, *Buddhism in Late Ch'ing Political Thought*. For assessments of Yogācāra in particular, see Eyal Eviv, "A Well-Reasoned Dharma," Erik J. Hammerstrom, "Yogācāra and Science in the 1920s," and Bing Chen, "Reflections on the Revival of

Yogacara." The *Introduction to Logic* has been translated into English by Tachikawa Musashi, "A Sixth-Century Manual of Indian Logic."

133. Sylvain Lévi, *Matériaux pour l'étude du système Vijñaptimātra*. On the collaboration between Japanese and European scholars and the history of Yogācāra studies in the West, see Hans Martin Krämer, "Orientalism and the Study of Lived Religions," and Dan Lusthaus, "A Brief Retrospective of Western Yogācāra Scholarship."

134. Jason Clower, "Chinese Ressentiment and Why New Confucians Stopped Caring about Yogācāra."

135. Rudyard Kipling, *Kim*, 11–12. The monk in Kipling's novel is on a quest for the "River of the Arrow," which has purificatory powers. This miraculous river issues from a spring created by an arrow shot by the Buddha when he was still a young prince in Kapilavastu. Its location is described in the records of both Faxian and Xuanzang.

136. Jean-Pierre Abel-Rémusat, *Foĕ Kouĕ Ki; ou, Relation des royaumes bouddhiques*. Julien Stanislas, *Histoire de la vie de Hiouen-Thsang* and *Mémoires sur les contrées occidentales*.

137. William Anderson, "An Attempt to Identify Some of the Places Mentioned in the Itinerary of Hiuan-Thsang." Alexander Cunningham, "Verification of the Itinerary of Hwan Thsang." Louis Vivien de Saint-Martin, *Mémoire analytique sur la carte de l'Asie centrale et de l'Inde*.

138. Max F. Müller. *Buddhism and Buddhist Pilgrims*, 42.

139. Alexander Cunningham, "An Account of the Discovery of the Ruins of the Buddhist City of Samkassa," 247.

140. Alexander Cunningham, *The Bhilsa Topes*, 368.

141. Aurel Stein, *Serindia*, 805.

142. Stein details his negotiations with Wang Yuanlu at the Mogao caves in *Serindia*, vol. 2.801–13, and in Stein, *Ruins of Desert Cathay*, 164–94.

143. Stein, *Serindia* II: 812–13.

144. Stein, *Ruins of Desert Cathay* II: 172.

145. Stein, *Ruins of Desert Cathay* II: 171.

146. Stein, *Serindia* II: 825.

147. Stein, *Ruins of Desert Cathay* II: 181.

148. Wang Jiqing, "Aurel Stein's Dealings with Wang Yuanlu," 5.

149. Stein, *Archaeological Reconnaissances in North-Western India and South-Eastern Īrān*: viii.

150. Langdon Warner and Theodore Bowie, *Langdon Warner through His Letters*, 118.

151. National Commission for the Preservation of Antiquities (China), "Statement from the National Commission for the Preservation of Antiquities, Peking, China, regarding Sir Aurel Stein's Archaeological Expedition in Chinese Turkestan." Shareen Brysac, "Sir Aurel Stein's Fourth 'American' Expedition," 18.

152. For more on the discovery and history of the relic in China, see Benjamin Brose, "Resurrecting *Xuanzang*," and the sources cited therein.

153. Zhongjian Sanzang Fashi Dinggu Ta Weiyuan Hui, *Song sheng ji*, 4–5.

154. Xu Xun, "A Convergence of Nations."

155. Hirayama Ikuo, "Xuanzang's Pilgrim on the Silk Road."

156. Takata, *Gandāra Daitō Seiikiki no tabi*.

157. The other known sites are Chōreitō at Chōshōji, Shorinji in Sasayama, Jōreiden at Kumedadera, Torii Kanon in Saitama.

158. Sakaida Yukiko, *Daremo shiranai Saiyuki*.

159. Sakaida, *Daremo shiranai Saiyuki*, 108.

160. Zeng Wusheng, *Jinian Xuanzang dashi linggu guiguo fengan zhuanji*, 22.

161. Yuan Puquan, "Husong Xuanzang fashi dinggu sheli fu Taiwan."

162. *Zhuan*, 277b18–20; *Biography*, 335.

163. *Xiyuji*, 934b21–23 and 933a13–18; *Record*, 333 and 326.

164. *Zhuan*, 267a25–27; *Biography*, 269.

165. *Zhuan*, 279a25–26; *Biography*, 344.

166. Translation slightly modified from Yi Ding, "By the Power of the *Perfection of Wisdom*," 675.

167. On the origin and evolution of Xuanzang images in China and Japan, see Liu Shufen, "Gaoseng xingxiang de chuanbo yu huiliu," "Tangdai Xuanzang de shenghua," and "Songdai Xuanzang de shenghua." In English, see Dorothy Wong, "The Making of a Saint."

168. On cults devoted to the monkey Sun Wukong and the pig Zhu Bajie, see Benjamin Brose, "The Pig and the Prostitute" and "Taming the Monkey."

169. The classic study of the novel's antecedents is Glen Dudbridge, *The Hsi-Yu Chi*. Anthony Yu's excellent four-volume translation is titled *The Journey to the West*; his one-volume abridgment is called *The Monkey and the Monk*.

170. M. Théodore Pavie, "Étude sur le Sy-Yéou-Tchin-Tsuén"; Dyer Ball, "Scraps from Chinese Mythology"; Timothy Richard, *A Journey to Heaven*"; and Helen M. Hayes, *The Buddhist Pilgrim's Progress*.

171. Arthur Waley, *Monkey*, 6.

172. Tansen Sen, "Taixu's Goodwill Mission to India," 330.

173. Lijun Chen, "Communist Party of China Embraces Virtues of Religion in Diplomacy."
174. Xuecheng, "The Modern Significance of Xuanzang's Spirit." Dong Leshuo, "Audience Treated to a Trip on Silk Road in Drama."
175. S. D. Muni, "Nalanda: A Soft Power Project." Bhanu Pratap, "India's Cultural Diplomacy."
176. *Zhuan*, 253b14–15; *Biography*, 178.

Abbreviations

Biography	Huili et al. *A Biography of the Tripiṭaka Master*
Record	Xuanzang. *The Great Tang Dynasty Record of the Western Regions*
T	Takakusu Junjirō and Watanabe Kaigyoku, eds. *Taishō shinshū daizōkyō*
Xiyu ji	Xuanzang. *Da Tang xiyu ji*
Zhuan	Huili et al. *Da Tang da Ci'en si Sanzang fashi zhuan*

Bibliography

Abel-Rémusat, Jean-Pierre. *Foë Kouĕ Ki; ou, Relation des royaumes bouddhiques: Voyage dans la Tartarie, dans l'Afghanistan et dans l'Inde, exécuté à la fin du IVe siècle, par Chy Fă Hian*. Paris: Imprimerie Royale, 1936.

Abramson, Marc S. *Ethnic Identity in Tang China*. Singapore: Institute of Southeast Asian Studies, 2014.

Al'baum, L. I. *Zhivopis' Afrasiaba*. Tashkent: Fan, 1975.

Anand, Deepak. "Retracing Bodhisattva Xuanzang Project." https://www.facebook.com/RetracingBodhisattvaXuanzang/. Accessed May 1, 2020.

Anderson, William. "An Attempt to Identify Some of the Places Mentioned in the Itinerary of Hiuan-Thsang." *Journal of the Asiatic Society of Bengal* 16 (December 1874): 1183–1211.

Asaṅga. *The Summary of the Great Vehicle*. Translated by John P. Keenan. Berkeley, CA: Numata Center for Buddhist Translation and Research, 1992.

Assandri, Friederike. "Yinming Logic and Dialogue in the Contact Zone." *Journal of Chinese Philosophy* 41, no. 3–4 (2014): 344–60.

Eviv, Eyal. "A Well-Reasoned Dharma: Buddhist Logic in Republican China." *Journal of Chinese Buddhist Studies* 28 (2015): 189–234.

Ball, Dyer. "Scraps from Chinese Mythology." *China Review* 13, no. 2 (1884): 75–85.

Barrett, Timothy H. *Taoism under the T'ang: Religion and Empire during the Golden Age of Chinese History*. London: Wellsweep, 1996.

Barrett, Timothy H. *The Woman Who Discovered Printing*. New Haven, CT: Yale University Press, 2008.

Bernstein, Richard. *Ultimate Journey: Retracing the Path of an Ancient Buddhist Monk Who Crossed Asia in Search of Enlightenment*. New York: Vintage Departures, 2002.

Blum, Mark L., trans. *The Nirvana Sutra (Mahāparinirvāṇa-sūtra)*. Berkeley, CA: Bukkyo Dendo Kyokai America, 2013.

Bregel, Yuri. *An Historical Atlas of Central Asia*. Leiden: Brill, 2003.

Brose, Benjamin. "The Pig and the Prostitute: The Cult of Zhu Bajie in Modern Taiwan." *Journal of Chinese Religions* 46, no. 2 (2018): 167–96.

———. "Resurrecting Xuanzang: The Modern Travels of a Medieval Monk." In *Recovering Buddhism in Modern China*. Edited by Jan Kiely and Brooks Jessup. New York: Columbia University Press, 2016, 143–76.

———. "Taming the Monkey: Reinterpreting the *Xi you ji* in the Early Twentieth Century." *Monumenta Serica* 68, no. 1 (2020): 1–28.

Brysac, Shareen. "Sir Aurel Stein's Fourth 'American' Expedition." In *Sir Aurel Stein: Proceedings of the British Museum Study Day*. Edited by Helen Wang. British Museum Occasional Papers 142 (2002): 17–22.

Burnes, Alexander. *Travels into Bokhara: being the account of a journey from India to Cabool, Tartary, and Persiam, also, narrative of a voyage on the Indus, from the sea to Lahore with presents from the King of Great Britain, performed under the orders of the Supreme Government of India, in the years 1831, 1832, and 1833*. London: J. Murray, 1834.

Chan, Sin-Wai. *Buddhism in Late Ch'ing Political Thought*. Hong Kong: Chinese University Press, 1985.

Chavannes, Édouard. "Voyage de Song Yun dans l'Udyāna et le Gandhāra." *Bulletin de l'Ecole française d'Extrême-Orient* 3, no. 1 (1903): 379–441.

Chen, Bing. "Reflections on the Revival of Yogacara in Modern Chinese Buddhism." In Kragh, *Foundation for Yoga Practitioners*, 1054–1076.

Chen, Lijun. "Communist Party of China Embraces Virtues of Religion in Diplomacy." *Global Times*, May 4, 2015. www.globaltimes.cn/content/920035.shtml.

Chu, William. "The Timing of Yogācāra Resurgence in the Ming Dynasty (1368–1643)." *Journal of the International Association of Buddhist Studies* 33, no. 1–2 (2010/2011): 5–25.

Clower, Jason. "Chinese Ressentiment and Why New Confucians Stopped Caring about Yogācāra." In Makeham, *Transforming Consciousness*, 377–411.

Cunningham, Alexander. "An Account of the Discovery of the Ruins of the Buddhist City of Samkassa." *Journal of the Royal Asiatic Society* 7 (1843): 241–47.

———. *The Bhilsa Topes: Buddhist Monuments of Central India: Rise, Progress and Decline of Buddhism*. London: Smith, Elder, 1854.

———. "Verification of the Itinerary of Hwan Thsang through Ariana and India, with reference to Major Anderson's Hypothesis of Its Modern Compilation." *Journal of the Asiatic Society of Bengal* 17 (1948): 476–88.

Daoxuan. *Ji gujin fodao lunheng.* T52, no. 2104.

———. *Xu gaoseng zhuan,* T50, no. 2060.

Deeg, Max. "Has Xuanzang Really Been in Mathurā? Interpretatio Sinica or Interpretatio Occidentalia—How to Critically Read the Records of the Chinese Pilgrim." In *Essays on East Asian Religion and Culture: Festschrift in Honour of Nishiwaki Tsuneki on the Occasion of His 65th Birthday.* Edited by Christian Wittern and Shi Lishan. Kyoto: Kyōto daigaku jinbun kagaku kenkyūjo, 2007, 35–73.

———. "'Show Me the Land Where the Buddha Dwelled…': Xuanzang's *Record of the Western Regions (Xiyu ji)*: A Misunderstood Text?" *China Report* 48, no. 1–2 (2012): 89–113.

Ding, Yi. "'By the Power of the *Perfection of Wisdom*': The 'Sūtra-Rotation' Liturgy of the *Mahāprajñāpāramitā* at Dunhuang." *Journal of the American Oriental Society* 139, no. 3 (July–September 2019): 661–79.

Dong Leshuo. "Audience Treated to a Trip on Silk Road in Drama." *China Daily Global*, January 29, 2019. https://www.chinadaily.com.cn/a/201901/29/WS5c4f293aa3106c65c34e6ee2.html.

Doniger, Wendy, and Harṣavardhana. *The Lady of the Jewel Necklace and The Lady Who Shows Her Love.* New York: New York University Press/JJC Foundation, 2006.

Dudbridge, Glen. *The Hsi-Yu Chi: A Study of Antecedents to the Sixteenth-Century Chinese Novel.* Cambridge: Cambridge University Press, 2009.

Errington, Elizabeth J., Piers Baker, and Charles Masson. *Charles Masson and the Buddhist Sites of Afghanistan: Explorations, Excavations, Collections, 1832–1835.* London: British Museum, 2017.

Faxian. *A Record of the Buddhistic Kingdoms: Being an Account by the Chinese Monk Fa-Hien of His Travels in India and Ceylon (A.D. 399–414) in Search of the Buddhist Books of Discipline Translated, Annotated and with a Corean Recension of the Chinese Text.* Translated by James Legge. Oxford: Clarendon Press, 1886.

Forte, Antonino. *Political Propaganda and Ideology in China at the End of the Seventh Century: Inquiry into the Nature, Authors and Function of the Tunhuang Document S.6502 Followed by an Annotated Translation.* Naples: Istituto Universitario Orientale, 1976.

Garfield, Jay L., and Jan Westerhoff. *Madhyamaka and Yogācāra: Allies or Rivals?* New York: Oxford University Press, 2015.

Ghosh, A. *A Guide to Nālandā*. New Delhi: Director of Publications, Archaeological Survey of India, 1986.

Green, Ronald S., and Cha'n-ju Mun. *Gyōnen's "Transmission of the Buddha Dharma in Three Countries."* Leiden and Boston: Brill, 2018.

Grenet, Frantz. "The 7th-Century A.D. 'Ambassadors' Painting' at Samarkand." In *Medieval Paintings of the Silk Road: Cultural Exchanges between the East and West*. Edited by Kuzuya Yamauchi. Tokyo: Archetype, 2007, 9–19.

Grenet, Franz, and Zhang Guangda, "The Last Refuge of the Sogdian Religion: Dunhuang in the Ninth and Tenth Centuries." *Bulletin of the Asia Institute*, n.s., 10 (1996): 175–86.

Grünwedel, Albert. *Alt-Kutscha: Archäologische und Religionsgeschichtliche Forschungen an Tempera-Gemälden aus Buddhistischen Höhlen der Ersten Acht Jahrhunderte nach Christi Gerburt*. Kyoto: Rinsen Books, 1997.

Hammerstrom, Erik J. "Yogācāra and Science in the 1920s: The Wuchang School's Approach to Modern Mind Science." In Makeham, *Transforming Consciousness*, 170–97.

Hanh, Thich Nhat, and Rachel Neumann. *Understanding Our Mind*. Berkeley, CA: Parallax Press, 2006.

Hansen, Valerie. *The Silk Road: A New History with Documents*. New York: Oxford University Press, 2017.

Hayes, Helen M. *The Buddhist Pilgrim's Progress*. New York: E. P. Dutton, 1930.

Hinton, David, trans. *Mencius*. Washington DC: Counterpoint, 1998.

Hirayama Ikuo. "Xuanzang's Pilgrim on the Silk Road." *The Silk Roads of Sanzohoshi Xuanzang: His Legacy and Our Future*. Silk Roads Nara International Symposium 1999 (record no. 5): 62–66.

Horner, I. B., trans. *Milinda's Questions*. London: Luzac, 1969.

Huili et al. *A Biography of the Tripiṭaka Master of the Great Ci'en Monastery of the Great Tang Dynasty*. Translated by Li Rongxi. Berkeley, CA: Numata Center for Buddhist Translation and Research, 1995.

———. *Da Tang da Ci'en si Sanzang fashi zhuan*. T50, no. 2053.

Keenan, John. *A Study of the Buddhabhūmyupadeśa: The Doctrinal Development of the Notion of Wisdom in Yogācāra Thought*. Berkeley, CA: Institute of Buddhist Studies and Bukkyō Dendō Kyōkai America, 2014.

Kipling, Rudyard. *Kim*. London: Macmillan, 1901.

Kotyk, Jeffrey. "Chinese State and Buddhist Historical Sources on Xuanzang: Historicity and the *Daci'en si sanzang fashi zhuan* 大慈恩寺三藏法師傳." *T'oung Pao* 105 (2019): 513–44.

Kragh, Ulrich T., ed. *The Foundation for Yoga Practitioners: The Buddhist Yogā-cārabhūmi Treatise and Its Adaptation in India, East Asia, and Tibet.* Cambridge, MA: Harvard University Press, 2013.

Krämer, Hans Martin. "Orientalism and the Study of Lived Religions: The Japanese Contribution to European Models of Scholarship on Japan around 1900." In *Scholarly Personae in the History of Orientalism, 1870–1930.* Edited by Christiaan Engberts and Herman J. Paul. Leiden: Brill, 2019, 143–71.

Kuwayama Shōshin. "Chinese Records on Bamiyan: Translation and Commentary." *East and West* 55, no. 1/4 (December 2005): 139–61.

———. "How Xuanzang Learned about Nālandā." *China Report* 48, no. 1–2 (2012): 61–88.

La Vaissière, Étienne de. *Sogdian Traders: A History.* Leiden: Brill, 2005.

———. "Sogdians in China: A Short History and Some New Discoveries." *Silk Road* 1, no. 2 (December 2003): 23–27.

———. "Note sur la chronologie du voyage de Xuanzang." *Journal Asiatique* 298, no. 1 (2010): 157–68.

La Vallée Poussin, Louis. *L'Abhidharmakośa de Vasubandhu.* Paris: P. Geuther, 1923–31.

———. *Vijñaptimātratāsiddhi: La Siddhi de Hiuan-Tsang.* Paris: P. Geuthner, 1929.

Le Coq, Albert von. *Chotscho: Facsimile-wiedergaben der wichtigeren funde der ersten Königlich preussischen expedition nach Turfan in Ost-Turkistan, im auftrage der generalverwaltung der Königlichen museen aus mitteln des Baessler-institutes.* Berlin: D. Reimer (E. Vohsen), 1913.

Lévi, Sylvain. *Matériaux pour l'étude du systeme Vijñaptimātra.* Paris: Bibliothèque de l'école des Hautes études, 1925.

Lin, Chen-Kuo "The Uncompromising Quest for Genuine Buddhism: Lü Cheng's Critique of Original Enlightenment." In Makeham, *Transforming Consciousness,* 317–42.

Liu Shufen. "Gaoseng xingxiang de chuanbo yu huiliu—cong 'Xuanzang fuji tu' tanqi." *Xu Pingfang xiansheng jinian wenji.* Shanghai: Shanghai guji chubanshe, 2012, 333–59.

———. "Songdai Xuanzang de shenghua: Tuxiang, wenwu he yiji." *Zhonghua wenshi luncong* 133 (2019): 161–219.

———. "Tangdai Xuanzang de shenghua." *Zhonghua wenshi luncong* 125 (2017): 1–57.

———. "Xuanzang de zuihou shinian (655–664)—jianlun zongzhang ernian (669) gaizang shi." *Zhonghua wenshi luncong* 95 (2009): 1–97.

Lusthaus, Dan. "A Brief Retrospective of Western Yogācāra Scholarship in the 20th Century." Paper presented at the Eleventh International Conference on Chinese Philosophy, Chengchi University, Taipei, Taiwan, July 26–31, 1999. http://www.acmuller.net/yogacara/articles/ISCP_99_Yogacara_retro2.html.

———. *Buddhist Phenomenology: A Philosophical Investigation of Yogācāra Buddhism and the Ch'eng Wei-Shih Lun.* London: RoutledgeCurzon, 2006.

———. "Xuanzang and Kuiji and Madhyamaka." In *Madhyamaka and Yogācāra: Allies or Rivals?* Edited by Jay L. Garfield and Jan Westerhoff. New York: Oxford University Press, 2015.

Makeham, John. *Transforming Consciousness: Yogācāra Thought in Modern China.* New York: Oxford University Press, 2014.

Minamoto Toyomune. *Genjō Sanzō e.* Tōkyō: Chūō Kōronsha, 1981–82.

Mizutani Shinjō. *Daitō Seiikiki.* 3 vols. Tokyo: Heibonsha, 1999.

Moro Shigeki. "Jayasena's Proof of the Authenticity of the Mahāyāna Scriptures." *Journal of Indian Philosophy* 46 (2018): 339–53.

Müller, F. Max. *Buddhism and Buddhist Pilgrims: A Review of Stanislas Julien's "Voyage Des Pélerins Bouddhistes."* London: Williams and Norgate, 1857.

Müller, F. Max, and Bunyiu Nanjio. *Buddhist Texts from Japan.* Anecdota Oxoniensia, Aryan Series. Oxford: Clarendon Press, 1881.

Mun, Chanju, and Ronald S. Green. "Xuanzang's Manual for Conferring the Bodhisattva Precepts." *Bulgyomun yeyeongu* 3 (2014): 245–69.

Muni, S. D. "Nalanda: A Soft Power Project." *Hindu,* August 30, 2010. https://www.thehindu.com/opinion/lead/Nalanda-a-soft-power-project/article16151885.ece.

Nara National Museum and Asahi Shinbunsha, eds. *Tenjiku e: Sanzō hōshi 3-man kiro no tabi* 天竺へ: 三蔵法師 3万キロの旅 [On to India! Xuanzang's thirty-thousand-kilometer trek]. Exhibition catalog. Nara: Nara Kokuritsu Hakubutsukan, 2011.

National Commission for the Preservation of Antiquities (China). "Statement from the National Commission for the Preservation of Antiquities, Peking, China, regarding Sir Aurel Stein's Archaeological Expedition in Chinese Turkestan [Fogg Art Museum archives: Confidential File on Sir Aurel Stein]."

Owen, Stephen. *The Great Age of Chinese Poetry: The High Tang.* Melbourne, Victoria: Quirin Press, 2013.

Pavie, M. Théodore. "Étude sur le Sy-Yéou-Tchin-Tsuén, Roman Bouddhique Chinois." *Journal Asiatique*, ser. 5, 9 (April–May 1857): 357–92.

Pelliot, Paul. "Autour d'une traduction sanscrite du Tao tö King." *T'oung Pao* 13, no. 1 (1912): 351–430.

Powers, John. *Hermeneutics and Tradition in the Saṃdhinirmocana-sūtra.* Leiden and New York: Brill, 1993.

Pratap, Bhanu. "India's Cultural Diplomacy: Present Dynamics, Challenges and Future Prospects." *International Journal of Arts, Humanities and Management Studies* 1, no. 9 (September 2015): 55–65.

Richard, Timothy. *A Journey to Heaven being a Chinese Epic and Allegory dealing with the Origin of the Universe: the Evolution of Monkey to Man: the Evolution of Man to the Immortal: and Revealing the Religion, Science, and Magic, which moulded the Life of The Middle Ages of Central Asia and which underlie the civilization of the Far East to this day, by Ch'iu Ch'ang Ch'un, A.D. 1208–1288, Born 67 years before Dante.* Shanghai: Christian Literature Society's Depot, 1913.

Richthofen, Ferdinand von. *China: Ergebnisse eigener Reisen und darauf gegründeter Studien.* 5 vols. Berlin: Reimer, 1877–1912.

Saito Tatuya. "Features of the Kongō-ji version of the Further Biographies of Eminent Monks 続高僧伝：With a Focus on the Biography of Xuanzang 玄奘 in the Fourth Fascicle." *Journal of the International College for Postgraduate Buddhist Studies* 16 (2012): 69–104.

Saiyūki no shiruku rōdo: Sanzō hōshi no michi: 西遊記のシルクロ-ド: 三蔵法師の道 [The Silk Road and the world of Xuanzang]. Tokyo: Asahi Shinbunsha, 1999.

Sakaida, Yukiko. *Daremo shiranai Saiyuki: Genjo Sanzo no ikotsu o meguru higashiajia sengoshi.* Tokyo: Ryukei shosha, 2013.

Salomon, Richard. *The Buddhist Literature of Ancient Gandhāra: An Introduction with Selected Translations.* Somerville, MA: Wisdom Publications, 2018.

Sandes, E. W. C. *The Military Engineer in India.* Vol. 2. Chatham, UK: Institution of Royal Engineers, 1935.

Saran, Mishi. *Chasing the Monk's Shadow: A Journey in the Footsteps of Xuanzang.* New Delhi: Penguin Books, 2008

Schmithausen, Lambert. *Alayavijñana: On the Origin and Early Development of a Central Concept of Yogācāra Philosophy.* 2 vols. Tokyo: International Institute for Buddhist Studies, 1987.

———. *On the Problem of the External World in the "Ch'eng wei shi lun."* Tokyo: International Institute for Buddhist Studies, 2005.

Sen, Tansen. *Buddhism, Diplomacy, and Trade: The Realignment of India-China Relations, 600–1400.* Lanham, MD: Rowman and Littlefield, 2015.

———. "Taixu's Goodwill Mission to India." In *India, China, and the World: A Connected History.* Lanham, MD: Rowman and Littlefield, 2017.

Śīlabhadra. *The Buddhabhūmi-sūtra and the Buddhabhūmivyākhyāna of Çīlabhadra.* Translated by Nishio Kyōo and J. Rahder. Tokyo: Kokusho Kankokai, 1982.

Stanislas, Julien. *Histoire de la vie de Hiouen-Thsang et de ses voyages dans l'inde, depuis l'an 629 jusqu'en 645.* Paris: Imprimerie impériale, 1853.

———. *Mémoires sur les contrées occidentales, traduit du sanscrit en chinois, en l'an 648, par Hiouen-Tshang.* Paris: Imprimerie Impériale, 1857–58.

Stein, Aurel. *Ancient Khotan Detailed Report of Archaeological Explorations in Chinese Turkestan.* Oxford: Clarendon Press, 1907.

———. *Ruins of Desert Cathay: Personal Narrative of Explorations in Central Asia and Westernmost China.* 2 vols. London: MacMillan, 1912.

———. *Serindia: Detailed Report of Explorations in Central Asia and Westermost China, Carried Out and Described under Orders of H.M. Indian Government by Aurel Stein.* Oxford: Clarendon Press, 1921.

Stein, Aurel, et al. *Archaeological Reconnaissances in North-Western India and South-Eastern Īrān.* Macmillan & Co: London, 1937.

Strong, John S. *The Legend of King Asoka: A Study and Translation of the Asokava-dana.* Princeton: Princeton University Press, 1989.

Sun Shuyun. *Ten Thousand Miles without a Cloud.* London: HarperPerennial, 2004.

Tachikawa Musashi. "A Sixth-Century Manual of Indian Logic." *Journal of Indian Philosophy* 1 (1971): 111–45.

Tagawa Shun'ei and Charles Muller. *Living Yogācāra: An Introduction to Consciousness-Only Buddhism.* Somerville, MA: Wisdom Publications, 2014.

Takada Kōin. *Gandāra Daitō Seiikiki no tabi.* Tokyo: Kōdansha, 1988.

Takakusu Junjirō and Watanabe Kaigyoku, eds. *Taishō shinshū daizōkyō.* Tokyo: Taishō issaikyō kankōkai, 1924–32.

Tatz, Mark. *Asanga's "Chapter on Ethics" with the Commentary of Tsong-Kha-Pa, The Basic Path to Awakening, The Complete Bodhisattva.* Lewiston, NY: Edwin Mellen Press, 1986.

Tiwald, Justin, and Bryan W. Van Norden. *Readings in Later Chinese Philosophy: Han to the 20th Century.* Indianapolis, IN: Hackett, 2014.

Tokiwa Daijō, et al. *Wan Qing Minguo shiqi Zhongguo mingsheng guji tuji* [Chinese historical sites of the Late Qing Dynasty and the Republic of China]. Vol. 9. Beijing: Zhongguo huabao chubanshe, 2017.

Tokyo National Museum. *Ancient Buddhist Treasures of Kōfukji Temple: In Commemoration of the Completion of the Heisei-era Grand Repairs of the Nan'endō Hall*. Tokyo: Tōkyō Kokuritsu Hakubutsukan, 1997.

Tucci, Giuseppe. *The Nyāyamukha of Dignāga*. Leipzig and Heidelberg: Otto Harrassowitz, 1930.

Vajirā, Sister, and Francis Story, trans. *Last Days of the Buddha: The Mahāparinibbāna Sutta*. Kandy: Buddhist Publication Society, 1998.

Vivien de Saint-Martin, Louis. *Mémoire analytique sur la carte de l'Asie centrale et de l'Inde, construite d'après le Si-yu-ki (Mémoires sur les contrées occidentales) et les autres relations chinoises des premiers siècles de notre ère, pour les voyages de Hiouen-Thsang dans l'Inde, depuis l'année 629 jusqu'en 645*. Paris, Imprimerie impériale, 1858.

Waley, Arthur. *Monkey: Folk Novel of China*. New York: Grove Press, 1943.

Wang Jiqing. "Aurel Stein's Dealings with Wang Yuanlu and Chinese Officials in 1907." In *Sir Aurel Stein Colleagues and Collections*. Edited by Helen Wang. London: British Museum Press, 2012, 1–6.

Wang, Zhihong. *Dust in the Wind: Retracing Dharma Master Xuanzang's Western Pilgrimage*. Taipei: Rhythms Monthly, 2006.

Warner, Langdon, and Theodore Bowie. *Langdon Warner through His Letters*. Bloomington: Indiana University Press, 1966.

Wertmann, Patrick. *Sogdians in China: Archaeological and Art Historical Analyses of Tombs and Texts from the 3rd to the 10th Century AD*. Munich: Philipp von Zabern 2016.

Westerhoff, Jan. *The Golden Age of Indian Buddhist Philosophy*. Oxford: Oxford University Press, 2018.

Wong, Dorothy. "The Making of a Saint: Images of Xuanzang in East Asia." *Early Medieval China* 1 (2002): 43–95.

Wu Cheng'en. *The Journey to the West*. 4 vols. Translated by Anthony Yu. Chicago: University of Chicago Press, 2012.

Wu, Jiang. "Buddhist Logic and Apologetics in 17th Century China: An Analysis of the Use of Buddhist Syllogisms in an Anti-Christian Polemic." *Dao: A Journal of Comparative Philosophy* 2, no. 2 (June 2003): 273–89.

Xu Xun. "A Convergence of Nations: Revered Monk of Shared History Again Symbol of IntraAsia Cooperation," *China Pictorial* (November 2011).

Xuanzang. *Da Tang xiyu ji*. T51, no. 2087.

284 BIBLIOGRAPHY

———. *The Great Tang Dynasty Record of Western Regions*. Translated by Li Rongxi. Berkeley, CA: Numata Center for Buddhist Translation and Research, 1996.

———. *The Scripture on the Explication of Underlying Meaning*. Translated by John P. Keenan. Berkeley, CA: Numata Center for Buddhist Translation and Research, 2000.

Xuecheng. "Xuanzang jingshen de xiandai yiyi xue" [The Modern Significance of Xuanzang's Spirit]. *Fayin* 370 (June 2015): 6–7.

Yang Xuanzhi. *Record of Buddhist Monasteries in Lo-Yang*. Translated by Yi-tung Wang. Princeton, NJ: Princeton University Press, 2016.

Yijing. *Buddhist Monastic Traditions of Southern Asia: A Record of the Inner Law Sent Home from the South Seas*. Translated by Li Rongxi. Berkeley, CA: Numata Center for Buddhist Translation and Research, 2000.

Yoshimura Makoto. "Genjō no nenji mondai ni tsuite." *Komazawa Daigaku Bukkyōgakubu ronshū* 46 (2015): 183–205.

———. "The Weishi School and the Buddha-Nature Debate in the Early Tang Dynasty." In Kragh, *Foundation for Yoga Practitioners*, 1234–53.

Yu, Anthony C. *The Monkey and the Monk: An Abridgment of "The Journey to the West."* Chicago: University of Chicago Press, 2006.

Yuan Puquan. "Husong Xuanzang fashi dinggu sheli fu Taiwan." *Zhongshan fengyu* 6 (2011): 22–23.

Zeng Wusheng, et al. *Jinian Xuanzang dashi linggu guiguo fengan zhuanji.* Huweizhen: Xingtai chubanshe, 1957.

Zhongjian Sanzang Fashi Dinggu Ta Weiyuan Hui, eds. *Song sheng ji (Datang Sanzang Xuanzang fashi jinian ce)*. Nanjing: Mucun yinshua suo, October 10, 1944.

Index

Map and illustration page numbers indicated with italics.

LIVES OF THE MASTERS

"Since the time of Buddha Shakyamuni himself, Buddhists have been accustomed to recollect the lives of great teachers and practitioners as a source of inspiration from which we may still learn. The Lives of the Masters series continues this noble tradition, recounting the stories, wisdom, and experience of many accomplished Buddhists over the last 2,500 years. I am sure readers will find the accounts in this series inspirational and encouraging."

HIS HOLINESS THE DALAI LAMA

"The lives of the most important Buddhist masters in history written by the very best of scholars in elegant and accessible prose—who could ask for more?"

JOSE CABEZÓN, *Professor of Tibetan Buddhist Studies, University of California Santa Barbara*

BOOKS IN THE SERIES

Atiśa Dīpaṃkara: Illuminator of the Awakened Mind
Dogen: Japan's Original Zen Teacher
Gendun Chopel: Tibet's Modern Visionary
Maitrīpa: India's Yogi of Nondual Bliss
S. N. Goenka: Emissary of Insight
The Third Karmapa Rangjung Dorje: Master of Mahāmudrā
Tsongkhapa: A Buddha in the Land of Snows
Xuanzang: China's Legendary Pilgrim and Translator

*Please visit www.shambhala.com
for more information on forthcoming titles.*

01 14